CAMBRIDGE STUDIES
IN ENGLISH LEGAL HISTORY

Edited by

HAROLD DEXTER HAZELTINE, LITT.D., F.B.A.

Of the Inner Temple, Barrister-at-Law;
Downing Professor of the Laws of England in
the University of Cambridge

THE EQUITY OF REDEMPTION

ITS NATURE, HISTORY AND CONNECTION WITH EQUITABLE ESTATES GENERALLY

by

R. W. TURNER

M.A., LL.M. CAMBRIDGE

Tutor in Law
University College of the South-West
Exeter

CAMBRIDGE
AT THE UNIVERSITY PRESS
1931

CAMBRIDGE UNIVERSITY PRESS
Cambridge, New York, Melbourne, Madrid, Cape Town,
Singapore, São Paulo, Delhi, Mexico City

Cambridge University Press
The Edinburgh Building, Cambridge CB2 8RU, UK

Published in the United States of America by Cambridge University Press, New York

www.cambridge.org
Information on this title: www.cambridge.org/9781107695443

© Cambridge University Press 1931

This publication is in copyright. Subject to statutory exception
and to the provisions of relevant collective licensing agreements,
no reproduction of any part may take place without the written
permission of Cambridge University Press.

First published 1931
First paperback edition 2013

A catalogue record for this publication is available from the British Library

ISBN 978-1-107-69544-3 Paperback

Cambridge University Press has no responsibility for the persistence or
accuracy of URLs for external or third-party internet websites referred to in
this publication, and does not guarantee that any content on such websites is,
or will remain, accurate or appropriate.

CONTENTS

General Preface by H. D. Hazeltine . . *pages* vii–lxiii

Author's Preface lxv

Index of Cases lxvii

Index of Statutes lxx

Index of Year Books lxxii

Chap. I Introduction: The Common Law Conception of an "Estate" . . .   I

  II The Foundation of the Equity of Redemption   17

  III Hale and Nottingham: The Equity of Redemption as a Thing, an Interest in Land   43

  IV Hardwicke: The Equity of Redemption as an Estate in Land   65

  V The Nature of the Mortgagor's Possession   88

  VI The Influence of Roman Law and the Movement towards *Hypotheca* . .   III

  VII The Equity of Redemption and Rights *in Rem* and *in Personam*   138

 VIII A. Incidents of Analogy with the Trust   157

  B. The Mortgagee as a Trustee . .   166

  C. The Theory of Clogging the Equity of Redemption   175

  D. The Mortgagor and the Franchise .   183

Appendix   186

Index   190

THE ROMAN *FIDUCIA CUM CREDITORE* AND THE ENGLISH MORTGAGE

A COMPARISON, WITH SPECIAL REFERENCE TO THE RIGHT OF REDEMPTION

I

THE trust and the mortgage are both notable illustrations of that duality of legal and equitable rights which has been so marked a feature of English law from medieval times to the present day. In his monograph on the history of the equity of redemption Mr Turner has considered one aspect of this dualism of rights by taking into account both the legal and the equitable bases of the mortgage. By his study of the common-law conception of an estate in land, as well as by his investigation of the early common-law forms of security on property, he has laid a solid foundation for his examination of equitable jurisdiction over mortgages, with special reference to the origin and development of the mortgagor's equity of redemption. He has explained the slow growth of judicial doctrine respecting the nature of the equity of redemption; he has traced the evolution of the equity in the age of Hale and Nottingham and has shown us how, in the time of Hardwicke, it ultimately emerged clearly as an equitable estate in land.[1] In dealing with the growth of chancery's doctrine in regard to the juridical nature of the mortgagor's right, Mr Turner has also studied some of the other equities of English law, notably the equity of the *cestui que trust*; and, indeed, throughout his essay he has kept steadily in view the parallel development of the equitable estate of the beneficiary under a trust and the equitable estate of the debtor under a mortgage. Consideration has been given,

[1] The conception of the equity of redemption as an estate in equity seems to be implicit in some of the early doctrines of chancery in regard to mortgages, such as the doctrine of tacking. In the latter part of the seventeenth century, more than half a century before Hardwicke's time, this doctrine, which assumes that the mortgagor could give a second mortgage, had already been partly developed. See *March* v. *Lee*, (1670) 1 Ch. Ca. 162; *Edmunds* v. *Povey*, (1683) 1 Vern. 187; Holdsworth, *History of English Law*, 3rd ed. VI, 663–665. Cf. chaps. III and IV, *infra*.

viii   GENERAL PREFACE

moreover, to another outstanding feature of the history of the English mortgage: its transformation from a form of security with creditor's possession of the *res* into a form of security wherein the debtor retains possession until default in payment. Nor has this evolution of the mortgage into a form of *hypotheca* been studied in isolation; it has been viewed as an integral part of the growth of the mortgagor's equitable right as an estate in land. Mr Turner has not neglected, furthermore, the jurisprudential aspect of his subject, as the chapter on *iura in rem* and *iura in personam* bears witness.

A knowledge of the universal legal history of securities on property helps us to grasp with greater clearness the significance of the English evolution which Mr Turner has sketched. From the age of antiquity down to our own day the conditions of economic and social life, ever in constant process of change, have created various forms of security on property; and in respect of these forms, which have been combined and modified from time to time, rules and doctrines comparable to those developed by our own courts concerning English forms, including the mortgage, have made their appearance. In all, or nearly all, of the world's legal systems there has been a general progress from the forfeit idea to the conception that the gage or pledge is merely collateral security. In many countries, again, the law has recognized not only forms of security where possession of the property is delivered at once to the creditor, but also forms where the debtor remains in possession of the *res* until his default in payment of the loan. It may be pointed out, moreover, that the distinction between *vifgage* and *mortgage* has made its appearance in most laws; and that, side by side with the gage or pledge proper, a form of security known as "sale for repurchase" (*Verkauf auf Wiederverkauf, vente à rémére*) has usually arisen. These aspects of the history of securities on property do not exhaust the long list of common developments; but they adequately illustrate the point that the pledge idea has been evolved on parallel lines in many diverse legal systems.[1]

---

[1] See Wigmore, "The Pledge Idea: A Study in Comparative Legal Ideas", *Harvard Law Review*, x, 321–350, 388–417, xi, 18–39, in which the Chaldean, Jewish, Greek, Roman, Mohammedan, Hindu, Japanese, Slavic, Germanic, Scandinavian and French systems of law have been brought under review.

GENERAL PREFACE ix

Some of the forms of security known to ancient law, together with the doctrines that surrounded them, have had a continuous history down to our own times. In many respects Roman law inherited the legal traditions of earlier ages and transmitted them, with modifications, to the medieval and modern world; and of this continuity in legal history the *hypotheca* is sometimes mentioned as a striking illustration. In the middle of the nineteenth century it was in fact held by some civilians that the Roman *hypotheca* was borrowed from the Greek ὑποθήκη.[1] But this view, suggested by the name of the security, appears to be discarded by all scholars of the present day; and, indeed, so far as Roman law is concerned, the term *hypotheca* was applied to a native Roman security some centuries after it had taken its place in the legal life of the Romans.[2] Although, therefore, one may not now safely hold that the Greek security was received into Roman law, it is nevertheless true that the Roman *hypotheca* not only largely displaced the old Roman *fiducia* as a form of security, but also influenced some of the forms of gage in European countries during later ages.[3] That the history of the Roman security has a bearing on the history of the English mortgage will be apparent to the reader of Mr Turner's chapter on the influence of Roman law and the movement towards *hypotheca*.

In addition to continuity there has also been parallelism in the history of securities on property. When closely related to continuity parallelism in the growth of forms within two or more systems may be due to common legal origins and reciprocal legal influences. As already observed, comparative studies have shown us that, in response to similar economic and social developments, essentially the same forms of security take their place in each of many legal systems, and that, underlying the evolution of the forms of each system, the security idea has gradually displaced the earlier and more primitive idea of the forfeiture of the property for non-payment of debt. But, while there has been this marked development of similar forms and

---

[1] E.g., Dernburg, *Pfandrecht*, I, 50–95.
[2] See, e.g., Joers, *Römische Rechtswissenschaft der Republik*, pp. 108 *seq.*; Cuq, *Manuel des Institutions juridiques des Romains*, 2nd ed. pp. 663 *seq.*; Girard, *Manuel élémentaire de Droit Romain*, 8th ed. pp. 816 *seq.*
[3] For German law, see Dernburg, *op. cit.* I and II, *passim.*

TER

GENERAL PREFACE

doctrines in many systems, parallelism in the history of the "pledge idea" has not always been accompanied by continuity; and it is not to be assumed that the forms and ideas of later ages are merely the modification of those of earlier times. Hypothecations of property—that is, forms of security where the debtor remains in possession until default—offer a notable example of parallelism; but since, in the course of world history, these forms make their appearance in many diverse legal systems, eastern as well as western, it cannot be held, in the present state of our knowledge, that all these forms of hypothecation have been derived from a common source in one of the ancient systems of law. It is not true, as we have already seen, that the Greek ὑποθήκη was the source of the Roman *hypotheca*; but it is an established historical fact that the Roman *hypotheca* helped to shape the hypothecary forms known to Germanic systems. At the same time it should be observed that before the spread of Romanic legal influence in the West early Germanic law had already developed the *jüngere satzung*, a form of security by which, in contrast with the *ältere satzung*, the debtor retained possession. The *jüngere satzung* was a Germanic parallel to the hypothecary forms of Greek and Roman law; and after the Reception of Roman law it was transformed into the modern *hypothek* of German law. This modern *hypothek*, as Gierke has remarked, "hat nicht nur den Namen, sondern auch einen Teil ihres Wesens dem fremden Rechte entlehnt. Allein die schöpferischen Gedanken, denen sie ihre äussere und innere Bildung verdankt, entstammen der jüngeren Satzung und dem Rentenkauf".[1] Thus, in the history of the German *hypothek* we have a striking illustration of parallelism without continuity combined with parallelism based on continuity; and it is possible that the history of our English forms of security, if carefully examined from this special view-point, might present us with further examples. Several forms of hypothecation were known to English law before the chancery transformed the common-law mortgage into a security fundamentally similar to the Roman *hypotheca*.[2] It would seem that some of

[1] Gierke, *Deutsches Privatrecht*, II, 829.
[2] See Hazeltine, *Geschichte des englischen Pfandrechts*, pp. 261–305.

GENERAL PREFACE

these English hypothecations, including the mortgage itself in this form, have their historical roots in Germanic custom and that they have been subjected to at least an indirect influence of the Roman *hypotheca*. If further research should prove conclusively that English hypothecations have been the result of both Germanic and Roman factors in legal growth, the English development, not less than the German, would present us with an illustration of parallelism based on a combination of native and foreign elements.

Before the rise of the chancery the early common-law courts developed a rudimentary equity which, although it was in decay by the early fourteenth century, left its traces in the later law. In the time of Henry II an equity of redemption and a decree of foreclosure were incident to the form of gage described by Glanvill,[1] but this early equity of the debtor, which appears not to have been regarded as in the nature of an estate in the land, had become obsolete by the time of Edward I;[2] and, moreover, in this connection, it is to be remembered that the Glanvillian gage was a conveyance on condition precedent,[3] while the Littletonian or common-law mortgage was a conveyance on condition subsequent.[4] One of the most distinctive features of the history of the common-law mortgage has been the gradual development of the debtor's right of redemption into an equitable estate in the land. At any rate since Lord Hardwicke's time, as Mr Turner explains, the debtor's equity of redemption has been treated, not less than the equity of the beneficiary in a trust, as an equitable estate; and, since this concept has become so much a part of English juridical thought, its place in universal legal history, as a special manifestation of the spirit of English law, has not always received due consideration. In one of its main aspects the debtor's right of redemption, viewed in

---

[1] Glanvill, x, 6–8.
[2] Britton, Book III, Chap. xv, 6 (Nichols' ed. II, 128).
[3] See Hazeltine, "Early English Equity" (*Essays in Legal History*, ed. Vinogradoff, pp. 261–285), at pp. 265–267.
[4] Both these forms of conditional conveyance for purposes of security were known to Germanic law on the Continent; and like the securities described by Glanvill and Littleton they were forms of property-gage, as distinct from usufruct-gages. See Huebner, *History of Germanic Private Law* (Continental Legal History Series), pp. 375–377.

b 2

GENERAL PREFACE

equity as an estate, is a mitigation of the rigour of the common-law conception of a mortgage; for, even after the legal day for redemption has passed and the land has been forfeited at law for non-payment of the debt, the chancery allows redemption. Are there, we may now ask, similar developments in any of the other legal systems known to history? Are there foreign parallels to the English right of redemption as an equitable estate of the mortgagor? If we were seeking merely for mitigation of legal rigour, a relief granted to the debtor in order to prevent the forfeiture of his *res* for non-payment of the debt at a fixed time, our question would be ridiculously easy to answer. Studies in comparative legal history have revealed to us that in many legal systems, at an earlier or a later stage of their development, clemency has been shown to debtors in the matter of redemption. Indeed, in some early systems of security on property the debtor has not been tied to any time for payment and has been free to redeem his *res* whenever he saw fit.[1] But, apart from this feature of some of the forms of security known to legal history, there are many instances where the law has not allowed final forfeiture of the *res* on default in payment at a fixed day, but has given to the debtor liberal additional times for redemption.[2] When we look for parallels with the English equity of redemption we are seeking to find not only a softening of strict law on principles of natural justice, but, in addition, a duality of law and equity with its resultant duality of both personal and proprietary rights. What we are really trying to discover, in other words, are legal systems which, like the English, display a legal ownership in the creditor and an equitable ownership in the debtor; and it is precisely this duality of ownerships, a duality comparable to the legal estate of the mortgagee and the equitable estate of the mortgagor in English law, which seems to elude us. It is true that duality of laws and duality of rights are found in systems other than the

---

[1] See, e.g., Kohler, *Pfandrechtliche Forschungen*, p. 123 n. 1. In the case of the Roman *fiducia cum creditore*, as we shall see presently, the debtor's right to redeem the *res* was not, apart from special agreement, originally restricted to any definite point of time. Undue delay, however, might result in legal process by the creditor.

[2] See, e.g., Kohler, *op. cit.* pp. 30–34, 99, 123–128, 137.

GENERAL PREFACE

xiii

English; but when in these systems the rights of the creditor and of the debtor, in respect of the *res*, are examined with care, it is found that only in a restricted sense can they be regarded as analogous to the legal and equitable estates of the parties in the English mortgage. While, however, no other system of justice seems to have evolved a proprietary interest exactly parallel with the mortgagor's equity of redemption in English law, the study of these other systems, from the special view-point of the debtor's right, will throw at least some illumination upon the nature of the equity of redemption itself; for not alone the contrasts, but also the similarities, between the debtor's right in foreign securities and the debtor's right in the English mortgage seem only to emphasize the point that, as gradually shaped by the English chancery, the equity of redemption is unique in the legal history of the world. It is, indeed, as unique as the trust concept of English law, and for a like reason. Just as the trustee's legal estate in the land existed side by side with the equitable estate of the *cestui que trust*, similarly equity regarded the mortgagor's interest as an equitable estate existing side by side with the legal estate of the mortgagee.

History presents us with many forms of property-gage similar to the common-law mortgage: and one of these, the Roman *fiducia*, has been frequently mentioned by scholars as analogous to the English form. Comparisons of the mortgage and the *fiducia* have been, however, somewhat superficial; they have failed to take into account the fundamental differences between the two forms. A short account of the *fiducia*, on historical and juristic lines, may help us, therefore, to envisage the English mortgage on the background of this Roman form of security; and, above all, a study of this character, even though it be brief, should cause the equitable estate of the mortgagor to stand out in clearer relief as one of the most notable of all the English contributions to legal thought.

II

In some of its many applications the *fiducia* of Roman law bears, in fact, a striking resemblance both to the trust and the

xiv GENERAL PREFACE

mortgage of English law.[1] In the *ius rerum* its applications, according to Gaius, fell into two classes—*fiducia cum creditore* and *fiducia cum amico*. *Fiducia cum creditore* was the most ancient of the Roman forms of security for loan; and, while it survived long after the classical age, it had then been largely superseded by *pignus* and *hypotheca*, to both of which it had contributed some of its features.[2] *Fiducia cum creditore* was a dual transaction, or, to be more precise, a combination of two separate and distinct transactions. The first of these was a conveyance from the debtor to the creditor of the quiritarian ownership of the *res* by either *mancipatio* or *in iure cessio*, but not by *traditio*; while the second, known to civilians as the *pactum fiduciae*, was an agreement between the debtor and the creditor governing the ultimate disposition of the *res* as security for the loan.[3] As a result of the conveyance the *fiduciarius* became at once *dominus*, or owner, of the *res*; and as such he had all the rights of ownership, including the right of sale. He also acquired, in the case of movables, immediate possession of the *res*; and although the form of conveyance usually employed, the

[1] M. Pierre Lepaulle, in "Civil Law Substitutes for Trusts", an article recently published in the *Yale Law Journal*, has drawn attention to the fact that the *fiducia*, dormant for centuries, may still be regarded as an institution of the civil law and could be employed as a real substitute for the trust in civil law jurisdictions. He points out that in the province of Quebec, where the civil law prevails, the *fiducia* now serves the purposes of the trust, and he proposes that in other regions of civil law the *fiducia*, which has recently been recognized by courts as perfectly legal, should be revived and developed on lines similar to the trust of English law.

[2] It should be mentioned in passing that between *pignus* and *hypotheca* there was "in strictness no legal difference". See, further, Buckland, *Roman Law from Augustus to Justinian*, p. 475.

Since *fiducia cum creditore* was the most ancient of the Roman forms, it might be thought that it was also more distinctively Roman than either *pignus* or *hypotheca*. But this can hardly be true; for, as Dr Buckland has reminded the present writer, the Roman *hypotheca*, fundamentally different from the Greek ὑποθήκη, was at least as different from the Greek form as the *fiducia* was from its Greek parallel, and in neither case was there direct affiliation.

[3] On the *fiducia cum creditore*, see Oertmann, *Die Fiducia im römischen Privatrecht*, §§ 10–30; Dernburg, *Pfandrecht*, I, 7–26; Karlowa, *Römische Rechtsgeschichte*, II, 1, 560-575; Puchta, *Institutionen*, 10th ed. (Krüger), II, § 247; Esmein, *Manuel élémentaire de Droit Romain*, 3rd ed. pp. 514-520; Buckland, *op. cit.* pp. 427-430, 470-478.

Normally *fiducia cum creditore*, as a juristic entity, is a combination of *three* separate legal transactions: (1) the debt obligation, protected by action; (2) the conveyance of the *res*; (3) the *pactum fiduciae*.

GENERAL PREFACE

mancipatio, did not require delivery of possession in the case of immovables, in general the debtor placed the creditor in possession, save when, as frequently happened, the creditor left the *res* in the debtor's hands as a *precarium.*[1] Since by force of the conveyance the creditor acquired full *dominium,* any restrictions on his proprietary rights, being matter of contract, were embodied in the *pactum fiduciae,* a parasitic *obligatio* distinct from the conveyance but attaching to it. The creditor, in other words, was under the obligation of exercising his proprietary rights in consonance with the *pactum fiduciae;* and in truth it was this agreement between the parties which gave *fiducia cum creditore* its distinctive features as a form of security on property.

Based on the *pactum fiduciae* was the debtor's right to redeem the *res* by due payment of the debt;[2] and for the protection of this right he had the personal *actio fiduciae,* which enabled him to compel a reconveyance of the *res* by the creditor. The *fiducia* itself was *bonae fidei negotium;* and hence the debtor's *actio fiduciae* was not *stricti iuris,* but perhaps the oldest of the *bonae fidei actiones.* Since the debtor's action was *bonae fidei* the judge possessed a wide discretion; and in large measure it was the exercise of this judicial discretion which gave to the *fiducia,* more and more, the character of a security on property. Although the debtor could bring his *actio fiduciae,* to compel a reconveyance of the *res,* only after full payment of the debt, *satisfactio* was treated as equivalent to *solutio.*[3]

Originally, apart from special agreement, the debtor's right

---

[1] See Dernburg, *op. cit.* I, 17. Cf. Oertmann, *op. cit.* § 21. The question may be raised as to whether, in *mancipatio,* there was any difference between movables and immovables as to the need of transfer of possession. It is likely that in very early times it had to pass in both cases; in the time of the classical law it does not seem that it need pass in either.

[2] It should be pointed out that in the following account of the debtor's right to redeem, including the restriction of this right by inserting clauses, such as the *lex commissoria* and the *pactum de vendendo,* in the *pactum fiduciae,* the writer has relied chiefly on Dernburg, *op. cit.* I, 13–22. In these pages Dernburg may have read some things into the *fiducia* that are true of the *pignus:* but at the same time it must be remembered that many rules of *fiducia cum creditore* had been applied to *pignus.* See Buckland, *op. cit.* p. 428.

[3] Dernburg, *op. cit.* I, 13–16. On the *actio fiduciae,* see also Oertmann, *op cit.* § 30.

xvi   GENERAL PREFACE

of redemption was not restricted to any set day, but when the debtor was so much in delay with his payment as to cause hardship to the creditor, the creditor could, by legal process, free himself from his obligation to reconvey the *res* to the debtor. In addition to his proprietary rights in the *res*, the creditor had a personal claim against the debtor for the repayment of the loan, and indeed, by the *pactum fiduciae*, the creditor held the *res* merely as security for the loan. When, therefore, the debtor failed to pay, the creditor could bring his personal action on the debt claim, and by process of execution in this action, which resulted in a sale of the *res* to some third party, not only was the creditor relieved of his obligation to reconvey to the debtor, but the debtor's right of redemption was extinguished.[1]

Owing to inconveniences attaching to the security in this form it gradually became usual to insert clauses in the *pactum fiduciae* restricting the debtor's right of redemption. In the simplest of these clauses the redemption of the *res* was limited to a definite period of time: and in such case the failure of the debtor to pay within the fixed period resulted both in the absolute forfeiture of the *res* to the creditor and in the extinguishment of his personal claim against the debtor. This forfeiture clause, known as *lex commissoria*, was not an essential part of *fiducia cum creditore*, as some of the older civilians had thought, but it was very generally employed in the republican era. Since his slightest failure to pay by a set day resulted in absolute forfeiture of the *res* to the creditor, the *lex commissoria* was hard on the debtor; and, owing to the growth of the principle that the creditor could avail himself of only one of two remedies, either the forfeiture of the *res* or the personal action against the debtor, the clause as to forfeiture also proved to be, on the whole, disadvantageous to the creditor himself.[2]

These considerations led to a further development. It became usual to insert in the *pactum fiduciae* a clause, known as the

---

[1] Dernburg, *op. cit.* I, 18, 19.
[2] Dernburg, *op. cit.* I, 19, 20. On the *lex commissoria* see also Oertmann, *op. cit.* § 27.

GENERAL PREFACE

pactum de vendendo, which empowered the creditor, on non-payment of the debt at the fixed time, to sell the *res*;[1] and in such case the proceeds of the sale were reckoned, in accordance with their amount, either as a total or a partial extinguishment of the debt. In case the proceeds of the sale exceeded the amount of the debt, the creditor was obliged to pay the surplus to the debtor; and, where the proceeds of the sale were not sufficient to cover the entire debt, the creditor was permitted to bring his personal action against the debtor for the payment of the balance. The elaboration of these and other legal principles in regard to the *pactum de vendendo*, a development which appears to have fallen in the last centuries of the republican age, proves to us that the law concerning *fiducia cum creditore* had passed beyond the stage of strictness, represented by the *lex commissoria*, and had entered into a period of greater flexibility. Not only was the *pactum de vendendo* much fairer than the *lex commissoria* to both parties, but as developed by the law it transformed the *fiducia* into a true security on property. While this process of growth made for greater complexity in the relations of the parties, it expressed at the same time a milder temper in the law itself; and in no respect is this more noticeable than in the law's more equitable treatment of the debtor. Thus, in effecting a sale of the *res* the creditor could proceed either by private sale or by public auction; but in either case, before the sale could take place, he was required to give the debtor notice (*denuntiatio*), probably at three different times. Even though the period fixed in the *pactum de vendendo* had passed without payment by the debtor the creditor was obliged, therefore, to permit him further opportunity to redeem the *res*; and, to all seeming, if on payment, or tender of payment, the creditor refused to reconvey, the debtor could bring his *actio fiduciae* against the creditor and compel him to remancipate the *res*. If after *denuntiatio* the debtor still failed to redeem, the creditor could then sell the *res*; but, before doing so, he was

---

[1] It should be pointed out that a *pactum de vendendo* was not necessary to enable the fiduciary to give a good title; but, while it was immaterial for this, a *pactum de vendendo* would prevent the sale from being a breach of contract. No doubt the restrictions on sale introduced in post-classical times applied also to *fiducia*; but in that late age *fiducia* was in decay.

xviii GENERAL PREFACE

required to give public notice of the sale (*proscriptio*).[1] In the interests of the debtor the further principle was laid down that the creditor, who already had the *dominium*, was not allowed to buy the *res*, free from the *fiducia*, either directly or indirectly; and hence, when the *res* was sold to a third person acting as an intermediary on behalf of the creditor, the debtor could treat the sale as without legal significance, and, on tendering payment of the debt, require a conveyance of the *res* to himself. Frequently, however, the debtor gave his permission for such a sale; and in all such cases he renounced his right to recover the *res*.[2]

Attention has been drawn to the point that before the debtor could compel a reconveyance of the *res* by means of his *actio fiduciae*, he must have paid his debt in full (*solutio*) or otherwise rendered its equivalent (*satisfactio*). Although in strict law the creditor in possession, since he was *dominus*, was entitled to the fruits of the *res*, it is possible that even in the earliest times they were treated as equivalent to the interest on the loan.[3] However this may have been, in the later development of the *fiducia* it was a definite rule that the creditor in possession was required to reckon the fruits of the *res* towards principal and interest; and as soon as they covered both these sums the debtor could then compel, by means of his *actio fiduciae*, a remancipation of the *res*.[4] Although this rule is instructive as showing us that the Roman *fiducia* and certain forms of security in other systems, such as the English *vivum vadium* in its later development,[5] possessed a common element in the reckoning of fruits towards the extinguishment of both debt and interest, its chief significance in the present connection concerns the debtor's fiduciary right of redemption. The existence of the rule is in fact further evidence that the law regarded the *res* as only a security; for as soon as the creditor had received the principal and interest

[1] Puchta, *op. cit.* II, § 247 (at p. 247 n. 1); Dernburg, *op. cit.* I, 20, 21. Cf. Roby, *Roman Private Law*, I, 99. It should be pointed out that the textual authority for *denuntiatio* and *proscriptio* is very slight.

[2] On the *pactum de vendendo*, see Dernburg, *op. cit.* I, 20–22; Oertmann, *op. cit.* § 26.

[3] When the debtor was in possession, under a lease or a *precarium*, the fruits belonged to him.   [4] Dernburg, *op. cit.* I, 18.

[5] See Hazeltine, *Geschichte des englischen Pfandrechts*, p. 209.

GENERAL PREFACE

by any mode, whether it be *solutio, satisfactio*, or usufruct, the debtor was then entitled to a reconveyance.[1]

The treatment of the *res* as a mere security is evidenced by other rules applied to the *fiducia cum creditore*. Thus, although the creditor was the owner of the *res*, he was responsible to the debtor in the *actio fiduciae* for *culpa, diligentia diligentis patrisfamilias*, and, possibly, *custodia*;[2] while, on the other hand, he was not answerable in case of accident. The risk of accident was borne entirely by the debtor; and when the *res* was accidentally injured or destroyed, as by water or fire, the loss fell upon him. In case the *res* was totally destroyed by accident the debtor's right of redemption appears to have been regarded as completely extinguished. Despite loss by accident, however, the creditor's personal action of debt remained unaffected; and by its means he could recover from the debtor the full amount of the loan.[3] These principles resulted from the fact that the *fiducia* was treated as *bonae fidei negotium*; and they illustrate in a striking manner the distinction between strict law and *aequitas*.[4] At law the *res* was in the ownership of the creditor; and yet in *aequitas*, since the risk of loss by accident fell on the debtor, it was treated as in some measure belonging to him.[5]

The debtor's right to redeem the *res* was strengthened, or intensified, by the rule that under certain circumstances the creditor might be punished by *infamia*. When the debtor, having paid the debt, brought the *actio fiduciae* for a reconveyance, the creditor was obliged to restore the thing *in natura*, and, if before condemnation in the action he had failed to remancipate, he was liable to *infamia*, with its resulting disqualifications.[6] This rule further illustrates the point that the

---

[1] Dernburg, *op. cit.* I, 16, 18.

[2] Although Dernburg, *op. cit.* I, 14, states that the fiduciary was liable for *custodia*, this may be questioned. Dr Buckland has drawn the attention of the present writer to the point that Seckel, who finds *custodia* very readily, expressly excludes it in *fiducia*, though he finds it in *pignus*. See Heumann-Seckel, *Handlexicon, s.v.* Custodia.

[3] Dernburg, *op. cit.* I, 13, 14.

[4] See Buckland, *op. cit.* p. 55, on the several meanings of *aequitas*. The term was applied by the classical jurists to that part of the law in which the *iudices* had a freer hand, as, for example, in *bonae fidei iudicia*.

[5] See Dernburg, *op. cit.* I, 14.

[6] Dernburg, *op. cit.* I, 16.

GENERAL PREFACE

law treated the *fiducia* as *bonae fidei negotium*; and it also shows us that the convèyance to the creditor was merely as a security for debt.

With this rule as to the creditor's *infamia* should be contrasted the astounding fact that in the case of the *fiducia* the Romans did not treat the unauthorized asportation of the *res* by the debtor, in circumstances in which he could usucapt, as *furtum*.[1] It is true that by the taking the debtor had infringed the creditor's proprietary right and that the creditor could legally recover the *res* from him; but yet the debtor was not regarded by the law as a thief. The explanation of this somewhat strange principle is to be found, perhaps, in the antagonism between the strictly legal and juristic construction of the *fiducia* on the one hand and the customary view of the transaction taken by the parties and by society on the other hand. In strict legal theory the *res* belonged to the creditor; while in the mind of the debtor and of the community it was regarded as still the debtor's *res*. In the rule as to *furtum* the law itself gave expression to this popular conception.[2]

Closely related to the rule in regard to *furtum* is *usureceptio ex fiducia*,[3] a form of acquisition analogous to *usucapio* which shows us that, although the debtor had parted with all rights *in rem*, he could reacquire them by a mode other than reconveyance by the creditor, namely, possession of the *res* for a certain time.[4] Fully stated the rule was that "a *res* conveyed subject to *fiducia* could be reacquired by getting possession without good faith and holding for a year".[5] Not only in cases where the debtor wrongfully retook possession of the *res* by asportation, but also where, after the mancipation to the creditor, he remained in possession, he was allowed, unless he

[1] If the debtor held the thing *precario*, and made away with it, he was guilty of *furtum*.

[2] See Dernburg, *op. cit.* 1, 24, 25. Dernburg makes the statement that the debtor, in the case of the *fiducia*, was not guilty of *furtum*: this is somewhat too sweeping. All that his authority says is that it was not *furtum* for the debtor to take the *res* in circumstances in which he could usucapt.

[3] See Gaius, 2. 59–60; *ibid.* 3. 201; Dernburg, *op. cit.* 1, 23–26; Buckland, *op. cit.* p. 245.

[4] Gaius, 2. 59: "quae species usucapionis dicitur usureceptio, quia id quod aliquando habuimus recipimus per usucapionem".

[5] Buckland, *op. cit.* p. 245.

GENERAL PREFACE

held the *res* on hire or as a *precarium*, to become *dominus* by *usureceptio*. On the basis of his former *dominium* he was regarded as holding possession *pro suo*; and hence his possession was not treated, socially, as one in which *mala fides* was present.[1] For the acquisition of *dominium* by *usureceptio* it was immaterial whether the debtor had or had not paid the debt, but where he obtained possession from the creditor by hiring or *precarium*, either at the date of mancipation to the creditor or later, he could not reckon time against the creditor for purposes of *usureceptio* during the period of the hiring or the *precarium*, for during such period he held for the creditor. Although *precarium* was much employed as a means of preventing *usureceptio*, payment of the debt terminated the *precarium*; and from that moment onwards time could be reckoned towards the period required in order to obtain title by *usureceptio*. While, therefore, as already mentioned, the law allowed acquisition of title by *usureceptio* irrespective of the payment of the debt, that fact was nevertheless material in respect of the *causa possessionis*. If the debt had been paid, the *usureceptio* was effective, whatever may have been the debtor's *causa possessionis*; but, when the debt had not been paid, possession derived from the creditor prevented, during the continuance of such possession, the running of time in favour of the debtor.[2] While it seems surprising that the law allowed *usureceptio* in cases where the debt had not yet been paid, this feature of *usureceptio*, and indeed *usureceptio ex fiducia* in general, can hardly be explained as a manifestation of early Roman *aequitas*.[3] The debtor was merely recovering by *usureceptio* his own former *dominium*; and in his favour, it is true, there was a mitigation of the general principles of *usucapio*. At the same time, unless the creditor's interests were safeguarded by a *precarium*, which would prevent *usureceptio*, the debtor's recovery of the *res* by this mode unquestionably worked injustice to the creditor by depriving him of the

---

[1] Dernburg, *op. cit.* I, 25. Dr Buckland, *op. cit.* p. 245, treats *usureceptio ex fiducia* as one of several cases, under the general heading of *usucapio*, where *bona fides* was not required.

[2] Gaius, 2. 60.

[3] Dr Buckland, *op. cit.* p. 245, rightly regards the *restrictions* on *usureceptio ex fiducia* as an expression of *aequitas*.

xxii GENERAL PREFACE

res which he had acquired as security for the debt. In still another respect the law favoured the debtor. *Usucapio* proper required uninterrupted possession for one year of movables, two years in the case of land; but for *usureceptio* one year's possession, which apparently need not be continuous,[1] was enough in the case of both movables and immovables alike. While one reason for this clemency to debtors may well have been the interpretation placed upon the wording of the Twelve Tables in regard to *usucapio*,[2] no doubt, as Dernburg suggests, it is also to be explained as proceeding from a general desire of society to benefit the debtor class at the expense of creditors. Whatever the reason lying back of them may have been, the rules in regard to *usureceptio* enabled the debtor, irrespective of the payment of the debt, to reacquire *dominium* within a comparatively short period of time, namely, one year.[3]

Even before reconveyance or usureception, both of which modes revested the *dominium* in the debtor, he had the right not only to sell the *res*, but also to leave it as a legacy *per praeceptionem* to one of his heirs. Both of these rights, startling as they may seem at first sight, are to be looked upon, however, as being merely incidental to the debtor's right of redemption. Subject to restrictions imposed by the *pactum fiduciae*, notably the *lex commissoria* and the *pactum de vendendo*, the debtor had the right to redeem the *res* at any time. There was nothing in Roman law to prevent the sale of a third person's property; but in such case the vendor was obliged to acquire title from the third person or induce him to convey to the purchaser.[4] If, therefore, the debtor found a purchaser, he could contractually sell the *res* to him. Out of the proceeds of the sale, or with other funds at his disposal, the debtor could then exercise his right of

---

[1] See Dernburg, *op. cit.* I, 25.

[2] I.e. the *res*, itself known as *fiducia*, was regarded not as *fundus*, but as falling among the *caeterae res*.

[3] Dernburg's remarks on *usureceptio ex fiducia*, *op. cit.* I, 25–26, are partly vitiated by the fact that when he wrote, in 1860, no one knew that *bona fides* was not an original part of the law of *usucapio*. As Dr Buckland has remarked, *op. cit.* p. 245: "It is difficult to see why [the rule as to *usureceptio ex fiducia*] was allowed at all, or rather, as no doubt it antedates the rule of *bona fides*, why it was allowed to survive in a time when, unlike *usucapio pro herede*, it served no useful purpose, but was a mere injustice".

[4] Buckland, *op. cit.* p. 481.

GENERAL PREFACE xxiii

redemption by paying the debt, insist on a reconveyance to himself, and, since he was once more *dominus*, transfer the *res* to his purchaser.[1] Again, as already observed, even when *dominium* was still in the creditor, the debtor might by his will leave the *res* to one of his heirs *per praeceptionem*, which was one of the several recognized forms of legacy. While it was the opinion of the Sabinians that in general nothing could be left as a legacy by preception that was not the property of the testator, Gaius, who belonged to the school, tells us that there is one case in which they admit that "what belongs to a third party may be legated by preception, namely, when a man has legated a thing, which he has fiduciarily mancipated to a creditor; for they hold it to be within the powers of the judge to require the co-heirs, by payment of the debt, to release the thing in question, that so he to whom it has been legated may take it by preception".[2]

The view has been expressed by a modern civilian that the debtor who had conveyed a *res* to his creditor, under a *fiducia*, "was regarded still as owner, potential if not actual; he could bequeath his 'equity of redemption' as we should call it, by the form called *praeceptio*";[3] while still another Romanist of our own time has said that "even before reconveyance or usureception, the debtor had thus far still an equitable interest in [the *res*],—that if he legated it by preception to one of several heirs, the others had to redeem it".[4] These explanations of the legacy *per praeceptionem* in terms of English equitable estates and interests may easily be misleading; for too much is thereby imported into the debtor's right to redeem the *res* held by the creditor as quiritarian owner under a *fiducia*. The *legatum per praeceptionem*, the precursor of the *praelegatum* of later law, was a benefit given to one heir over the rest in addition to his share of the inheritance. The donee was both an heir, and, as regards his co-heirs, also legatee: and he was entitled to the legacy before the estate was divided. The true explanation of the legacy in question, in the case of *fiducia*, appears to be merely this: The

---

[1] Roby, *op. cit.* II, 100; Buckland, *op. cit.* p. 471.
[2] Gaius, 2. 220.
[3] Roby, *op. cit.* II, 100.
[4] Muirhead, *Institutes of Gaius*, 1904, p. 497.

xxiv GENERAL PREFACE

debtor's right of redemption devolves on the legatee's co-heirs and they may be compelled to exercise the right by paying the debt and securing a conveyance of the *res* to the legatee. This is in essence only what Gaius himself, our principal authority on the matter, tells us. The gift to the legatee is not direct, for the donor has no *dominium* in the *res*. The gift is in a sense indirect; and it is effected through the imposition of an obligation on the co-heirs to redeem the *res* for the benefit of the legatee. The description of the Roman debtor's right as an "equity of redemption", or as an "equitable interest", is not misleading only if we hold in mind the true nature and meaning of the fiduciary transaction and refuse to import into it English equitable ideas that are foreign to the Roman system. The use of the terms "equity of redemption" and "equitable interest" in reference to the debtor's fiduciary right of redemption is in fact a rhetorical flourish on the part of jurists to indicate the parallel to be found in the English mortgagor's equity of redemption as an estate in land. There are striking similarities between the Roman *fiducia cum creditore* and the English mortgage; and, indeed, even the Roman debtor's right of redemption and the English debtor's right or "equity" of redemption possess features in common. The differences between the *fiducia* and the mortgage, and not least of all the distinctions which affect the nature of the debtor's right of redemption in the two forms of security, are, however, not less striking than their similarities. Only by comparison, and comparison, moreover, which proceeds on historical as well as theoretical lines, are these similarities and differences revealed.

III

In speaking of the *fiducia cum creditore*, Roby has remarked that "the English mortgage forms a striking analogy to the Roman and was probably derived from it".[1] While no doubt the analogy is close, it can hardly be true that the English mortgage was modelled on the Roman *fiducia*. Two facts alone should serve to dispel any notion of copying; for not only was the juridical basis of the two forms of security different, as we

---

[1] Roby, *op. cit.* II, 99 n. I.

GENERAL PREFACE xxv

shall see presently, but the English mortgage has passed through the same stages of historical development as those which marked the evolution of the Roman *fiducia*.[1] Neither of these forms of security originated in a very early period of legal development: both of them have been regarded as largely the product of juristic speculation.[2] In each of them the *res* itself was the subject-matter of the security: both of them were forms of property-gage or substance-gage, as opposed to pure usufruct-gages. In each of them existing modes of conveyance, already well recognized for other purposes, were used for the vesting of ownership in the creditor; and in each of them, moreover, contract was combined with conveyance in order to give legal effect to the idea of security for debt. In the case of each of these forms of security, again, the narrowness of the legal basis, which consisted of a transfer of ownership to the creditor, and also the strictness with which that basis was viewed by the lawyers, necessitated an elaborate superstructure with its resultant complication of legal rules. Not only in the Roman *fiducia*, but also in the English mortgage, the mode of conveyance employed was one that required formality and publicity;[3] and yet in each instance, by a species of fiction, these characteristics were ultimately retained only in a vastly attenuated form by the use of a document.[4] The gradual transformation of both

[1] Franken, *Französisches Pfandrecht*, p. 167: "Aus inneren Gründen kann das Mortgage des Littleton kein Abkömmling der römischen Pfandfiducia sein, weil es eben selbst alle historischen Phasen derselben wiederholt. Es ist original englisch—wenn es sich auch nicht ohne Befruchtung mit römischer Rechtslogik entwickelt hat".

[2] Dernburg, *op. cit.* I, 10, stresses this point in reference to the *fiducia cum creditore*. For the English mortgage, see Holdsworth, *op. cit.* 3rd ed. III, 130. There can be little doubt, however, that, in the case of the *fiducia* and the mortgage alike, practice preceded speculation. In the case of the *fiducia* it would seem that the praetor gave sanction to a common practice and that then the lawyers began the process of elaboration. See Girard, *op. cit.* p. 556. Similarly, the mortgage appears to have been in use before the courts began to weave theories in regard to it.

[3] In the case of the *fiducia* these features were incident to *mancipatio* and *in iure cessio*, the forms of conveyance employed. See Dernburg, *op. cit.* I, 8–10. Similarly in the case of the mortgage they were incident to the conveyance, namely, feoffment with livery of seisin. See Holdsworth, *op. cit.* III, 219–234.

[4] See Dernburg, *op. cit.* I, 93–95; Franken, *op. cit.* pp. 92, 156, 160–162, 168; Holdsworth, *Historical Introduction to the Land Law*, pp. 110–116;

GENERAL PREFACE

forms of security proceeded, in fact, on similar lines. In the case of the *fiducia*, not less than in that of the mortgage, the principles of *ius strictum* were modified by *aequitas*. In both forms the creditor in possession was obliged to reckon the fruits of the *res* in reduction of the debt and interest; and in both, again, the creditor, ·although entitled to possession, usually permitted the debtor to retain it, *precario* in the one case and "at sufferance"[1] in the other. Moreover, both in the *fiducia* and in the mortgage the principle of forfeiture for non-payment at a fixed time was ultimately eliminated: in the case of the *fiducia*, as indeed for all forms of security on property, the *lex commissoria* was forbidden by Constantine,[2] while in the case of the mortgage the forfeiture, although it continued to be theoretically operative at law, was prevented in practice by means of the equity of redemption. Although in their earlier history both the *fiducia* and the mortgage were forms of forfeiture-gage, in course of time each of them was transformed into a sale-gage. As already remarked, a power of sale was incident to the *dominium* which the fiduciary had acquired and he could give a good title quite apart from any express power of sale; while, similarly, the mortgagee, being seized in fee, needed no express power of sale to enable him to convey title to a purchaser. In the *fiducia* and the mortgage alike, however, an express power of sale, based on the contract of the parties, was introduced; and in each case a power of sale was ultimately regarded as implied.[3]

Williams, *Law of Real Property*, 24th ed. (Eastwood) pp. 210–249, 653–663. On the question as to whether, even in classical law, the *mancipatio* as a form of conveyance had ceased to be real and was practically replaced by the written document, see Buckland, *op. cit.* pp. 237–8. Dernburg's remarks *loc. cit.*, on the use of a documentary *mancipatio* in *fiducia cum creditore* refer to a very late period when the *hypotheca* had almost completely displaced the earlier form of security. In England the statute 8 & 9 Victoria, c. 106, § 2 (1845), providing that corporeal as well as incorporeal things should lie in grant as well as in livery, was the result of a long historical development.

[1] See pp. 92 *seq.*, 124, *infra*.

[2] Puchta, *op. cit.* II, 248.

[3] On the power of sale in the *fiducia*, see Dernburg, *op. cit.* I, 20–22, Franken, *op. cit.* p. 169; on the mortgagee's power of sale, see Williams, *op. cit.* pp. 669–673. In the case of the *fiducia* one must distinguish (1) the creditor's power of sale incident to his *dominium*, (2) his power of sale based on the *pactum de vendendo*, (3) his implied power of sale in the absence of a *pactum de vendendo*.

GENERAL PREFACE

xxvii

These striking similarities in the history and structure of the *fiducia cum creditore* and the mortgage might easily create the impression that the English form is essentially a copy of the Roman and that in consequence the mortgage represents a marked Romanic influence on the development of English law. Any such idea, however, would violate historical truth. If English conveyancers and judges had consciously followed the pattern of the *fiducia* in the development of the mortgage they would have taken the Roman form of security in its later and not in its earlier structure as their guide; they would, for example, have passed at once to the idea of sale without going through the stage of absolute forfeiture. The mortgage is not Roman; it is a form of security which has its roots in the Germanic middle ages, and not in Roman antiquity, and, while it displays the influence of Roman juristic thought, it represents, not alone in its basis, but also in much of its super-structure, ideas that are foreign to the *fiducia cum creditore*, and also to the *pignus* and *hypotheca*, of the Romans. The differences between the *fiducia* and the mortgage represent fundamental contrasts between Roman and Germanic legal thought, and in any broad comparison of the two forms these distinctions must serve as the starting-point.[1] Without, however, entering this larger realm of jurisprudential contrasts, in which the basic distinctions between Roman law and Germanic law find expression, at least three essential differences between the Roman *fiducia* and the Anglo-Germanic mortgage may be mentioned and briefly considered. These important structural differences concern the form of the conveyance to the creditor, the nature of the debtor's right of redemption, and the transformation of the security into a form of hypothecation.

IV

The conveyance to the creditor by Roman *mancipatio* or *in iure cessio* was absolute; the conveyance to the creditor by English feoffment with livery of seisin was conditional. In the

[1] See, e.g., Carl Adolf Schmidt's enlightening book, *Der principielle Unterschied zwischen dem römischen und germanischen Rechte* (1853); and also Röder, *Grundgedanken und Bedeutung des römischen und germanischen Rechts* (1855). Many later works deal with the same subject.

xxviii   GENERAL PREFACE

period of the development of the *fiducia* the Roman law did not admit forms of conveyance of *dominium* until a fixed day or, in general, under a condition. It is true that *traditio* admitted conditions; but *traditio* could not be used in the case of *fiducia*. In the solemn conveyances by *mancipatio* and *in iure cessio*, the forms used for *fiducia*, such limitations were not permissible: and, as a result, the creditor was given all the rights *in rem* incident to full and unlimited *dominium*. As already remarked, the *pactum fiduciae*, concluded at the time of the conveyance, was an entirely separate transaction and formed no part of the transfer of title. It was not called a contract and it did not figure in the list of contracts; it may be called a *pactum*, but, as Dr Buckland has observed, "it differed from the actionable pacts known in the time of Gaius in that it had an *actio in ius*, a *bonae fidei iudicium*, so that it was not merely pretorian".[1] It was in fact, as we have seen, parasitic in character; it was never an independent transaction, but always an appendage to a conveyance. Its main purpose was the regulation of the ultimate destination of the property conveyed, but it might also contain subsidiary provisions, such as those dealing with the surplus arising from a sale of the *res* conveyed. While the *pactum fiduciae* made it clear that the conveyance to the creditor, legally absolute, was not intended as a sale, but merely for purposes of security, the *pactum* itself was only an *obligatio*; it created only rights *in personam*, as opposed to rights *in rem*. Since it had no *dingliche Kraft*, no proprietary effect, it imported into the conveyance nothing in the nature of a condition; after as before the conclusion of the *pactum* the conveyance itself remained absolute. By force of the conveyance alone, therefore, there could be no talk of a reversion of the *res* to the debtor, *ipso iure*, on payment of the debt; the conveyance was absolute, not conditional. The effect of the *pactum*, however, was to bind the creditor and his successors personally. Their obligation was to reconvey the *res* to the debtor on due payment of the debt; and this obligation could be enforced by the debtor

---

[1] Buckland, *op. cit.* p. 428. Dr Buckland has drawn the present writer's attention to Lenel's view. Lenel now holds that the action was never more than an *actio in factum*, but was nevertheless *bonae fidei*. Cf. Buckland, *op. cit.* p. 429.

GENERAL PREFACE   xxix

by means of his *actio fiduciae*, an action *in personam* based on the *pactum*.[1]

When we turn to the common-law mortgage we find that the conveyance to the creditor was not absolute, but conditional. One of the most distinctive characteristics of English medieval common law was its early, rapid, and fruitful development of conditional gifts;[2] and upon its earlier doctrines in regard to conditions the Italian civilians appear, through Bracton and otherwise, to have exercised some influence.[3] For our present purposes there is no need to penetrate into the earlier history of gages of property in England.[4] Let it be remarked merely that by Littleton's time, and indeed much earlier, a form of security had come into use which was destined to be the classical mortgage of the common law. "If a feoffment be made upon such condition", says Littleton, "that if the feoffor pay to the feoffee at a certain day, etc., £40 of money, that then the feoffor may re-enter, etc., in this case the feoffee is called tenant in mortgage...and if he doth not pay, then the land which is put in pledge upon condition for the payment of the money is taken from him for ever, and so dead to him upon condition, etc. And if he doth pay the money, then the pledge is dead as to the tenant".[5] The essence of the Littletonian mortgage of the fee simple is a conveyance on condition subsequent; and it is in marked contrast with the gages described by Glanvill and Bracton, which were conveyances on condition precedent. In the mortgage explained by Littleton the creditor acquires at once an estate in fee, subject, however, to a condition

---

[1] See Dernburg, *op. cit.* I, 10, 11.
[2] See Pollock and Maitland, *History of English Law*, 2nd ed. II, 17–29.
[3] See Holdsworth, *History of English Law*, 3rd ed. II, 276, 281.
[4] See Pollock and Maitland, *op. cit.* II, 117–124; Holdsworth, *op. cit.* II, 194, 336; III, 128–132; Hazeltine, *op. cit.* pp. 114–115, 164–305.
[5] Littleton, § 332. Littleton, § 333: "Also, as a man may make a feoffment in fee in morgage so a man may make a gift in tayle in morgage, and a lease for terme of life, or for terme of yeares in morgage. And all such tenants are called tenants in morgage, according to the estates which they have in the land, &c." In the present paragraphs attention will be focussed on the "feoffment in fee in morgage", that is, the mortgage of an estate in fee simple. Mortgages of estates tail, life estates, and terms for years demand special consideration. Many principles apply equally, however, to all forms of the Littletonian mortgage.

xxx GENERAL PREFACE

subsequent. If the debt be paid on the day fixed by the parties, the debtor-feoffor, or his heirs, may re-enter, but, if the debt be not so paid, the freehold estate of the creditor-feoffee is freed for ever from the condition and becomes thereby absolute.

The history of conveyance on condition subsequent for purposes of security reaches back to a distant past. Transfers of land on condition subsequent, as security, were part of old Germanic custom. The Anglo-Saxons knew and used a form of gage in which the land was conveyed to the creditor on condition subsequent; and although Glanvill and Bracton do not mention securities containing this form of condition, probably because they fell under the general heading of conditional gifts, they are found, nevertheless, in Bracton's Note Book, the early year books, and other sources long before the time of Littleton.[1]

Nor are these early examples of feoffments on condition subsequent, as security for debt, uninteresting from the point of view of our comparison of the Roman *fiducia cum creditore* and the English mortgage. In some of the charters of feoffment from this pre-Littletonian period there is nothing to indicate that the conveyance was conditional: on the face of the document the conveyance appears to have been absolute. The conditional character of the conveyance, the condition subsequent based on the idea of security for debt, is only revealed by other documentary evidence. In some instances the condition appears in a clause of annulment or defeasance written on the back of the charter which evidences on its face a feoffment absolute in terms; and in still other cases the conditional nature of the feoffment is disclosed only by a second document distinct from the charter of feoffment itself.[2] In these cases we seem to have

[1] References will be found in Hazeltine, *op. cit.* pp. 239–241. There is one brief passage in Britton's account of gage which seems to picture to us the pre-Littletonian mortgage, that is, a conveyance on condition subsequent for purposes of security.

[2] In Edward III's time it appears to have been the custom to employ two deeds. First a deed of feoffment was made; and then by a separate deed it was agreed that if the money was paid within a specified period the feoffment should be void, but that if the money was not so paid the land was to belong to the feoffee and his heirs. An example of one deed, with the condition endorsed on the back, comes to us from the year 1401, while in the nineteenth year of Henry VI's reign a mortgage deed was executed in the modern form. See Holdsworth, *op. cit.* III, p. 130 n. 3.

GENERAL PREFACE

an analogy to the *mancipatio* and the parasitic *pactum fiduciae*; and yet it would be altogether rash to take this semblance of analogy too seriously. Like the *mancipatio* the feoffment, as evidenced by the face of the charter of feoffment, is absolute; and like the *pactum fiduciae* the clause of defeasance, the security agreement, appears as something extraneous to this absolute conveyance, something that is as parasitic as the *pactum fiduciae* itself. Especially when it is written on the back of the charter the clause of defeasance may well appear as something parasitic, something in the nature of a contract which clings to a conveyance that is absolute; and even when the clause of defeasance is contained in a separate instrument it is possible to think of this as a contract independent of, but in a sense annexed to, the conveyance evidenced by the charter of feoffment. In truth the analogy of the *pactum fiduciae* vanishes completely when we recall that after all the deeds are only evidence of the feoffment and that, although on the back of a charter of feoffment, or in a separate instrument, the defeasance forms an integral part of the feoffment itself. By reading the documentary evidences together it is clear that we are in the presence of a feoffment that is far from being absolute; for, both in fact and in law, it is a feoffment subject to a condition subsequent.

The Littletonian mortgage is a feoffment: but not all of the early English conveyances on condition subsequent for purposes of security were feoffments. The Anglo-Saxon gage of land on condition subsequent was a conveyance by land-book; and although the exact point of time at which feoffment took the place of the book may not now be discoverable, it is possible that it was employed long before the time of Bracton, even as early as the Norman age.[1] Without, however, pursuing this problem of origins, let it be observed that the Littletonian security, the earliest form of the classical common law mortgage, embodied a clause of defeasance: failure on the debtor's part to pay on the set day freed the creditor's estate from the condition and made it absolute, whereas due payment at the agreed time defeated the creditor's estate and thus enabled the debtor to

---

[1] See Hazeltine, *op. cit.* pp. 141–145, 239 *seq.*

xxxii   GENERAL PREFACE

re-enter. This early form of mortgage by conveyance on condition subsequent long persisted and was sometimes used as
late as 1840; but it had been obsolete many years before the
recent Property Acts placed the law of mortgage on a new
basis.[1] Although the clause of defeasance long survived it was
practically superseded at a fairly early time, partly as a result of
the growth of equity jurisdiction over mortgages, by a different
form of conveyance. The transfer of the fee to the creditor was
made subject to an express "proviso for redemption", or, in
other words, "proviso for reconveyance": upon payment of the
debt and interest at an appointed day the mortgagee shall
reconvey to the mortgagor.[2] It is clear that in Littleton's time
the earlier form, that is, the one containing a clause of defeasance, was still in general use; for in his account of mortgage
in fee Littleton speaks only of this form.[3] It would seem, in
fact, that the second form, in which on redemption at the set
day the mortgagee shall reconvey, came into use after Littleton
wrote his *Tenures*.[4]

It is true that the gage of land in Anglo-Saxon times, when it
assumed the form of a conveyance upon condition subsequent,
may be viewed as a security which embodied, or implied, a
provision for reconveyance. In this form of "property-gage"
(or, "substance-gage"), not less than in the form known as
"usufruct-gage", possession of the land was delivered to the
creditor; but at the same time, in the case of the property-gage,
the debtor conveyed title to the land, upon condition subse-

[1] The objection to this form was stated by Chitty, L.J., in *Durham
Brothers* v. *Robertson*, [1898] 1 Q.B. at p. 772.
[2] See Butler's note (1) to Co. Litt. 205 a; Leake, *Law of Property in Land*,
2nd ed. pp. 202–203.
[3] Littleton, §§ 332–340.
[4] Cf., however, Holdsworth, *op. cit.* III, 129–130, VII, 375. In the first of
these passages it is stated that the mortgage in fee on condition subsequent,
in the period Henry III—Edward III, involved "a proviso that if the debt
was paid by a fixed date the land should be reconveyed, and this condition
was strictly construed". In the same passage it is also stated that in the early
common-law mortgage in fee the mortgagee "took an estate defeasible upon
condition subsequent". It is submitted that this latter statement correctly
expresses the nature of the common-law mortgage down to Littleton's time:
that is, re-entry by the mortgagor, and not reconveyance by the mortgagee.
After Littleton's time reconveyance could be enforced, and was enforced, by
the chancery.

GENERAL PREFACE

xxxiii

quent, by the delivery of the land-book to the creditor. In outward form the conveyance to the creditor was sometimes absolute; it differed in no respect from a sale. The land-book employed in fact the terminology of sale; it spoke, for example, of the price (*pretium*) paid for the land. In substance, however, the transaction was a conveyance upon condition subsequent for purposes of security; for at the time of the conveyance the parties entered into an agreement that by the repayment of the *pretium* the debtor could redeem the land. On repayment, or redemption, at the time fixed by the parties the creditor not only delivered possession of the land, he also transferred the instrument of title, the land-book, to the debtor. Since in Anglo-Saxon times title to book-land passed by the delivery of the land-book, we may, therefore, look upon this security-transaction as a form of conveyance upon condition subsequent which embodied a provision for reconveyance; in fact the condition was that, on payment by the debtor, the creditor should reconvey the land.[1]

Germanic laws on the Continent, it may be remarked in passing, recognized forms of conveyance on condition subsequent, as security, which embody features strikingly similar to the clause of defeasance and the proviso for reconveyance of the classical common-law mortgage.[2] In what appears to have been the older of two forms, the one which corresponds to the Littletonian mortgage, due payment by the debtor resulted in a defeasance of the ownership which had been conveyed to the creditor on condition subsequent; while in the second form there was at least an approach to the main feature of many of the later common-law mortgages, namely, the embodiment in the security of a "proviso for redemption", which, as Maitland has observed,[3] in strictness were better called a "proviso for reconveyance". Thus, on the Continent it not infrequently happened that the security transaction was concluded by the use of two documents which were, in outward form, independent of each other. In Italy, for example, the debtor

[1] See, further, Brunner, *Zur Rechtsgeschichte der Römischen und Germanischen Urkunde*, pp. 193–199; Hazeltine, *op. cit.* pp. 140–145.
[2] See Brunner, *op. cit.* pp. 193–194.
[3] *Equity*, p. 267.

xxxiv GENERAL PREFACE

sometimes gave the creditor an instrument of conveyance which in terms was absolute,[1] while at the same time the creditor executed in favour of the debtor a document, known to legal historians as the *pfandrevers*, wherein he bound himself on redemption to return the instrument of conveyance to the debtor.[2]

Not only in form, but also in essential character, the Anglo-Saxon and Italian securities now under consideration are much alike. When the terminology of sale is employed they are both easily confused with the transaction known as "sale for repurchase"; and, indeed, the older civilians would have construed the Anglo-Saxon transaction, not less than the Italian, as a sale for repurchase. To view either the Italian or the Anglo-Saxon transaction as a sale for repurchase would, however, do violence to its character as a conveyance on condition subsequent for purposes of security; for the debtor, as Brunner has observed, has not only a right *in personam* against the creditor, a contractual right to buy back the land, but he has also a right *in rem*, an absolute right to redeem the land, which he can enforce against third parties. In other words, the conveyance from the debtor to the creditor is not absolute, but conditional.[3]

The period of the Norman kings marks the transition from the Anglo-Saxon gage of book-land on condition subsequent to the feoffment on condition subsequent for purposes of security, or, in other words, the mortgage as described by Littleton in a later age.[4] For a long time, however, other forms of security on land held the ascendancy, chiefly the gage for a term of years. In Glanvill's time the gagee for a term had *seisina ut de vadio*, whereas in the age of Bracton he had the *possessio* of a termor. There was, moreover, another marked

---

[1] The document was usually couched in the terminology of sale; sometimes in that of gift.

[2] Illustrations of the *pfandrevers*, or of a provision corresponding to it, are found in English medieval instruments of conveyance. For an example of a covenant by the mortgagee that, upon payment of the debt, he will redeliver the writings, see Bridgman, *Conveyances*, p. 13.

[3] See Brunner, *op. cit.* p. 197. Cf. also Franken, *op. cit.* pp. 178 *seq.*

[4] While the sources of the Norman age dealing with gage are vague, some of them seem to indicate the existence of the mortgage.

GENERAL PREFACE xxxv

difference between the Glanvillian and the Bractonian gage for a term; for in the latter form of security failure of the gagor to pay the debt at the end of the term resulted in the shifting of the fee to the gagee and the sudden transformation of his *possessio* into *seisina* in fee.[1] The enlargement of a term of years into a fee, characteristic of the Bractonian gage, raised no difficulties for the lawyers of that age; as yet the *forma donationis*, wide and flexible, had not been fettered by strict rules as to the difference between *possessio* and *seisina* and by fine distinctions between the term for years and the freehold.[2] Nor is it unimportant to remember that both the Glanvillian and the Bractonian gage for years long persisted. For a time they both existed side by side with the gage in fee on condition subsequent, or, in other words, the common-law mortgage;[3] and they both contributed some of their characteristics to this latter form of security.[4] The mortgage in fee appears in fact to have developed very slowly in the environment of the other two forms; and while it was in use at an early day, possibly as far back as the Norman age, it seems to have emerged as a usual form of security only towards the latter part of the fourteenth century. From the point of view of the fee both the Glanvillian and the Bractonian gage for years differed materially from the mortgage; for while they were both conveyances of the fee on condition precedent, the mortgage was a transfer of the fee on condition subsequent.[5] From year book cases of the fourteenth century we can see that there was something in the nature of a struggle between these two kinds of condition. In several cases counsel for the gagee presented arguments to the effect that

---

[1] See Hazeltine, *op. cit.* pp. 214–238.

[2] See Pollock and Maitland, *op. cit.* II, 122–123.

[3] The Bractonian gage for years is found in year book cases of the fourteenth century; and there are forms of security in the same period which at least remind one of the Glanvillian gage.

[4] The most striking illustration is the inclusion, in the mortgage by feoffment, of a term for years, that is, the definite period from the feoffment to the set day for payment of the debt. As the mortgage developed, drawing some of its features from the Glanvillian and Bractonian forms of gage, the notion that the mortgagee, even though seised in fee, had also a term for years persisted; and, as a result, the mortgagor was allowed to bring the writ of entry *ad terminum qui praeteriit*. See Fitzherbert, *Natura Brevium*, 9th ed. 201 I.

[5] See Hazeltine, *op. cit.* pp. 214, 233, 239.

xxxvi GENERAL PREFACE

the conveyance was on condition subsequent, while, on the other hand, counsel for the gagor contended that the condition attaching to the conveyance was a condition precedent. Some of the gage transactions in these cases were in fact on the border-line between the Bractonian gage for years and the pre-Littletonian mortgage.[1]

V

Without inquiring further as to the early history of the common-law mortgage, it may be asserted with some confidence that, as already suggested, down to and including Littleton's time the condition subsequent attaching to the feoffment was one of defeasance: due payment at the set day defeated the mortgagee's estate and gave the mortgagor a right to enter, whereas failure to pay freed the mortgagee from the condition and made it absolute. When one examines the documents by which the oral and formal feoffment is evidenced, chiefly the charter of feoffment and the parties' indenture, one finds that the usual terms employed are that on payment the land shall "revert", or "return", to the mortgagor, and that on non-payment it shall "remain" to the mortgagee.[2] The terms "revert" and "remain" have undergone a change of meaning in the course of legal development. In its original signification "revert" was used to indicate what would happen when one man's enjoyment of the land had come to an end: the land would "revert" or "return" or "come back" to the donor or his representatives. Similarly, the term "remain" originally meant

---

[1] See, e.g., *Erdingstone* v. *Burnel*, Y.B. 6 Ed. II (Selden Society), 234; *Rye* v. *Tumby*, Y.B. 8 Ed. II (Selden Society), 36.

The great importance of the lease for years in the history of English securities on property cannot be too strongly emphasized. A striking illustration of this is found in the present-day law of real property. Although the Bractonian gage for years, with its enlargement of the term into the fee on default in payment, fell into desuetude, this mode has been revived, in substance if not in form, by the recent Property Acts. In the case of a legal mortgage by lease, under the new statutory law, the mortgagee has express power, on the realisation of the security by sale, to vest in the purchaser not merely the mortgagee's own legal term of years, but the whole legal fee simple vested in the mortgagor. See, further, Cheshire, *Modern Law of Real Property*, 2nd ed. pp. 557, 558, 585.

[2] See, e.g., Madox, *Formulare Anglicanum*, Nos. DLX, DLXII, DLXIX.

GENERAL PREFACE

xxxvii

that the land, instead of reverting or returning, stays out or remains away from the grantor. It was only in later times, with the growth of a doctrine of estates in land, that the original meaning of these terms was obscured; and it was then thought that "reversions" and "remainders" were known as such for the reason that they were estates left over after a lesser estate had been carved out of a greater estate.[1] In the thirteenth century the terms "revert" ("return") and "remain" still possessed their original meaning. They had not yet come to indicate a "residue" and a "remnant"; they did not as yet express, as Maitland has pointed out in reference to remainders, the notion of subtraction or deduction; they did not, in this early meaning, indicate "that quantitative conception of 'an estate' which is so remarkable a feature in the real property law of a somewhat later time, the conception that an estate has size".[2] When, therefore, we find the terms "revert" and "remain" in documents executed by gagors and gagees in the thirteenth and fourteenth centuries, we seem to be safe in concluding that the parties used these terms in their original signification; and we may indeed discover some confirmation of this in the striking fact that the parties, in employing these terms, always spoke of the *land* and never of an *estate* in the land. While it would take us too far from our main purpose to enter into the intricate learning of determinable fees, perhaps it may not be too bold to suggest that in its early history the common-law mortgage, as a feoffment on condition subsequent in which the terms "revert" and "remain" were used in their original meaning, was cast in the mould of a determinable fee: that is, that payment at the set day *ipso facto* defeated or determined the fee simple vested in the mortgagee on condition. In the later common law one of the main distinctions between a "conditional limitation" and a "condition" is that while a conditional limitation operates, by the intrinsic force of the limitation, to determine the estate *ipso facto*, a condition, on the other hand, makes the estate voidable merely,

---

[1] See Co. Litt. 22 *b*, 143 *a*.

[2] See, further, Pollock and Maitland, *op. cit.* II, 21–22; Maitland, *Collected Papers*, II, 174–181; Holdsworth, *op. cit.* III, 132–133.

xxxviii GENERAL PREFACE

and not void. The performance of the condition, in other words, does not of itself determine the estate, it merely gives the grantor or his heirs the right to avoid, or defeat, the estate by re-entry or by some other mode: until entry, or claim under the condition, the estate of the grantee continues.[1] But, while this was the established doctrine of the later common law, it may be gravely doubted whether the courts of the thirteenth century drew this sharp distinction between conditional limitations and conditions. However this may have been, there is much in the phraseology of the documents executed by mortgagors and mortgagees in the thirteenth and fourteenth centuries to indicate that in the view of early conveyancers the performance of the condition subsequent, by payment of the debt at the set day, *ipso facto* determined the feoffment to the mortgagee. On payment, so the documents read, the land shall "revert" or "return" to the feoffor; and, in this event, so the documents further declare, the feoffee's seisin, the charter of feoffment, and the bond shall all be null and void. The documents contain no support for the view that payment made the mortgagee's estate voidable merely and that entry was essential to its determination; on the contrary they expressly provide for its nullity or voidness as soon as payment has been made by the mortgagor at the fixed time. No doubt the mortgagor may enter as soon as he has paid the debt; but his entry seems not to be essential to the reverting of the fee. Although, therefore, it may well be true that by Littleton's time, when the law in regard to conditions had reached a maturer state, re-entry was regarded as essential, or, in other words, that an estate subject to a condition subsequent was not destroyed until the right of re-entry had been exercised,[2] there is nevertheless much evidence for the view that at least in the case of the mortgage, a special form of "estate upon condition", entry was not required in earlier periods.[3] To determine the accuracy of this

---

[1] See Leake, *op. cit.* pp. 162, 168; Challis, *Law of Real Property*, 3rd ed. pp. 260, 261.

[2] See Litt. § 347; Co. Litt. 214 *a*–215 *b*; Challis, *op. cit.* pp. 219, 261.

[3] In Littleton, § 332, where the mortgage is defined, there seems to be a reminiscence of earlier law. Littleton tells us that, if the feoffor pay the debt to the feoffee at the set day, "then the pledge is *dead* as to the tenant"; and

GENERAL PREFACE

xxxix

view, which is suggested here in passing, further research will be necessary. In the pursuit of such studies the remedies open to the mortgagor and his representatives, when the mortgagee insists on keeping possession after payment of the debt, will need to be subjected to careful review; for in the light thrown upon the problem by a knowledge of the mortgagor's remedies, his substantive rights, contractual, possessory, and proprietary, should appear in greater clearness.

If it be true, as suggested, that in the early history of the mortgage the performance of the condition, by payment, *ipso facto* determined the mortgagee's estate, some explanation of this phenomenon may be found in the fact that the mortgage was in essence a complex of two conveyances, a feoffment in fee and a lease for a term of years. That the leasehold part of the transaction had significance in the common law may be seen from the fact, which has already been noticed, that the mortgagor, even as late as Fitzherbert's time, could bring a writ of entry *ad terminum qui praeteriit*.[1] At common law, moreover, there was, as Coke mentioned, a "diversitie between a condition annexed to a freehold and a condition annexed to a lease for years": a freehold estate on condition could not cease before entry, whereas a leasehold estate on condition could determine *ipso facto* without entry.[2] When we remember that

that, on payment, "the feoffor may re-enter". If, on the other hand, says Littleton, the feoffor does not pay, then the land is "taken from him forever and so *dead* to him". Littleton's stress seems to be laid, not upon the question of re-entry, but upon the *deadness* of the land that results in one case from payment and in the other case from non-payment. Is not this notion of *deadness* at least partly based on the fact that, in the earlier history of the mortgage, performance of the condition *ipso facto* caused the mortgagee's estate to cease and determine, to become null and void, and that non-performance, causing forfeiture, *ipso facto* transformed the mortgagee's "estate on condition" into an absolute estate, freed forever from the condition?

[1] See p. xxxv n. 4, *supra.*

[2] Co. Litt. 214 *b.* It is noticeable that the precedents of mortgages for long terms drawn by Bridgman usually contain a proviso to the effect that on payment the lease shall be void. See Bridgman, *op. cit., s.v.* "Mortgage" (in both Tables). Thus, for example, an indenture of mortgage for five hundred years contains the following proviso: "And it is provided, conditioned and agreed [that upon payment] this present indenture, and the grant, bargain, sale and demise hereby made, shall cease, determine and be void; any thing herein before contained to the contrary notwithstanding". See *op. cit.* pp. 96 *seq.* (at pp. 97–98).

GENERAL PREFACE

the early development of the mortgage fell within a period when the *forma donationis* was not fettered by elaborate technical distinctions between freehold and leasehold estates, and when the doctrine of conditions had not been very clearly formulated, we need not be surprised to find that in the case of the mortgage, a transaction *sui generis* which has always held a unique place in our system, some of the more primitive legal notions, such as the early meanings of "revert" and "remain", long persisted. At the time when the mortgage was first coming into prominence gages for terms had already reached a stage of maturity; and since the mortgage involved not only a feoffment in fee, but also a lease for a term, it was but natural that both conveyancers and courts should lay special emphasis upon the leasehold ingredient in the mortgage and give its colour to the transaction as a whole. Although this view of the matter may not explain all of the peculiarities attaching to the pre-Littletonian mortgage, it nevertheless draws our attention to features of the early mortgage deeds and mortgage cases which would otherwise be even more difficult to grasp. The truth is that the early mortgage embodied archaic features which long persisted; and of these more primitive characteristics the determination of the mortgage's fee *ipso facto* on the performance of the condition, without entry, seems to be one of the most striking. By Littleton's time stricter notions as to the mortgage prevailed. Whereas in the earlier period stress had been laid on the leasehold aspect of the mortgage, emphasis came to be placed on the feoffment in fee; and, since the mortgagee's estate was now viewed as primarily a freehold estate on condition, it was brought into conformity with other similar estates by holding that not the mere performance of the condition by payment determined the mortgagee's estate, but only the entry of the mortgagor in accordance with the right of entry which had accrued to him from his payment.

VI

While the clause of defeasance is medieval in origin and character, the proviso for redemption, or, more properly, the proviso for reconveyance, is essentially a modern feature of the

GENERAL PREFACE

common-law mortgage. Although its early history is still largely a matter of conjecture, it may be confidently assumed that it did not begin to displace the clause of defeasance until chancery had developed its jurisdiction *in personam* and was thus able to compel the mortgagee, on payment at the day named, to reconvey the property to the mortgagor. The history of the proviso falls, in fact, within the period when chancery was developing its own conception of the mortgage transaction by the construction of the equity of redemption.

One main difficulty in approaching the proviso for reconveyance is that its history has never been carefully investigated by writers on the law of mortgage; nor have they been concerned to deal with this feature of the mortgage transaction from a theoretical or jurisprudential point of view. In general text-writers assume, without explanation, that the introduction of the proviso for reconveyance did not alter the fundamental character of the common-law mortgage. They take it for granted, in other words, that the proviso for reconveyance, not less than the clause of defeasance, resulted in making the mortgage a conveyance on condition subsequent; they imply, rather than expressly state, that while the proviso for reconveyance may be viewed as a contract between the parties, it nevertheless had a proprietary effect by subjecting the conveyance to a condition subsequent. There are some writers, on the other hand, who neglect the proprietary aspect of the proviso and treat it purely as an agreement between the mortgagor and the mortgagee.

This difference of opinion as to the nature of the proviso for reconveyance is in many respects an inheritance from the middle ages. Feoffment is a species of the great genus Gift; and the gift or grant of English medieval law, not less than the gift or grant of Germanic law in general, is a mixture of conveyance and contract. Especially in conditional gifts, including the conveyance of conditional estates, such as the mortgage, the two elements of conveyance and contract are present. To use the language of jurisprudence, rights *in rem* and rights *in personam* are intermingled in conditional gifts: and this general characteristic of all conditional gifts is illustrated in a striking manner

GENERAL PREFACE

by the conveyance on condition subsequent for purposes of security.[1] Since English law has persistently retained this duality of rights, within the sphere of grant or gift, it is but natural, perhaps, that some writers on the law of mortgage should stress the proprietary aspect of the proviso for reconveyance and that other writers should lay emphasis on its contractual features.

The true view would seem to be that at common law the proviso for redemption, or reconveyance, introduced a condition subsequent into the feoffment in fee. The words which import a condition in legal conveyances are *sub conditione, proviso semper, ita quod, quod si contingat,* and the like.[2] In his account of estates upon condition Littleton deals with cases where the words *proviso semper* stand alone, without words of covenant; and he holds that these two words of themselves create an estate upon condition in the feoffee.[3] Coke, in his commentary on Littleton, draws attention to the point that where the words *proviso semper* are accompanied by other words, namely, "and it is covenanted and agreed between the parties, etc.", there is a condition by force of the *proviso semper* and a covenant by force of the other words.[4] In Coke's time, in fact, the common-law courts devoted much attention to the problem as to the effect of the word *proviso* when accompanied by words of covenant; and some of the general principles relative to this aspect of conveyancing were then adjudged. Thus, in *Lord Cromwell's Case*,[5] where the authorities were reviewed, the court held that the word "proviso being a condition ought to do the proper office of a condition, and that is to make the estate conditional; and therefore in what place soever it be put, it, having the force of a condition, shall have reference to the estate, and shall be annexed to it: and it was said, *quod proviso est providere praesentia & futura, & non praeterita*". The court also laid it down as a principle that neither a precedent

---

[1] On the Germanic Gift, see the present writer's "Comments on the Writings known as Anglo-Saxon Wills" (Whitelock's *Anglo-Saxon Wills*, pp. vii–xl, at pp. xviii–xxi).

[2] Litt. §§ 328–331; Leake, *op. cit.* 2nd ed. p. 169. See also *Doe* v. *Watt*, 8 B. and C. 308.   [3] Litt. §§ 328, 329.

[4] Co. Litt. 203 *b*. See also Leake, *op. cit.* p. 170.

[5] 2 Co. Rep. 69 *b*.

GENERAL PREFACE

nor a subsequent covenant takes away the force of the proviso; "for although words of covenant had been contained in the same clause of the proviso itself, yet the proviso being in judgment of law, a word of condition, shall not lose its force". These general principles in regard to the effect of the word "proviso" are applicable to the "proviso for reconveyance" in mortgages. Its "proper office", in the language of *Lord Cromwell's Case*, "is to make the estate conditional".

More than a little confusion in regard to the nature of the proviso for reconveyance has been caused by a failure on the part of certain writers to distinguish one from another three essential elements in the mortgage transaction as it has developed in modern times. These three essential elements are (1) a conveyance of the legal estate in the property that is mortgaged, (2) a covenant for the payment of the loan, with interest, on a day named, (3) a proviso for reconveyance of the legal estate on repayment being made in accordance with the covenant.[1] It is the proviso for reconveyance which affects the conveyance of the legal estate to the mortgagee and makes it a conditional conveyance.[2] But, apart from this proprietary effect of the proviso, it should be observed that the "proviso", looked at as a whole, also contains words of covenant, namely, an agreement of the parties that if payment be made in accordance with the covenant, which is also contractual, the mortgagee shall reconvey the property to the mortgagor.[3] By a failure to see that the "proviso" has both proprietary and contractual effects some writers have been led into the error of thinking that it is merely a covenant, a contract; and by so doing they have neglected the main characteristic of the conveyance as a transfer of the legal title on condition subsequent.[4] So far

[1] White and Tudor, *Leading Cases in Equity*, 8th ed. p. 16. Cf. Maitland, *Equity*, p. 279.

[2] It appears to have been usual to provide in the *habendum* that the conveyance of the fee was subject to the proviso, thus: "To have and to hold the same unto and to the use of the mortgagee, his heirs and assigns, subject to the proviso for redemption hereinafter contained".

[3] See Maitland's *Equity*, pp. 266–282, for an analysis of a simple mortgage deed.

[4] Cf. Mr Turner's explanation of the nature of the proviso for reconveyance, pp. 18–19, *infra*, where he says, *inter alia*, that the proviso was "not properly a condition, but a covenant in the nature of a condition".

xliv

GENERAL PREFACE

as one can determine, after a somewhat superficial examination of the authorities, the chancery judges did not make this mistake. They do not appear to have drawn any material distinction, from the view-point of conveyance, between the clause of defeasance and the proviso for reconveyance; they seem in fact to have treated the proviso for reconveyance, not less than the clause of defeasance, as having the effect of introducing a condition subsequent into the conveyance itself.

The introduction of the proviso for reconveyance appears to have some historical connection with the attempt to treat the mortgage transaction as a sale of land with an option of buying it back.[1] In this attempt two instruments were employed. The first was a deed of the land, absolute in form, given by the debtor to the creditor; while the second instrument, executed concurrently with the deed of conveyance, was a bond given by the creditor to the debtor. When this second instrument took the form of a so-called bond of defeasance, it provided that if a certain sum of money were paid by a certain time the deed of conveyance should become inoperative. The second instrument could, however, assume a different form; it could provide that on payment of the money at the set day the creditor should reconvey to the debtor. If by means of these instruments the transaction could be treated as a sale with option of repurchase the debtor's rights would be lost immediately upon his default. On the principles of "once a mortgage, always a mortgage", it was held by the chancery, however, that if such a transaction was in fact intended merely as a security, it was nothing but a mortgage. Since it was treated as a mortgage, it fell within the principles of equity in regard to mortgages in general, including those which concerned the equity of redemption.[2]

Apart from this historical relation between the "sale for repurchase" and the introduction of the proviso for recon-

---

[1] For an example of a "sale for repurchase", see Bridgman, *op. cit.* pp. 56–58; and cf. Holdsworth, *op. cit.* VII, 376. In the precedent given by Bridgman, *loc. cit.*, the provision in regard to reconveyance is not a condition, but a covenant merely.

[2] See Chaplin, "Story of Mortgage Law", *Harvard Law Review*, IV, 11; Hazeltine, *op. cit.* p. 256.

GENERAL PREFACE

xlv

veyance, there was another development which seems to lie at the basis of the proviso historically. Mr Turner has pointed out that in the reigns of Henry VI and Edward IV chancery had already acquired a jurisdiction to compel the mortgagee, in cases where the debt had been duly paid at the set day, to reconvey the property to the mortgagor.[1] This jurisdiction, which arose at a time when payment at the set day resulted in defeasance of the mortgagee's estate and entry by the mortgagor, was independent of any contractual arrangement for reconveyance; and it was based, as Mr Turner has mentioned, on the idea of preventing a breach of faith on the part of the mortgagee by his refusal to allow the mortgagor to enter after defeasance.[2] The convenience of compelling a reconveyance by the mortgagee, as opposed to the entry of the mortgagor on defeasance, must have appealed to conveyancers who were drafting mortgage deeds; and it would appear that this early chancery practice, in the time of Henry VI and Edward IV, of ordering a conveyance where the debt had been duly paid in accordance with contractual and legal requirements, suggested to conveyancers the desirability of inserting either a proviso for reconveyance, or a mere covenant for reconveyance, in the mortgage deeds themselves.[3] Once established as a normal feature of mortgage conveyances the proviso for reconveyance, by force of its own virtue, gradually displaced the earlier mode of defeasance with entry by the mortgagor.

The point should not be overlooked that the conveyancing device of "sale for repurchase", in which two instruments are employed, outwardly presents a close resemblance to the Roman *fiducia cum creditore*. As in the case of the *fiducia*, the conveyance to the creditor is absolute in form, and again, like the

---

[1] See pp. 21–24, *infra*. It should be noted, however, that "the first cases where the Chancellor gave relief to a mortgagor who had failed to pay on the stated day (a relief which developed later into the mortgagor's equity of redemption) occurred in the reign of Elizabeth". See p. 23, *infra*.

[2] Cf. Bracton's Note Book, pl. 50, where a gagor sued in the Court Christian *de lesione fidei*, claiming that the gagee had pledged his faith (*affidavit*) to return the land at the end of ten years and that he had not done so: but the gagor was restrained by writ of prohibition. See Fry, *Specific Performance of Contracts*, 4th ed. p. 11.

[3] See, e.g., Bridgman, *op. cit.* pp. 9, 62; and cf. p. 354.

xlvi

GENERAL PREFACE

Roman security, the conveyance is accompanied by a contractual obligation on the part of the creditor to reconvey to the debtor: and it is possible that in devising "sale for repurchase" conveyancers were influenced by the *fiducia*, wherein the *mancipatio* was accompanied by the *pactum fiduciae*.[1] But, however close the resemblance between the "sale for repurchase" and the *fiducia cum creditore* may be, the analogy of the Roman security fails in the case of the mortgage: and for the simple reason, as already explained, that the English mortgage conveyance, in contrast with the Roman *fiducia*, was conditional. When either the clause of defeasance or the proviso for reconveyance was employed, the mortgagor's failure to pay the debt at the set day freed the mortgagee's estate from the condition and made it absolute. On the other hand, when the proviso for reconveyance was used due payment by the mortgagor did not, as in the case of the clause of defeasance, either *ipso facto* defeat the mortgagee's estate or give the mortgagor the right to defeat it by entry; it had the effect, however, of transforming the "estate on condition" into a species of trust estate. In the words of Lord Nottingham, "after payment of the money, the law keeps a trust for the mortgagor, which the heir of the mortgagee is bound to execute".[2] At law the estate of the mortgagee had become absolute; but, in equity, he held this estate in trust for the mortgagor. By suing in chancery the mortgagor could compel a reconveyance to himself as the one who was beneficially entitled.[3]

The proviso for redemption, or reconveyance, bears an outward resemblance to the *pactum fiduciae* in one important respect. The Roman debtor's right to redeem the *res* by due payment of the loan was based on the *pactum fiduciae*; and, as

[1] By some writers the "sale for repurchase" ("Verkauf auf Wiederverkauf") has been confused with, and even identified with, both the *fiducia cum creditore* and the mortgage. For one view that the "*fiducia* is the sale-for-resale form", see Wigmore, *loc. cit.* XI, 24, 31–32. For the legal distinctions between "sale for repurchase" and the *fiducia*, see Dernburg, *op. cit.* I, 12, 13; for the legal differences between "sale for repurchase", or "sale with option of repurchase", and the mortgage, see White and Tudor, *op. cit.* II, 31–35.

[2] *Thornbrough* v. *Baker*, 1 Ch. Ca. 283 (a). See also the remarks of Lord Hardwicke in *Casborne* v. *Scarfe*, 1 Atk. 603; Leake, *op. cit.* p. 216.

[3] Cf. pp. 166–175, *infra*. On the statutory power of the common-law courts to order reconveyance, see p. 120, *infra*.

GENERAL PREFACE

already observed, for the protection of this right he had the personal *actio fiduciae*, one of the *bonae fidei actiones*, by which he could compel a reconveyance of the *res*. Similarly, the English debtor's right to redeem the land was based on the proviso for redemption; and, if he duly paid the debt, he could compel a reconveyance of the land by suing in chancery. In both these forms of security, therefore, the creditor could be compelled, on redemption, to reconvey the *res* to the debtor; and in both of them, again, the proceedings brought by the debtor against the creditor were personal and equitable.[1] The parallel between the *pactum fiduciae* and the proviso for redemption, in respect of the right to compel a reconveyance, should not, however, be unduly emphasized; and for the simple reason that there are important differences between the *pactum* and the proviso. While the *pactum* is purely contractual and gives rise only to rights *in personam*, the proviso, as already observed, has both proprietary and contractual effects. In the case of the *fiducia* the debtor's right to compel a reconveyance rested entirely on the contractual *pactum*; and to the end it remained a right *in personam*. In the case of the mortgage, on the other hand, the debtor's right to compel a reconveyance depended not only on covenant, or contract, but also on the condition that was imported, by force of the proviso, into the conveyance to the creditor. In the case of the mortgagor's right to a reconveyance, furthermore, there are considerations associated with equitable as well as legal title. The growth of the mortgagor's equity of redemption as an estate in land, a development closely connected with, and partly based upon, the proviso for redemption in the legal conveyance to the mortgagee, gives to the proviso a proprietary character in equity as well as at law. For these reasons, if for no others, the parallel between the *pactum fiduciae* and the proviso for redemption, in the matter of reconveyance, is far from close. In large measure it is the dual character of the proviso, its proprietary as well as its contractual aspect, which distinguishes it from the *pactum*, a contract pure and simple.[2]

---

[1] The *actio fiduciae* was "equitable", in the Roman sense, owing to the fact that the *fiducia* was *bonae fidei negotium*.

[2] On the abolition of the need for reconveyance by recent statutory law, see pp. 127, 130, 132, *infra*; and cf. Cheshire, *op. cit.* pp. 578, 579.

xlviii GENERAL PREFACE

VII

The differences between the *fiducia* and the mortgage are not expressed completely, therefore, by saying that the *mancipatio* as a conveyance is absolute and that the feoffment as a conveyance is conditional; nor are these differences fully indicated by stating that the contractual element in the Roman form is contained in a separate *pactum fiduciae*, whereas in the English mortgage it is embodied in the deed of conveyance itself. The radical differences between the two forms of security in the matter of conveyance, that is, in respect of the rights *in rem* transferred to the creditor, materially affect the nature, scope, and effect of the rights *in personam* incident to the two transactions; and, on the other hand, the differences between the two forms in respect of rights *in personam* have a corresponding relationship, historically and theoretically, to the distinctions between the two transactions in the matter of rights *in rem*.[1] Both the *fiducia* and the mortgage, viewed as transactional entities, are in fact bundles of proprietary and personal rights: and in each of these bundles the two classes of rights are intertwined in a complicated and somewhat confusing network. These rights, protected by actions, are the weapons wielded by the debtor and the creditor in their legal struggle with each other. Both in the *fiducia* and in the mortgage the creditor is in a strong position, for, in addition to his personal right arising out of the debt, he has proprietary rights as security, whereas the debtor in both forms relies chiefly, at least in the earlier history of the struggle, on rights that are personal in character. To a certain extent the inner meaning of the struggle between the two parties may be expressed by saying that the creditor is fighting, by means of his rights *in personam* and *in rem*, to recover the money which he has loaned to the debtor, while the debtor on his side is fighting, by the weapon of his rights *in personam*, to recover the *res* which he has transferred to the creditor as security. The history of the *fiducia* and the history of the mortgage both show us the several stages in this

---

[1] Cf. Butler's note (1) to Co. Litt. 205 *a*, on the differences between the *pignus*, or *hypotheca*, of Roman law and the mortgage of the English common law.

GENERAL PREFACE

continual struggle between the creditor class and the debtor class; and while at the beginning, both at Rome and in England, the creditors are in a position of advantage, the later stages of the struggle prove that the debtors have been gaining ground. Forfeiture and sale of the *res* mark victories for the creditor; but the right of redemption, ever the chief weapon of the debtor, gives him as time goes on more and more control over his adversary. There is this important distinction, however, between the Roman debtor and the English debtor. Apart from certain incidental rights, such as the right to acquire *dominium* by *usureceptio*, rights which are in truth unconnected with the security itself, the debtor under a *fiducia* is obliged to rely, throughout the whole history of the security, on purely personal rights arising out of the *pactum fiduciae*: the debtor's right of redemption is more and more safeguarded by the law, but to the very end it remains a right *in personam* only.[1] The mortgage debtor's right of redemption has, on the other hand, a different history. Owing to the conditional character of the conveyance to the creditor, the debtor always retains, even in the early history of the mortgage, something which is more than a purely personal right of redemption; and, as time goes on, this right of redemption is so shaped by chancery that it ultimately takes its place in English law as an equitable estate in the land. In addition to his legal and contractual right of redemption at the set day, he has an equitable right of redemption that is invested, so far as it can be invested, with proprietary character.

Indeed, it is when we come to study the history of the debtor's right of redemption that the chief differences between the Roman *fiducia* and the English mortgage emerge clearly. In the history of the mortgage one of the cardinal features of later growth is this doctrine of the equity judges that the debtor's right of redemption is an equitable estate in the land; and, from a jurisprudential point of view, the existence of two estates in the land, the legal estate of the creditor and the

[1] It is worthy of emphasis, in this connection, that originally the *mancipatio* to the creditor was quite absolute. The debtor had at one time no remedy at all: he was obliged to trust the creditor. See p. lv, *infra*.

GENERAL PREFACE

equitable estate of the debtor, is of great interest. In their development of the equity of redemption as an estate the judges of chancery always kept the legal estate in mind as a model; and so far as possible they gave to this equitable estate the qualities of a legal estate. On the question, however, whether the mortgagor's equity is a true proprietary right, a species of ownership, or, on the other hand, merely a bundle of personal rights against certain individuals, theorists have long disputed.

Leaving these theoretical problems on one side for the moment, let us examine briefly the nature of the Roman debtor's right in respect of the *res* which he has conveyed to his creditor by *mancipatio* and which, by the *pactum fiduciae*, the creditor has undertaken to reconvey on payment of the debt. Views have been expressed by certain writers to the effect that the element of *fiducia* is imported into the proprietary right of the creditor;[1] and the general result of this process of thought is not only to limit the proprietary right of the creditor, to make the creditor's *dominium* something less than full and absolute ownership, but also to enlarge the debtor's right of redemption from a pure right *in personam* into a species of right *in rem*. These writers, as Oertmann has observed, "auch in das dingliche Moment den fiduciarischen Character hineinspielen lassen wollen". Thus, Rudorff, Zachariae, and others regard the creditor's ownership as "prokuratorisches Eigenthum", an ownership based on the principles of *procuratio*, or general agency. L. von Stein speaks of the creditor's ownership as revocable, a "revokables Eigenthum", while Sintenis reaches the same result by holding that the creditor has "widerrufliches Eigenthum". Since on redemption the creditor is under the duty of remancipating the *res* Fuchs treats his ownership as "resolutiv-bedingt"; and, in accordance with this view, the *mancipatio* by the debtor to the creditor is a conveyance on condition subsequent similar to the English common-law mortgage. Sohm also gives to the fiduciary agreement a proprietary and not merely a contractual effect; he views the ownership of the creditor as something less than

[1] See Oertmann, *op. cit.* § 20, at p. 162, for a summary and criticism of some of these views.

GENERAL PREFACE

li

full and absolute *dominium*, namely, a "fiduciary owner-ship" ("Treuhänder-Eigenthum", "fiduciarisches Eigenthum"). "Der fiduciarische Vorbehalt", Sohm writes, "hatte nicht bloss verpflichtende, sondern dingliche Wirkung. Es war ein anderes Eigenthum, das Treuhänder-Eigenthum, als das normale Eigenthum. Daher die Möglichkeit der *usureceptio ex fiducia*, d.h. der Rückgewinnung des Eigenthums seitens des Veräusserers durch Ersitzung ohne *bona fides*, und eben daher die Möglichkeit, den Anspruch des Erwerbers bei *mancipatio* oder *in iure cessio* auf bloss fiduciarisches Eigenthum zu stellen."[1]

The history of all these juristic attempts to limit the proprietary right of the fiduciary creditor reaches back at least as far as Gothofredus. It was Gothofredus who maintained that after the conveyance to the creditor the *res* remained "*in bonis*" *debitoris* and that the *dominium* of the creditor was an ownership "*non proprie*"; and to this Thomasius justly replied, "*dominium improprie dictum plane dominium non esse*".[2] In our own time the doctrine of Gothofredus has been revived and elaborated. Indeed, it has been held by Scheurl that, although the creditor acquires quiritarian *dominium*, the bonitarian *dominium* remains in the debtor.[3] On this view, which constructs a dual ownership analogous to the legal estate of the creditor and the equitable estate of the debtor in the case of the English mortgage,[4] the creditor has a *nudum ius quiritium*;[5] and it is true that *dominium*, as "the ultimate right to the thing, the right which had no right behind it", might be a mere *nudum ius* with no practical content and still be *dominium ex iure quiritium*.[6] In support of the view that the creditor has merely a *nudum ius quiritium* an analogy drawn from the law of sale has been presented. In the classical law if the thing sold was a *res*

---

[1] Sohm, *Institutionen*, 7th ed. (1898) p. 61 n. 13.

[2] See Dernburg, *op. cit.* I, 24 n. 46; Oertmann, *op. cit.* p. 162.

[3] Oertmann, *op. cit.* p. 163: "Scheurl meint, die Sache sei nicht aus 'dem Vermögen' des Schuldners gekommen. Der Gläubiger habe daher nur ein 'eventuelles Verkaufsrecht'".

[4] Gaius (1. 54) speaks, but without reference to the *fiducia*, of quiritarian title and bonitarian title as *dominium duplex*.

Compare Scheurl's view with those expressed by Roby and Muirhead. See p. xxiii, *supra*.

[5] See Dernburg, *op. cit.* I, 23.

[6] See Buckland, *op. cit.* p. 189.

mancipi, traditio did not pass *dominium*, but only bonitary ownership. Although it was legally impossible to attach a *fiducia* to a conveyance by *traditio*,[1] it has been suggested that the analogy of such a conveyance helps us to understand the rights of the creditor and the debtor in the case of a conveyance by *mancipatio* for the purposes of *fiducia cum creditore*. The debtor, so it is said, stands in the same position as the purchaser who, before *mancipatio* on the part of the seller, has received possession of the *res* by *traditio*: the debtor, that is, has bonitary ownership, while the *nudum ius quiritium* is in the creditor.[2] Much the same view has been expressed by Huschke, who claims that although the creditor acquires *dominium*, the *res* nevertheless comes into his custody as *res alienae familiae*; with the result that, since his *familia* as such was inalienable, the debtor by *usureceptio* merely obtains the return of the *res* to himself out of the custody of the creditor.[3]

Finally, attention may be drawn to the view held by Manigk: in the later law, he says, the rules of *fiducia cum creditore* had been so much influenced, through reaction, by those of *pignus* that the fiduciary creditor had, in effect, only a limited ownership.[4] But, although Manigk's position may well represent the true state of the later law, it is now the prevailing view that in the earlier periods of legal development the fiduciary creditor acquired full and absolute *dominium*.[5] To import the *pactum fiduciae* into the conveyance itself, and thus contractually to transform the creditor's full and absolute *dominium* into a limited or a conditional *dominium*, is to disregard elementary juristic distinctions. As Oertmann has remarked[6] in reference to the theory that the creditor acquires a *dominium* on condition subsequent: "Eine nur obligatorisch wirkende Resolutivbedingung ist doch nimmermehr eine wahre Bedingung und eigentlich ein Nonsens". Nor is the theory that the bonitary ownership

---

[1] Buckland, *op. cit.* p. 231. See p. xxviii, *supra.*
[2] See Dernburg, *op. cit.* I, 23; Oertmann, *op. cit.* p. 163.
[3] See Dernburg, *op. cit.* I, 23, 24; Oertmann, *op. cit.* p. 163.
[4] See Buckland, *op. cit.* p. 471 n. 8.
[5] I.e., the conveyance was abstract and disregarded the *causa*: so far as the *dingliche Wirkung* of the conveyance was concerned the *pactum fiduciae* was irrelevant. See Oertmann, *op. cit.* p. 162.
[6] *Op. cit.* p. 162.

GENERAL PREFACE

liii

remains in the debtor legally sound.[1] The theories of Scheurl and Huschke rest, as Dernburg has explained, on a mingling of two distinct and different elements in the *fiducia cum creditore*: the legal and formal element on the one hand and the material and natural element on the other. In legal contemplation the *res* is in the *dominium* of the creditor; it forms a part of his property (*Vermögen*)[2] not less than the *dos* forms a part of the property of the husband, even though materially and *naturaliter* it is the wife's. But although legally the *res* was the creditor's, the debtor regarded it as still his own; and, in truth, the Roman juridical construction given to the *fiducia* went somewhat beyond the intention of the parties themselves.[3] Even the law, however, recognized to a certain extent the material and natural element in the *fiducia*, as in the rules, already considered, with reference to *infamia, furtum*, and *usureceptio*.

In order to grasp the nature of the *fiducia cum creditore*, from the standpoint of the law and of the parties alike, it is essential to regard the whole transaction as one of the *scheingeschäfte*, the "feigned transactions", of Roman law.[4] When *fiduciae causa* a thing was conveyed by *mancipatio* or *in iure cessio*, it was not the intention of the parties that the *res* should belong to the creditor permanently, as in the case of a sale, but that, on the contrary, it should be restored to the debtor in accordance with the agreement of the parties. *Mancipatio* and *in iure cessio* were transactions of the *ius strictum*: the agreement, which rested on *bona fides*, could find no place in the conveyance itself.[5] Both the *mancipatio* and *in iure cessio* were intensely formal modes of conveyance: not only was their ceremonial elaborate, but their binding force was derived from the form alone without regard to consent and without reference to any *causa*. Both of these

---

[1] See Dernburg, *op. cit.* I, 23, 24; Oertmann, *op. cit.* p. 163.

[2] Gaius (3. 201) appears to regard the *res*, from the standpoint of the debtor, as *aliena*.

[3] Dernburg, *op. cit.* I, 24.

[4] See von Ihering, *Geist des römischen Rechts*, II, 2 (5th ed.), § 46 (pp. 529–532), III, 1 (4th ed.), § 53 (pp. 141–142), § 58 (pp. 281–283).

[5] See von Ihering, *op. cit.* III, 1, pp. 141–142. We may, however, go further than this; for, as we shall see directly, the real reason why the agreement could find no place in the conveyance was that *mancipatio* and *cessio in iure* were *actus legitimi* which did not admit of modalities, such as express suspension or condition. See Buckland, *op. cit.* p. 190; p. xxviii, *supra*.

GENERAL PREFACE

modes of conveyance were, moreover, absolute; they could be subject to no conditions.[1] Although it was once asserted that the *pactum fiduciae* was included, or could be included, in the conveyance itself, this view has now been generally discarded.[2] Had the *pactum fiduciae* formed a part of the conveyance, it would have given rise to an *actio stricti iuris*; but, as is well known, the *actio fiduciae* was in fact an *actio bonae fidei*, and such an action, in von Ihering's picturesque phrase, "could not have grown on the hard stock of *mancipatio* any more than a rose can grow on an oak-tree".[3] The *fiducia*, therefore, both in its origins and development, was a feigned transaction. The customary formal modes of conveyance, *mancipatio* and *in iure cessio*, were employed to transfer *dominium* to the creditor; and, since by the *ius strictum* the conveyance was as absolute as an unconditional sale, the creditor was invested with all the rights of a *dominus* and he could, therefore, at once sell the *res* to a purchaser and pocket the money. The legal formalism of the conveyance did not, however, express the real intention of the parties; and it was used merely as a means to an end. This end, or purpose, found expression in the accompanying transaction, the *pactum fiducia*, and in that alone. The conveyance, although binding in *ius strictum*, was nevertheless a feigned, or pretended, transaction, a "juristische Nothlüge", a lie permitted by the law and yet a lie; and its function was purely technical, namely, by the use of a legal form to reach an end that was equally legal. Pretence, however, must actually be present; legal *decorum* must be preserved; the *mancipatio* or the *in iure cessio* must not outwardly appear to be pretended or feigned, it must be, and must seem to be, a proper conveyance. In von Ihering's words: "Wie bei jeder Comödie so durfte auch bei dieser juristischen die Illusion nicht gänzlich fehlen".[4] Whereas the conveyance was a part of the formalism of *ius strictum*, the *pactum fiduciae*, which embodied the purpose of the conveyance, was a part of

---

[1] Dernburg, *op. cit.* I, 11, draws attention to this point in relation to the conveyance to the fiduciary. See Buckland, *op. cit.* pp. 233–241, on *mancipatio* and *in iure cessio* as modes of conveyance.

[2] See Muirhead, *Historical Introduction to the Private Law of Rome*, 2nd ed. (Goudy) pp. 132–134.

[3] Von Ihering, *op. cit.* III, 1, p. 142.

[4] Von Ihering, *op. cit.* II, 2, p. 530; III, 1, p. 282.

GENERAL PREFACE

lv

the informalism of Roman law, and, as such, it represented an aspect of *aequitas*. Only by bearing in mind this marked contrast between the two distinct and different elements of *fiducia cum creditore*, the conveyance and the agreement, shall we understand the true nature of this Roman form of security. The conveyance represents *par excellence* the legal and formal element; the agreement represents the element that is material and natural, the spirit as opposed to the form. It is the combination, or mingling, of these two distinct and different elements in the *fiducia cum creditore* as a juristic entity which gives this form of security its complicated character; and it is only by disentangling some of the main threads in the web that we can gain a definite conception of the nature of the debtor's right of redemption.[1]

The rights of the debtor, including his right of redemption, are all founded, directly or indirectly, on the *pactum fiduciae*. In the words of Boethius, *res mancipatur, ut eam mancipanti remancipet*; but originally the *pactum* gave rise to no action[2] and the debtor was dependent entirely upon the *bona fides* of the creditor. Even after the debtor had been provided with his *actio fiduciae*, based on the *pactum*, he was not, however, fully protected in respect of the *res*. It is true that the action lay against the creditor and his heirs; and that by means of it the debtor could, on payment of the debt and interest, compel a reconveyance of the *res*. The action did not, however, lie against third parties who had acquired title to the *res* from the creditor. If, therefore, the debtor sold before the debt was due, or in any way contrary to the terms of the *pactum fiduciae*, he was of course liable to the debtor for breach of contract, but the sale was good; the buyer not only acquired a good title, but one that

---

[1] It would be interesting, if time served, to study the mortgage, in the several periods of its development, as a "feigned transaction". After the growth of the equity of redemption as an estate in land, the legal conveyance to the creditor becomes a formal part of the transaction which does not express the true intention of the parties. Indeed, as Maitland has remarked, owing to the action of equity the mortgage deed is "one long *suppressio veri* and *suggestio falsi*. It does not in the least explain the rights of the parties; it suggests that they are other than they really are". See Maitland, *Equity*, p. 269, and cf. Lord Bramwell's remarks in *Salt* v. *Marquess of Northampton*, 1892, A.C. pp. 18 and 19.

[2] Von Ihering, *op. cit.* III, 1, p. 142; and cf. II, 2, p. 531.

lvi GENERAL PREFACE

was not subject to the *fiducia*.[1] The debtor, in other words, could not follow the fiduciary *res* into the hands of a purchaser from the creditor, even though at the time of the purchase he had notice of the *fiducia*; and this fact alone should be sufficient proof that the debtor's right was purely personal and in no sense proprietary. Modern theorists who hold that the *fiducia cum creditore* is a legal institute involving *duplex dominium* are in reality reading the *aequitas* of the *pactum* into the *ius strictum* of the conveyance; essentially they are making the *pactum* an integral part of the *mancipatio* or the *in iure cessio*. Let it be noted in passing, moreover, that the theories, like those of Scheurl and Huschke, which would invest the debtor's right of redemption with the qualities of bonitary or some other species of limited ownership, arose at a time before scholarship had clearly differentiated between the conveyance and the agreement and had shown that the *pactum* was a distinct transaction. The view that the *pactum* formed a part of the conveyance has been justly described by von Ihering as *eine rechtshistorische Ungeheuerlichkeit*;[2] and, indeed, the *formula* of a fiduciary *mancipatio*, engraved on bronze, which was discovered in 1867 in Andalusia near the mouth of the Guadalquivir, proves beyond the shadow of a doubt that the *pactum fiduciae* was a separate "*pactum conventum*", or informal agreement, and was not incorporated in the *mancipatio*.[3] At the present day any theory as to the nature of the debtor's right of redemption must take this fact into account.

The only safe conclusion, it may be asserted with confidence, is that the debtor's right of redemption was merely a right *in personam* and that to call it a right *in rem* would do violence to well-established principles of law. It is possible, as we have seen, that in the latest phases of the history of the *fiducia* the debtor's right of redemption had become, under the influence of *pignus*, a species of limited ownership comparable to the

[1] Buckland, *op. cit.* p. 471.
[2] Von Ihering, *op. cit.* II, 2, p. 532 n. 688.
[3] For the text of the *formula*, which dates from the first or second century after Christ, and which all scholars agree cannot be later than the second century, see Girard, *Textes de Droit Romain*, 3rd ed. pp. 786–788. See also von Ihering, *op. cit.* II, 2, p. 532 n. 688; Karlowa, *Römische Rechtsgeschichte*, I, 789, 790.

GENERAL PREFACE

lvii

English equity of redemption; but for the period when the *fiducia* was developing on its own lines it may be gravely doubted whether the debtor's right was anything more than a right *in personam*, a right arising out of *obligatio*. A return to the English equity of redemption will be made presently; for the moment it may be useful to draw attention to certain rights of the Roman debtor which seem to intensify or strengthen his right of redemption, but without changing it into a right *in rem*. Thus, his right to reacquire *dominium* of the *res* by *usureceptio* was merely a special mode of *usucapio*; but at the same time the fact that he had his right of redemption led, as we have already noticed, to a shortening of the usual period of two years in *usucapio* of land to a period of only one year. While this special favour to the debtor is based indirectly on the *pactum fiduciae*, in the sense that but for the *pactum* the law would not have given the debtor the boon of a one-year period, it is nevertheless true to say that the principles of *usureceptio* do not alter, or otherwise affect, the principles applicable to the debtor's right of redemption. It is true that his possession was regarded as being *pro suo*; but this is merely saying that the law treated him as having a right of redemption, a personal right to recover his *dominium*. During the running of the period of *usureceptio* the creditor's rights in *rem* remained intact and the debtor's right *in personam* remained in full vigour. The fact that time was running against the creditor did not in any way enlarge the debtor's personal right of redemption into a right *in rem*; the rules as to *usureceptio* did not transform the right of redemption into ownership, but merely facilitated the debtor's acquisition of *dominium* by a title quite distinct from reconveyance by the creditor. Nor do the rules in regard to the debtor's sale of the *res* and his leaving it as a legacy *per praeceptionem* in any way enlarge the right of redemption into a right *in rem*. Both the contract of sale and the will leave the right of redemption intact as a right *in personam*. In the one case the debtor has contractually bound himself to a third person to redeem the *res* and convey it to the purchaser; in the other case the debtor has imposed an obligation on the legatee's co-heirs to redeem the *res* and convey it to the legatee. These obligations to redeem,

lviii GENERAL PREFACE

one arising by the debtor's contract and the other by his will, do not, however, in any way change the juridical nature of the right of redemption. After, as before, the creation of the obligation, the right of redemption itself remains a mere right *in personam*; it does not by force of the obligation to redeem become, as by magic, a right *in rem*.

Roman *aequitas*, in one or another of its several senses, indubitably influenced the history of the *fiducia cum creditore*; and, among other effects, it strengthened the debtor's personal right of redemption without enlarging it, except possibly at a very late stage of development, as we have seen, into a proprietary right, even of a limited character. In any comparison of the Roman *fiducia* and the English mortgage, from the viewpoint of redemption, the fact that the right of the fiduciary debtor was personal, as opposed to proprietary, must be borne in mind; and, indeed, there are those who hold that the mortgagor's equity of redemption, like all other equitable estates and interests in English law, is in reality not a true proprietary right, a right *in rem*, but merely a right *in personam*. An examination of the secure position of the *bona fide* purchaser for value without notice may in fact easily lead one to the view that, at the critical moment of the ultimate test of ownership as opposed to obligation, the "equitable estate" of the mortgagor reveals itself, stripped of its proprietary garb, as merely a *ius in personam*; and, if this be true, there is a close parallel between the fiduciary debtor's and the mortgage debtor's respective rights of redemption, for, as we have seen, the fiduciary debtor could not follow the *res* into the hands of a purchaser from the creditor. Whether or not this parallel is as close as it seems to be is a problem of great interest; but it is at the same time a problem of much difficulty, both as a matter of historical development and as a part of juridical theory.

To the English aspect of this problem in comparative legal history and theory Mr Turner has devoted much research of an illuminating character; and, by contrasting his statement of the nature of the English mortgagor's equity of redemption with the nature of the fiduciary debtor's right of redemption in Roman law, briefly outlined in the present paragraphs, the

GENERAL PREFACE

reader will be able to draw his own conclusions as to the presence or absence of closeness in the parallel suggested. Any comparative study of this suggested parallel must be based, however, on the fundamental difference between the *fiducia* and the mortgage; for in the mortgage, as contrasted with the *fiducia*, an essential element of the parties' contract, the element concerning defeasance or reconveyance, forms an integral part of the conveyance. Since the legal basis of the mortgage was a conveyance on condition subsequent, and not an absolute conveyance, it was easier for the chancery judges to envisage the equity of redemption as an "estate" in the land itself, an equitable right *in rem*, and not merely a right *in personam*.[1] The conditional character of the conveyance helped them as administrators of equity to revest in the mortgagor the title of which he had been devested by the common law's strict interpretation of the condition. As Mr Turner has shown, even the common lawyer had viewed the mortgage condition as "a condition to preserve the mortgagor's estate rather than a defeasance of that of the mortgagee;[2] for the mortgagor, on performance, was considered to be seised as of his former estate, paramount to all charges connected with the mortgagee". Hale, moreover, regarded the equity of redemption as a proprietary right, a right "inherent in the land", which was left to the mortgagor after he had made a feoffment of the land to the mortgagee on condition subsequent;[3] while to Hardwicke the ownership, and

[1] For the conflicting views as to the nature of equitable rights, including the equitable estate of the *cestui que trust* and the equitable estate of the mortgagor, see Maitland, *Equity*, pp. 111–155; Scott, "The Nature of the Rights of the *Cestui que trust*", *Columbia Law Review*, XVII, 269–290; Stone, "The Nature of the Rights of the *Cestui que trust*", *ibid.* 467–501; Hohfeld, *Fundamental Legal Conceptions*, pp. 23–114. In determining the nature of equitable rights, within the sphere of the law of property, it would seem that everything depends upon the definition of the terms "right *in personam*" and "right *in rem*".

[2] See Robbins, *Law of Mortgages*, I, 4.

[3] Chief Baron Hale's *dictum* in *Pawlett* v. *Attorney-General*, Hardres 465, that an equity of redemption is "an equitable right inherent in the land, and binds all persons in the post, or otherwise", is a generalization which may be taken to mean that the mortgagor can follow the land into the hands of all persons, even the *bona fide* purchaser for value without notice. But, as Mr Turner points out, the protection of such a purchaser, as against the *cestui que trust* and the mortgagor alike, has been, and still is, a principle of modern equity. See pp. 51–55, *infra*.

GENERAL PREFACE

apparently the same estate as he had before the mortgage conveyance, remained in equity in the mortgagor.[1] The fact that in England equity was administered, down to the time of the Judicature Acts, by a separate tribunal distinct from the common law courts, also assisted the growth of the equitable notion that the mortgagor's right was not merely a right of action against the mortgagee, but an equitable estate of the same nature as the equitable estate of the beneficiary under a trust.[2] By application of its basic principles, such as the maxims that "equity follows the law" and that "equity acts *in personam*", the chancery was able to erect its elaborate structure of equitable estates in analogy to the system of common-law estates; and one of the great benefits arising out of this theory of equitable estates was the tempering of the rigour of the law in the interest of the mortgagor and mortgagee alike. It was the mortgagor, however, who gained the larger share of advantage from the growth of equitable jurisdiction over mortgages; and his gain was enshrined in the doctrine that his equity of redemption was an estate in the land which left the mortgagee with a mere charge.

VIII

The development of English equitable jurisdiction led in fact to a complete transformation of the mortgage from a form of security where the creditor took possession until default to a security in the nature of the *hypotheca* of Roman law. In this there is a sharp line of distinction between the Roman *fiducia* and the English mortgage. The fiduciary creditor sometimes leased the *res* to the debtor or allowed him to be in possession under a *precarium*; but this possession of the debtor was in a sense something extraneous to the *fiducia* as such, it was at most merely an incident resting on agreement or understanding. The *fiducia* never developed into a *hypotheca*, although it contributed some of its rules to the evolution of both *pignus* and *hypotheca*; and, indeed, the *hypotheca* of Roman law represents a later stage of legal growth than the *fiducia*. In the case of the *fiducia* the creditor acquired both *dominium* and possession of

[1] See pp. 20–21, 53–54, 70–71, *infra.*
[2] *Casborne* v. *Scarfe,* (1737) 1 Atk. 603.

GENERAL PREFACE

the *res*; in the case of the *hypotheca* the debtor retained *dominium* and actual possession and the creditor was secured by his *ius in re aliena*.[1] In England the common-law mortgage itself, so similar in many other respects to the *fiducia*, was transformed by the equity judges into a *hypotheca*; in equity the mortgagor retained ownership and possession, while the creditor was protected by his charge, a right strikingly similar to a *ius in re aliena* of the Roman system.[2]

The legal basis for the wide divergence between the *fiducia cum creditore* and the mortgage, in the later stages of their development, lies in the fact, already strongly emphasized in these pages, that the *dominium* of the fiduciary was absolute and that the estate of the mortgagee was conditional. There are, however, other reasons why the two securities had different histories. The *fiducia*, partly owing to its sharp distinction between conveyance and contract and partly owing to its inelasticity in other respects, proved itself ill-adapted to meet most of the security needs of social and economic life in the imperial age; and, as a result, it gradually fell into decay, displaced in large measure, although not entirely, by *pignus* and *hypotheca*.[3] In at least two important respects the mortgage, under equitable influence, showed greater adaptability than the *fiducia* to economic and social change. The growth of the equity of redemption as an estate meant that the security-idea was fully victorious over the earlier idea of strict legal forfeiture of the *res* for non-payment at a set day; while the retention of possession by the debtor, on principles of hypothecation, further accentuated the conception of security for debt. These aspects of development improved the position of the debtor class; and, on the other hand, the state of creditors was bettered by the

[1] The creditor in hypothec had *possessio*, i.e., he had possessory remedies against the debtor and others.

[2] The present writer is indebted to Dr Buckland for the reminder that the expression *ius in re aliena* was not known to the Romans: it has been invented by modern civilians. Although pandectists call *pignus* (or *hypotheca*) a *ius in re aliena*, the Romans never did. They rarely called it a "*ius*" at all; and they never classed it with servitudes and the like.

[3] On some of the advantages of *pignus* and *hypotheca*, as opposed to the *fiducia*, see Buckland, *op. cit.* pp. 472, 473. On the other hand, *fiducia* was not completely superseded by the later forms of security; it had certain advantages for the creditor and was kept in use. See *op. cit.* p. 471.

lxii   GENERAL PREFACE

introduction of the express power of sale and the decree of
foreclosure, features of mortgage history which also brought
the security-idea into greater prominence. While preserving,
in accordance with the spirit of English legal conservatism,
some of its medieval characteristics, more particularly the legal
conveyance to the creditor, the mortgage had become, therefore,
prior to the changes introduced by the recent property legislation, a form of security comparable in many respects to the
hypotheca of later Roman law; and in assuming this form the
mortgage displayed, in contrast with the *fiducia*, a most remarkable flexibility. This difference between the *fiducia* and the
mortgage in respect of historical development—the difference
expressed by saying that while the *fiducia*, after a period of
growth, fell more and more into disuse, the mortgage, modified
and improved in the course of centuries, has survived, as the
leading form of English security, to our own day[1]—is one of
the most fascinating features of comparative legal history.

The historical causes of the different fates of two securities,
which bear several outward resemblances, are partly legal and
partly social and economic. Some of the legal causes, closely
related to causes of an economic and social character, have been
briefly considered in the present paragraphs; and they may be said
to consist, fundamentally, in the greater rigidity of the *fiducia* in
comparison with the mortgage. Not only was the *fiducia* tied
to antique modes of conveyance, but it was also fettered by
other archaic features which failed to express the true intention
of the parties. The spirit of security for debt was more and
more stifled by an ancient formalism inherent in the form of
security itself: and the *fiducia* proved itself, therefore, a weak

---

[1] While mortgages under the recent Property Acts fall outside the scope of
the present study, it may be mentioned in passing that the legal mortgage of
an estate in fee simple can be effected, by the new statutory law, only (1) by
a demise for a term of years absolute, subject to a provision for cesser on
redemption, or (2) by a legal charge by deed. In the case of a mortgage by
demise for a term of years absolute, the mortgagor remains owner of the legal
fee simple; and he has an equitable right to redeem the legal term of years
that is vested in the mortgagee. This equitable right to redeem is called the
"equity of redemption", but it is theoretically different from the equity of
redemption as an equitable estate in land, distinct from the legal estate, under
the old law. See, further, Cheshire, *op. cit.* pp. 573–580; and cf. Mr Turner's
remarks, pp. 186–189, *infra.*

GENERAL PREFACE lxiii

competitor with the *hypotheca*, a newer and more flexible form which represented *par excellence* the notion of security. Of the legal causes for the gradual decline of the *fiducia* and the vigorous persistence and continuous evolution of the mortgage the difference between Roman *aequitas* and English equity is of paramount importance. The Roman lawyers never developed a consistent theory as to the nature of *aequitas*; and, while in general *aequitas* operated as a mode of thought which permitted change in the law, it always held in the Roman system a subsidiary place and never became a dominating influence comparable to the equity of the English chancery. It was in fact the chancery, with its elaborate system of equitable rights, which enabled the mortgage to persist and flourish in modern times. In the hands of chancery the legal technicalities of the medieval mortgage, as, for example, in the matter of conveyance, were made subservient to the spirit of equity. By its development of the duality of estates, the legal estate of the mortgagee and the equitable estate of the mortgagor, and also by its transformation of the mortgage into a form of hypothecation, the chancery brought the old mortgage of Littleton's time into line with the general advance in juridical concepts, so moulding the transaction that more and more it adequately expressed the idea, ever present in the minds of the parties themselves, that the property had been merely charged for the repayment of the loan. Had Rome possessed a separate and independent court of equity, comparable with the English chancery, the fate of the *fiducia* might well have been different.

Mr Turner has written a most interesting, and also a very instructive, history of the equity of redemption; and this history forms, moreover, a valuable contribution to our knowledge of several other aspects of mortgage history closely related to the equity of redemption itself. The chapters which follow are based on much laborious, painstaking, and scholarly research. They deserve the careful attention of all who are interested in the legal and economic history of England.

H. D. H.

13. ix. 1930.

PREFACE

THIS treatise contains the substance of the Cambridge University Yorke Prize Essay 1923, the subject set being "The Equity of Redemption as an Estate in Land, considered with reference to its history and its place in legal science". The Essay has since been revised and is now published under a new title.

The subject-matter has been obtained by a study of every case on mortgages to be found in the Chancery Reports up to the year 1750, and numerous cases in the common-law reports found by reference. Having regard to the volume of the reports concerning mortgages after that date a selection by reference from text-books was made. It was necessary, for the sake of clearness, to devote some considerable attention to the common-law conception of an estate: this has been done by means of an introductory chapter. The views of well-known authorities on questions not directly connected with the subject in hand have been largely accepted; but that part of the work dealing directly with the equity of redemption represents my own conclusions, based upon research among the reports, or the adoption of the conclusions of others, verified by such research.

I have derived much benefit from a reading of the various standard text-books on mortgages, past and present; and I am greatly indebted to various members of the legal fraternity at Cambridge for their suggestion of fields for research and discussion with me of points of difficulty, but most of all for their encouragement during my research. In particular I wish gratefully to acknowledge the kind assistance of Professor Sir William Holdsworth, Professor P. H. Winfield, and Mr H. A. Hollond, in the labour of reading the proofs, during the course of which they made valuable suggestions; while to Professor H. D. Hazeltine, who has not only helped to prepare

lxvi PREFACE

the work for publication, but also contributed an introductory preface, I am specially indebted. I desire also to thank the Syndics of the Cambridge University Press for undertaking the publication of the work and the Staff for the care taken in printing it.

R. W. T.

22. x. 1930.

INDEX OF CASES

A.-G. v. Buller, 159
A.-G. v. Meyrick, 72, 158
A.-G. v. Pawlett, 46, 50, 51, 55, 151
A.-G. v. Sands, 163
Abington's Case, 45
Acton v. Pierce, 164
Allen v. Woods, 125
Amhurst v. Dawling, 168
Andrew Newport's Case, 93
Anon. Case, cited Balch v. Westall, 47
Ash v. Gallen, 45
Awlry v. George, 36

Bacon v. Bacon, 29, 176
Baden v. Earl of Pembroke, 164
Banner v. Berridge, 171, 173
Barthrop v. West, 163
Bennett v. Box, 46, 163, 164, 165
Bennett v. Davis, 47
Bevant v. Pope, 47
Biggs v. Hoddinott, 179
Birch v. Wright, 96
Bodenham v. Halle, 21
Bowden's Synd. Ltd. v. Smith, 125
Bowen v. Hall, 151
Bradley v. Carritt, 181
Braybroke v. Inskip, 160
Brettel, Ex parte, 159
Bridgman v. Tyrer, 63
Bromley v. Dorell, 27
Browne v. Richards, 36
Browne v. Wentworth, 25
Brydges v. Brydges, 46, 78
Brydges v. Chandos, 123
Burgess v. Wheate, 47, 72, 74, 76, 78, 121
Burgh v. Francis, 47, 54, 168

Calvin's Case, 116
Casborne v. Scarfe, xlvi, lx, 47, 66, 69, 70, 74, 77, 82, 94, 157 et seq., 168
Chambers v. Goldwin, 182
Cheetham v. Williamson, 123
Chester v. Chester, 157
Child v. Stephens, 161
Cholmondeley v. Clinton, 83, 98, 169, 174

Christophers v. Sparke, 97, 98
Chudleigh's Case, 45
Clarke v. Abbot, 158
Clay v. Willis, 166
Clench v. Witherby, 62
Cliffe v. Cliffe, 36
Cole v. Warden, 60, 163
Coll v. Wood, 28
Colt v. Colt, 46, 47
Colvin's Case, 116
Compton v. Compton, 162
Cook v. Gregson, 166
Copland v. Bartlett, 184
Cornbury v. Middleton, 45
Corsellis v. Corsellis, 63
Coryton v. Helyar, 7
Cotterell v. Purchase, 183
Cotton v. Iles, 60
Courthope v. Heyman, 45
Courtman v. Convers, 26
Creditors of Sir C. Cox, Case of, 164 et seq.
Creed v. Colville, 47, 163, 164
Cricklade Case, 184
Crisp v. Heath, 161
Crosbie-Hill, v. Sayer, 130

Darby's Estate, In re, Rendall v. Darby, 64
Davie v. Dabinett, 163
Davis v. Dendy, 182
Davis v. Thomas, 40
Deg v. Deg, 166
Dent's Case, 184
Dixon, In re, 40
Dobson v. Land, 171, 173
Doe d. Fisher v. Giles, 99
Doe d. Marriott v. Edwards, 124
Doe d. Parsley v. Day, 108
Doe d. Roby v. Maisey, 102
Doe v. Rock, 174
Doe v. Watt, xlii
Dowdenay v. Oland, 122
Drummond v. Sant, 174
Duchess of Hamilton v. Countess of Dirlton, 56
Duke of Norfolk's Case, 163
Durham Brothers v. Robertson, xxxii

lxviii INDEX OF CASES

Earl of Carlisle *v.* Gower, 56
Eaton *v.* Jacques, 121
Edmunds *v.* Povey, vii
Emmanuel College *v.* Evans, 27, 28, 37, 38
England *v.* Codrington, 62
Evans *v.* Elliot, 108
Evans *v.* Thomas, 92

Fairclough *v.* Marshall, 125
Fentiman *v.* Smith, 93
Finch's Case, 44, 45
Finch *v.* Earl of Winchelsea, 47, 54, 69
Flack, *Re*, 64
Foord *v.* Hoskins, 44
Forth *v.* Duke of Norfolk, 161
Freeman *v.* Banes, 91, 106
Freeman *v.* Edwards, 109
Freeman *v.* Taylor, 163

Gale *v.* Burnell, 108
Garrard *v.* Tuck, 91
Gibbs *v.* Cruikshank, 107
Gird *v.* Toogood, 29, 52
Goring *v.* Bickerstaff, 45
Grenville *v.* Blyth, 78
Greswold *v.* Marsham, 161
Grey *v.* Colvile, 47, 60, 163
Guy *v.* Donald, 104
Gwinne *v.* Hobbes, 36

Hale *v.* Sparry, 36
Hales *v.* Hales, 27, 31, 89
Hall *v.* Dench, 60
Hall *v.* Doe d. Surtees, 101
Hanmer *v.* Lochard, 26, 50
Harding *v.* Hardrett, 54
Harmood *v.* Oglander, 71, 78, 85, 168
Hartwell *v.* Chitters, 165, 166
Hickman *v.* Machin, 102
Hide *v.* Chowne, 25
Hitchman *v.* Walton, 99, 101, 102
Hobart *v.* Selby, 168
Holles *v.* Wyse, 177, 182
Holloway *v.* Pollard, 44
Holman *v.* Vaux, 26
Hook *v.* Hoffman, 147
Hopkinson *v.* Chamberlain, 128
How *v.* Vigures, 27, 28, 49
Howard *v.* Harris, 62, 176, 177, 182
Howell *v.* Price, 63
Hyde *v.* U.S., 104

Jane Tyrell's Case, 44

Jason's Case, 62
Jennings *v.* Jordan, 79, 84
Jennings *v.* Ward, 177, 182
Jory *v.* Cox, 168

Keebel *v.* Powell, 31
Keech d. Warne *v.* Hall, 94, 95, 96
Kemp *v.* Kemp, 46
King *v.* Ballett, 166
Kirkwood *v.* Thompson, 171, 173
Kreglinger *v.* New Patagonia Meat Co., 180

Langford *v.* Barnard, 26, 182
Langstaffe *v.* Fenwick, 182
Lapworth *v.* Smith, 50
Lee *v.* Hutchinson, 184
Leeds *v.* Munday, 159
Leman *v.* Newnham, 97
Litchfield *v.* Ready, 102
Littleton's Case, 62, 157
Litton *v.* Russell, 158
Lloyd *v.* Lander, 82
Locking *v.* Parker, 171, 173
Lord Cromwell's Case, xlii
Lumley *v.* Gye, 151
Lyster *v.* Dolland, 161

Mamford *v.* Oxford, 124
March *v.* Lee, vii, 57
Marlow *v.* Smith, 157, 159, 160
Mathews *v.* Usher, 125
Maxwell *v.* Montacute, 62
Megod's Case, 44
Melbourne Banking Co. *v.* Brougham, 183
Melling *v.* Leak, 91
Mellor *v.* Lees, 178
Merest *v.* James, 187
Mole *v.* Franklin, 161
Moor *v.* Hawkins, 20
Morgan, *Ex parte*, 160
Moss *v.* Gallimore, 95, 96, 98

Nash *v.* Preston, 50
Nelson *v.* Nelson, 36
Newcomb *v.* Bonham, 62, 63, 176, 177, 182
Newman, *In re*, 40
Noakes *v.* Rice, 178
Noel *v.* Jevons, 46, 50
Northampton *v.* Salt, 178, 181

Orby *v.* Trigg, 177, 182

INDEX OF CASES

lxix

Osborn's Mortgage, *Re*, 174
Oxfordshire Case, 184

Paget *v.* Ede, 82
Partridge *v.* Bere, 99
Pawlett *v.* Attorney-General, lix
Peachey *v.* Duke of Somerset, 40
Pearson *v.* Pulley, 58
Perkins *v.* Walker, 58
Pit *v.* Hunt, 47, 160
Plucknet *v.* Kirk, 60
Plunkett *v.* Penson, 161, 163, 165, 166
Pockley *v.* Pockley, 63, 164
Porey *v.* Juxon, 44
Porter *v.* Emery, 28, 49, 55
Powsely *v.* Blackman, 14, 19, 31, 89, 92, 108
Prat *v.* Colt, 46, 163
Preston *v.* Christmas, 122
Price *v.* Perrie, 177, 182

Quarrell *v.* Beckford, 83

R. *v.* Baker, 103, 183
R. *v.* Daccombe, 44
R. *v.* Holland, 46, 52, 80
Rand *v.* Cartwright, 50
Ratcliffe *v.* Davies, 38
Reeves *v.* Lisle, 183
Reynell *v.* Peacock, 44
Richards *v.* Syms, 167, 174
Roe *v.* Jones, 20
Roscarrick *v.* Barton, 23, 56, 58
Rowell *v.* Walley, 50
Roylance *v.* Lightfoot, 103, 183
Ryall *v.* Rolle, 71

Salt *v.* Marquess of Northampton, lv, 118
Sambach *v.* Dalston, 44
Samuel *v.* Jarrah Timber Co., 118, 179
Sands to Thompson, 105
Saunders *v.* Hord, 58
Scaldewell *v.* Stormesworth, 43
Scobie *v.* Collins, 102
Scott *v.* Brest, 182
Sedgwick *v.* Evan, 26
Sergison, *Ex parte*, 159
Sharpe *v.* Scarborough, 166
Shirley *v.* Watts, 162
Shrapnel *v.* Vernon, 183
Sibson *v.* Fletcher, 31, 89
Silvester *v.* Jarman, 168
Sish *v.* Hopkins, 162

Smartle *v.* Williams, 93
Smith *v.* Doughtie, 36
Solly *v.* Gower, 163, 164, 166
Sparrow *v.* Hardcastle, 71
Starling *v.* Hickson, 63
Stileman *v.* Ashdown, 162
Stokes *v.* Russell, 123
Stone *v.* Grubham, 89
Stonehewer *v.* Thompson, 162
Strode *v.* Parker, 177, 182
Strode *v.* Russell, 62, 157
Sutton's Hospital, Case of, 44
Sweetapple *v.* Bindon, 75

Talbot *v.* Braddill, 177, 182
Tanner *v.* Heard, 173
Tarn *v.* Turner, 84
Taylor *v.* Russell, 172
Thetford *v.* Rowe, 27
Thornbrough *v.* Baker, xlvi, 38, 58, 59, 61, 157
Thorne *v.* Thorne, 60
Thorpe *v.* Thorpe, 122
Thunder *v.* Belcher, 102
Toomes *v.* Conset, 178
Toplis *v.* Baker, 97
Trash *v.* White, 97
Trent *v.* Hunt, 124
Trevor *v.* Perryor, 62, 163
Tucker *v.* Thurston, 54, 83
Turner *v.* Barnes, 102
Turner *v.* Walsh, 125
Tyler *v.* Court of Registration, 147

Venables *v.* Foyle, 167
Vernon *v.* Bethell, 62, 178, 180

Wallingford *v.* Mutual Society, 182
Walsingham's Case, 5
Warmer *v.* Jacob, 173
Warmstrey *v.* Tanfield, 45
Wetherell *v.* Hall, 185
White *v.* Ewer, 58
Wickham *v.* Dighton, 36
Wilkey *v.* Dagge, 26
Willet *v.* Sanford, 7
Williams *v.* Owens, 78
Williams *v.* Wray, 75
Wilton *v.* Dunn, 102
Winnington's Case, 89
Witham's Case, 44, 46
Wolstan *v.* Ashton, 50, 63
Wright, *In re*, 40
Wynn *v.* Littleton, 158

INDEX OF STATUTES

13 Ed. I, c. 1, De Donis, 3
18 Ed. I, c. 1, Stat. of Westminster, II (Quia Emptores), 3
 6 Ed. I, Stat. of Gloucester, 4
20 Ed. III, c. 5, Subpoena, 43
 7 Rich. II, c. 12, Stat. of Provisors, 7
 8 Hen. VI, c. 7, Franchise, 7
 1 Rich. III, c. 1, Subpoena, 7
21 Hen. VIII, c. 15, Fines, 4
23 Hen. VIII, c. 5, Statute of Sewers, 1531, 103
27 Hen. VIII, c. 10, Statute of Uses, 1535, 7, 9, 43, 44, 47, 48, 69, 91, 126
40 & 41 Eliz. c. 5, Fraudulent preference, 89
21 Jac. I, c. 16, Limitation Act, 1623, 58, 60
 —   c. 19, Bankruptcy Act, 1623, 28, 55, 71, 72
12 Car. II, c. 24, Statute of Tenures, 1660, 60
22 & 23 Car. II, c. 25, Game Act, 1670, 185
29 Car. II, c. 3, Statute of Frauds, 1677, 47, 60, 161, 163, 164, 166, 174
 3 & 4 W. and M. c. 14, Bonds, 165, 166
 7 & 8 Will. III, c. 25, Parliament (Election of Members) Act, 80, 185
 8 & 9 Will. III, c. 2, Bonds, 121
 4 & 5 Anne, c. 16, Bonds, 121
 7 Geo. II, c. 20, Mortgage Act, 1733, 120
 9 Geo. II, c. 36, Mortmain Act, 1735, 72
17 Geo. III, c. 26, Annuity Act, 1776, 83
28 Geo. III, c. 36, Franchise, 184
53 Geo. III, c. 141, Annuities, 83
 2 & 3 Will. IV, c. 45, Representation of the People Act, 1832, 80
 —   c. 104, Administration of Estates Act, 1833, 165, 184
 3 & 4 Will. IV, c. 27, Real Property Limitation Act, 1833, 174
 6 & 7 Vict. c. 17, Parliamentary Voters Registration Act, 1843, 80, 184
 8 & 9 Vict. c. 106, Real Property Act, 1845, xxvi
11 & 12 Vict. c. 48, Equitable Estate, 84
12 & 13 Vict. c. 77, Equitable Estate, 84
13 & 14 Vict. c. 60, Trustee Act, 1850, 174
17 & 18 Vict. c. 90, Usury Laws Repeal Act, 1854, 178, 179, 180
 —   c. 113, Real Estate Charges Act, 1854, 64
21 & 22 Vict. c. 72, Equitable Estate, 84
 —   c. 98, Equitable Estate, 84

INDEX OF STATUTES

lxxi

23 & 24 Vict. c. 38, Law of Property Amendment Act, 1860, 121
30 & 31 Vict. c. 69, Real Estate Charges Act, 1867, 64
32 & 33 Vict. c. 46, Administration of Estates Act, 1869, 165
36 & 37 Vict. c. 66, Judicature Act, 1873, 124, 125
38 & 39 Vict. c. 87, Land Transfer Act, 1875, 127, 133
40 & 41 Vict. c. 34, Real Estate Charges Act, 1877, 64
41 & 42 Vict. c. 31, Bills of Sale Act, 1878, 127
44 & 45 Vict. c. 41, Conveyancing Act, 1881, 112, 121, 122, 124, 125, 126, 160
45 & 46 Vict. c. 43, Bills of Sale Act, 1882, 127
—   c. 38, Settled Land Act, 1882, 127
47 & 48 Vict. c. 26, Yorkshire Registry Act, 1884, 127
54 & 55 Vict. c. 64, Middlesex Registry Act, 1891, 127
56 & 57 Vict. c. 53, Trustee Act, 1893, 174
57 & 58 Vict. c. 60, Merchant Shipping Act, 1894, 127
59 & 60 Vict. c. 35, Judicial Trustees Act, 1896, 174
60 & 61 Vict. c. 65, Land Transfer Act, 1897, 127, 133
15 Geo. V, c. 20, Law of Property Act, 1925, 105, 117, 124, 128 *et seq.*, 186 *et seq.*
16 & 17 Geo. V, c. 11, Law of Property Amendment Act, 1926, 134

INDEX OF YEAR BOOKS

20 & 21 Ed. I, 39 (status in fee and for life), 2
— 12, 34, 38, 50, 500 (meaning of status), 2
— 125 (gage by term of years), 18
— 422 (mortuum vadium), 20
30 & 31 Ed. I, 208–12 (mortuum vadium), 20
32 & 33 Ed. I (R.S.), 474 (termor's action on the covenant), 3
6 Ed. II (S.S.), 234 (conditions in gages for years and mortgages), xxxvi
8 Ed. II (S.S.), 36 (conditions in gages for years and mortgages), xxxvi
5 Hen. VI, 3, 6 (tenancy of cestui que use), 91
11 Hen. VI, Mich. 11 (termor's action on the covenant), 3
22 Hen. VI, 57, pl. 7 (common law conditions), 20
33 Hen. VI, Mich. 19 (termor's action on the covenant), 3
5 Ed. IV, 18, pl. 7 b (no remedy against creditor, etc. of feoffee to uses), 43
7 Ed. IV, 3, 4, pl. 7, 10 (common law conditions), 20
8 Ed. IV, 4 (breach of faith), 18
— 6 (use), 43
9 Ed. IV, 25 (satisfied mortgage), 22
22 Ed. IV, 6 (protection of use), 43
7 Hen. VII, 10, pl. 2 (satisfied mortgage), 22
14 Hen. VIII, 4, 7, 8 (purchaser without notice), 43

CHAPTER I

INTRODUCTION:
THE COMMON LAW CONCEPTION OF AN "ESTATE"

THE legal term "estate" has been evolved out of the Latin word, *status*, which had no reference to proprietary rights, but meant personal condition. In this latter sense only it was used by Bracton, writing as late as the thirteenth century.[1] A favourite maxim of his was that a man's free or villein tenure does not affect his free or villein status. The conception that an estate had size, that, for example, a fee tail was larger than a life estate, but smaller than a fee simple, and that smaller estates might be "carved" out of larger estates, was not then in existence.

During the early period after the Norman Conquest, the division between free and villein tenure probably corresponded accurately with the division of status, viz. free or bond men. This connection did not last long. Soon we find that a free man does not lose his freedom by accepting lands to be held by villein tenure;[2] and the grant by the lord to the villein of any estate greater than a tenancy at will, or of anything, such as an annuity, whereby the villein could maintain an action in the King's Courts against his lord, operated as an enfranchisement of the villein himself.[3] These rules may be explained by the general leaning in favour of free status to be found from the earliest times in the English common law,[4] a leaning no doubt largely due to the fact that the King's Courts assumed juris-diction over freemen only, and hence were only too ready to regard a suitor as of free status.

From its connection with political status, that species of tenure which came under the cognizance of the King's Courts in their administration of the common law acquired the name of free or frank tenure, and the tenant holding by such tenure was said to have an "estate" of "freehold". The common law of that

---

[1] Maitland, *Collected Papers*, II, 181; Bract. 26 a, 199 b; see also Glanv. v, 1; *Fleta*, IV, c. 11.

[2] Litt. §§ 172, 174.   [3] Litt. §§ 205–208.   [4] Co. Litt. 124 b.

TER   I

2 INTRODUCTION: THE COMMON LAW

day recognized no proprietary interest in land less than free-hold. The only other proprietary right in land was a sort of tenancy at will, which later came to be designated an "estate" at will, a tenancy which seems originally to have corresponded with the status of bondman, the tenant holding by what was soon to be called villein tenure, in opposition to the free or frank tenure of the freeman.

At some subsequent date, instead of speaking simply of the land which one person held of another, men came to speak of the "estate", or status, in such land. The tenant was conceived as having an estate in the land, an interest which, though capable of descending to heirs *ad infinitum*, was something short of absolute ownership. The lord still retained his feudal rights, and a possibility of the land reverting to him, which the tenant could not defeat, save where the lord granted to his tenant all his estate by substitution. These feudal rights were regarded as of a different nature from an "estate", and became less and less important as the centuries rolled by. Exactly when this change took place is uncertain, but soon after Bracton's death we hear in the Year Books of a man having a status in fee simple and a status for life;[1] so the change was probably completed within a century of his decease.

At first an "estate" was an interest in land of a peculiar nature, viz. a "freehold". To the early English lawyers legal possession and seisin meant the same thing, and, so far as real property was concerned, they recognized neither unless accompanied by an "estate" of "freehold".[2] For instance, Britton defines a *liberum tenementum* as the possession of the soil by a freeman,[3] and St German, writing at a later date, says, "the possession of the land is called, in the law of England, the frank tenement, or freehold".[4] The expression, "estate", in its early days of development from "status", was still closely connected with the parent word. It was an interest in land of a particular type, one which conferred upon the holder the status of a freeman. Incidentally it was an interest which was limited

---

[1] Y.B. 20–21 Ed. I, 39; see, for meaning of "status" at this time, Y.B. 20–21 Ed. I, 12, 34, 38, 50, 500.
[2] Maitland, "Seisin", *L.Q.R.* I, 324.   [3] Britton, c. 32.
[4] *Doctor and Student*, b, 3 d, 22

CONCEPTION OF AN "ESTATE"

in point of time, i.e. as long as the tenant had heirs, for his life, etc. Soon this limitation in duration was to supersede the idea of "status" in the conception of an "estate".

How far the notion of proprietary right entered into this early conception of an "estate" is not clear. The change from "status" to "estate" seems to have been completed soon after the tenant had successfully established a right of alienation as against his heirs, and had been finally confirmed in a similar right against his lord by the Statute of *Quia Emptores*.[1] It is easy to understand that, as long as the tenant in fee was unable to alienate his land as against his lord, the King was not only technically, but largely in fact, owner of the land; but as soon as the tenant had established a right of alienation it was possible to regard him as having a much larger proprietary interest. It is not to be supposed, however, that in the formation of the conception of an "estate" there was any conscious consideration of proprietary rights. A "freehold" conferred a "status". It was the tenant's "estate". The conception was one of "status".

At first there were only three estates in number, the fee simple, the estate for life, and the estate *pur autre vie*. The Statute *De Donis* added the estate tail. From time to time various new interests in land arose, such as the term of years, and later the tenancy by *elegit*, by statute merchant or by statute staple. The term of years was at first considered merely a personal agreement between the freeholder and the termor, often a convenient mode of pecuniary investment at a time when usury was discountenanced as sinful; and a tenancy by *elegit* or statute was a mere security for the debt due under the judgment or statute, a tenancy which ceased upon payment of the debt. None of these interests imposed a status, bond or free, upon the holder of them. They were mere chattel interests. The owner of them had no seisin, i.e. legal possession, and hence was unable to make use of the possessory assizes. They did not descend to his heir, but passed to his executors or the ordinary as the case might be. For a while the termor had no remedy at all save by action on the covenant against his lessor,[2] but about 1235

---

[1] Stat. Westminster, II, 13 Ed. I, c. 1.
[2] P. and M. *Hist.* II, 106; Y.BB. 32–33 Ed. I (R.S.), 474; 11 Hen. VI, Mich. 11; 33 Hen. VI, Mich. 19.

4 INTRODUCTION: THE COMMON LAW

William Raleigh invented the writ *Quare ejecit infra terminum*, whereby the tenant could recover the land itself from a purchaser of the lessor. The tenant's holding was further secured him by the Statute of Gloucester, 6 Ed. I, which prevented the lessor ejecting him by collusive action; and finally, from Edward II's reign onwards he was protected against all ejectors by that form of the action of trespass known as *De ejectione firmae*, though in this action the tenant could not always obtain possession of the land itself. Subsequently the tenant by *elegit* or statute was allowed to make use of the freeholder's remedies for the protection of his interest. Later still the termor's position was further strengthened by the statute 21 Hen. VIII, 15, which enabled termors to falsify collusive recoveries obtained on feigned titles, a new method of avoiding the lease.[1]

Some time before the end of the sixteenth century these chattel interests had come to be regarded as estates in land. The change was brought about by an alteration, both in the conception of the interests themselves, and also in the meaning of the word "estate". The holder of these chattel interests was now recognized as having the legal possession, and was firmly protected in that possession by the law of the land, though he was not regarded as having seisin. Seisin had ceased to be synonymous with possession and had come to be limited to that possession which was connected with an "estate" of freehold. Littleton spends some time in attempting to prove that a tenure exists between the termor and his lessor. He bases his argument on the fact that the lessee does fealty to the lessor, a custom which had long been in general practice; and further, on the words of the writ of waste when brought by the lessor against the lessee, which "shall say that the lessee holds his tenements of the lessor".[2] His reasoning is not so convincing as usual, but his opinion has been generally accepted and acted upon ever since; and therefore, as Challis remarked after a telling historical criticism of this extension of the term "estate" to the leasehold interests, "It is too late now, in the face of Littleton and Coke", to dispute it.[3]

[1] 2 *Inst.* 321, 322; Co. Litt. 46 a.   [2] Litt. § 132.
[3] Challis, *Real Property*, Appendix, p. 426 (3rd ed.).

CONCEPTION OF AN "ESTATE"

The most important part of the change, however, is that of the meaning of the word, "estate". Littleton frequently uses it instead of its French or Latin equivalent, and Coke says of it:

state or estate signifieth such inheritance, freehold, term for years, tenancy by Statute Merchant, staple, Elegit, or the like, as any man hath in Lands or Tenements etc. And by the grant of his estate etc. as much as he can grant shall pass.[1] Tenant for life, the remainder in tail, the remainder to the right heirs of the tenant for life; tenant for life grants *totum statum suum* to a man and his heirs; both estates do pass.

Here Coke does not give a definition so much as an enumeration of the various kinds of interests in land which were regarded as estates. The general conception of an estate at the end of the sixteenth century is better gathered from Plowden. He reports an argument submitted to the Court that "The land itself is one thing, and the estate in the land is another thing; for an estate in the land is a time in the land, or land for a time; and there are diversities of estates, which are no more than diversities of time".[2] Similarly Lord Chancellor Bacon writes, "There are two substantial and essential differences of estates, the one limiting the times for all estates are but times of their continuences. And the other maketh difference of possession as remainder: all other differences of estate are but accident".[3]

It had long been possible to create successive interests in land by way of remainder, and the operation of the Statute of Uses extended this by bringing executory interests within the jurisdiction of the common law. In Coke's day all notions about status, bond or free, had long ceased to exist in connection with the theory of "estate". The term "estate" was applied to the quantum of the interest of the tenant, instead of to the quality of the tenure. The bondman was now the copyholder with his estate at will, the custom of the manor being enforced at common law. The termor was said to have an estate in the land, and likewise a vested remainderman whose interest had not yet come into possession; but the holder of a contingent interest was said to have a mere possibility of an estate upon the

---

[1] This was also pointed out by Littleton. Co. Litt. 345 a.
[2] *Walsingham's Case*, (15 Eliz.) Plow. 555 b.
[3] Bacon, *Law Tracts*, 337.

6 INTRODUCTION: THE COMMON LAW

fulfilment of the contingency, and no estate in the land until the interest became vested upon the fulfilment thereof.

An estate in land was now an interest in land which gave a right to the possession and enjoyment of it, either immediately or at some future date, such right being limited merely in point of time. The law now recognized the phenomenon of a number of persons having various interests in the same piece of land at the same time, the difference between each being merely the time of enjoyment. There might be in the same land a fee simple in remainder, an estate tail waiting to take effect on the determination of the estate of a tenant for life, and one or more estates for life, with seisin, but in enjoyment subject to an estate for years. Each estate was limited in point of time. The fee simple did not come into actual possession until the determination of all the prior estates, and even the fee simple did not last for ever, but only so long as the last purchaser thereof had heirs.

This conception of an estate is peculiar to English law. Our early lawyers were unable to grasp the idea of a legal right apart from the thing over which that right exists. To-day we know that ownership is a bundle of rights; but the distinction between a right and the subject of that right was a feat of which they were incapable. The tenant in possession was the only person who had a present right to the land; but the remainder-men also had rights over the land, rights to possession of it at a future time. To surmount the difficulty the ownership was first detached from the land itself, and then attached to an imaginary thing called an "estate". This enabled it to be dealt with in a much more fanciful way than if it were attached to the soil. An "estate" was treated as something out of which any number of smaller estates might be carved; and the estates so carved might be conferred upon different persons, each of whom, though he might have to wait a long time for his enjoyment of the property, was considered to have a present right, an estate, which would descend to his heirs or personal representatives, as the case might be, even though the estate itself might be only *in futuro*.

Estates in land were not the only estates known to the com-

CONCEPTION OF AN "ESTATE"

mon law. Estates, analogous to those in land, which supplied the model for them, were regarded as existing in some incorporeal hereditaments, such as rent charges. The Court of Chancery also borrowed the common law theory of estates and applied it to uses and trusts. These "estates" did not give a right to the enjoyment of the land itself, but a right to the enjoyment of the "thing" in which the "estate" existed, e.g. in the rent charge or use respectively. A rent charge issuing out of the land was treated in the same manner as the land itself, and by analogy it was conceived that the enjoyment of the rent might be split up into estates of the same various types as those permitted of the land itself. The owner of an "estate" in a rent charge could grant any number of smaller "estates" in that rent charge just as if it were an estate in the land.

Some time between the rise of the use (about Edward III's reign[1]) and the Statute of Uses, we find the Court of Chancery, among the many other doctrines which it borrowed from the common law, applying the theory of estates to this creature of equity, the use, and thus establishing estates in fee, in tail, or for life, etc., in the use, similar to the like estates in the land at law.

Exactly when this notion of an "estate" in the use first made its appearance it is difficult to say, as there is very little material upon which to base an opinion. The idea was well established before the Statute of Uses, for the Statute itself speaks of "estates" in the use. Section 1 enacts that all such persons etc., "That have...etc., any such Use Confidence or Trust, in Fee-simple...etc., shall from henceforth stand and be seised deemed and adjudged in lawful Seisin estate and Possession...etc., of and in such like Estates as they had or shall have in Use, Trust or Confidence of or in the same". All the evidence, including the opinions of lawyers of later periods, such as Hardwicke,[2] points to the prevalence of the notion long before the Statute of Uses. The statute 1 Rich. III, c. 1., intended to give the *cestui que use* an alienable power over the seisin and possession as well as the use, enacts "that every Estate, Feoff-

---

[1] See Statute of Provisors, 7 Rich. II, c. 12.
[2] *Coryton* v. *Helyar*, (1745) 2 Cox, 342; *Willet* v. *Sanford*, (1748) 1 Ves. 186.

8 INTRODUCTION: THE COMMON LAW

ment, Gift...of Lands...shall be good and effectual to him to whom it is so made, had or given, and to all other to his Use". This would seem to speak of "estates" in the use. Indeed, it may well be that the idea appeared as a matter of course at the same time as the use itself, before ever the latter had been brought to the notice of the Chancellor.

It may seem strange that this theory of estates was applied to rent charges and such "things in action" "in Chancery only", as uses and trusts were then regarded, and yet was not applied to such interests in land as easements and rights of entry. It is sometimes pointed out that these latter are interests not limited in point of time. This is begging the question. Had estates been allowed in these interests they would then have been so limited. The true cause of the distinction was a difference in the conception held of these latter interests. An easement at common law could only be held as an appendage or appurtenance to some dominant tenement, and was not a thing which could exist of itself apart from such tenement. Hence its enjoyment could only be limited in duration by a limitation of the estate in the dominant tenement; otherwise an easement *in gross* would be created, a thing unknown to the common law.

Again, a right of entry, not in the nature of an easement, could only be created as incident to some estate larger than that against which the right existed, or by being reserved on the grant of an estate such as a fee upon condition, or by disseisin. It was an incident of the estate in remainder, or all that was left of an estate transferred or lost. It would descend to heirs, etc., as incident to the remainder or the smaller estates into which that remainder might be carved, or would pass to the heirs, etc., of the grantor or disseisor as the ghost of the estate lost or transferred, or would pass to those who would have been entitled to possession but for the disseisin. Its duration depended solely on the estates or possibilities of estates it represented, and it passed to heirs in accordance therewith.

A rent charge, on the other hand, was not the shadow of an estate now lost or in the hands of another, nor was it appurtenant to an estate in some other land. It was a right to the enjoyment

CONCEPTION OF AN "ESTATE" 9

of a fixed sum out of the rents and profits, together with a security for the same in a right of distress, appointment of a receiver, sale or mortgage of the land, etc. It never could become an estate in the land as could a right of entry, but issued out of the land as an entirely new "thing". These "things", uses and rent charges, could not be made to last longer than the estate in the land out of which they were created. Out of an estate for life in the land the greatest use that could be created was for life only. The estate in the land itself could then be divided into estates of smaller duration all bearing the burden of the rent or use in proportion to the "times of their continuences". There could be a rent or use of fee simple duration imposed on what had become a series of estates into which the fee simple of the land had been carved, or a rent charge *pur autre vie* imposed upon a life estate in the land. It was then an easy matter to allow the owner of a rent charge or use to divide it up into "estates" which would represent the duration of his previous interest. Thus the rent or use came to be limited in a series of estates different from that in which the land itself was limited, and the whole theory of estates was finally applied.

At this time uses and trusts were not regarded even as interests in land. They were considered mere "things in action in equity" until well into the seventeenth century. The theory of estates was thus extended from the land itself to "things", which were not then regarded as interests in the land, though the "things" to which the theory was applied all had, in fact, some connection therewith. This application of the system to things other than land did not in any way alter the conception of what was meant by an "estate" as an interest of a limited duration, a test to which it now still conforms. All it did was to widen the application from interests in land only to interests in "things" connected with the land.

When the Statute of Uses turned the majority of uses into legal estates, there was very little alteration, if any, in the common law conception of an estate. The estates and interests in the use were of the same nature as those of the common law save for some new future interests, such as springing and shifting uses, which had been permitted in the Courts of Equity but had

10   INTRODUCTION: THE COMMON LAW

not previously been enforceable at law. The Courts of Common Law after some hesitancy enforced these new interests, but did so without altering their conception of an estate. They admitted springing uses, which offended the common-law rules as to abeyance of seisin, by adopting the doctrine of the resulting use. Likewise shifting uses were allowed by giving the holder a mere right of entry on the happening of the contingency at law and no estate until such right had been exercised, the position before exercise being similar to that of disseisee and disseisor. All that the shifting use gave the holder was the possibility of an estate, as did a contingent remainder; and the common-law rule that there could be no estate limited after the limitation of a fee simple was preserved intact. There was thus no disturbance of the common-law theory of estates.

It must be remembered that, at the time of these developments in the theory of estates, lawyers and jurists were concerned rather with the administration of justice and the difficulties of the various concrete problems brought before them, than with the erection of a theoretical jurisprudence. Their jurisprudential conceptions were of a rough and ready nature. There was no jurisprudence worked out, as it is to-day, so as to fit in with a comparatively rigid system of law, but merely a number of working rules and theories, with which new problems had to be continually compared and dovetailed. As a result they applied what theories they already possessed to the problems before them, as in the application of "estates" to the rent charge and the use; and, where difficulty arose in attaining a desired result, recourse was had to what may seem to the lawyers of to-day somewhat fictitious reasoning.

Again, it must not be supposed that they had any clear-cut notion of what was meant by an "estate". The law was developing rapidly in a time of national peace and prosperity. The lawyers of the sixteenth century had no definition of an estate as "the enjoyment of a thing limited in duration". Both the idea of enjoyment and that of limitation in time were vaguely present, as can be seen in the passages quoted from Bacon and Plowden, though considered but little and indefinitely expressed. At an earlier period the exact notions

CONCEPTION OF AN "ESTATE"

involved were so little considered, and legal phraseology was so weakly set, that, as in the case of both "estate" and "seisin", the ideas conveyed were from time to time extended, limited, and even completely changed.

From the time of Coke to the present day, the chief characteristic of an estate has been the limitation of the enjoyment in point of time. The other important feature, the enjoyment of the "thing" in which the estate exists, is so obvious that it has rarely been brought out in all its essential importance by those judges and text-writers who have paused to examine its true meaning. An estate in land implies a right to the enjoyment of the rents and profits accruing therefrom for a limited period, subject to the limitations which may have been imposed upon such enjoyment by the grantor or by present or former owners, and, if only of small duration, subject also to this, that the holder must do nothing to waste, sell or destroy the thing itself, and so prevent its being passed on unimpaired in due course to the next limited owner.

This explains why easements and rights of entry have never been regarded as an estate in land. An easement was not a right to enjoy the land, but a right to do something concerning the land, which operated as a limitation of the interest of those who had the possession and enjoyment of it. The latter have the "estates" in the land. Unless there is a right to enjoy the land, or the rents and profits therefrom, either immediately or *in futuro*, there is no "estate". Again, immediately on the death of a tenant for life the remainderman next entitled was considered as having an estate in possession, and no actual entry was necessary to give him the remedies incident thereto. This was not so where a grantor created or parted with an estate, but reserved a right of entry exercisable at will or on certain conditions, as in an estate upon condition, or where there had been a disseisin. Here he had lost his estate, and all that remained to him was this right of entry. Before it could be exercised and possession of the land obtained, recourse might have to be made to the Court, for his entrance might be disputed and forcible entry was a criminal offence; or, again, the right might never be exercised, or he might fail to obtain

12 INTRODUCTION: THE COMMON LAW

possession owing to some technical defect. The grantee or disseisor had an estate in the land. The grantor or disseisee had no estate by reason of the right of entry, but merely the possibility of obtaining enjoyment by peaceful persuasion or by recourse to law. This was not an estate, but what was called "the possibility of an estate".

Preston points this out very clearly. He says:

Every estate confers the right of enjoyment at present or in future. This right may be interrupted as to the possession and estate. After such interruption, the estate is turned to a right, and as to the person whose possession or estate is thus affected, cannot be re-covered or regained, without an entry or an action (1 *Inst.* 345 a, b): and in the meantime, this person has not an estate in the property; he has merely the right to an estate. In some cases the law, by its own operation, remits the party to his estate; hence the doctrine of disseisin, discontinuance, and remitter. These rights of entry and of action are descendible to the heir, are releasable to the terre-tenants, or any person who has any estate of freehold, but they are not...assignable to a stranger, and the better opinion is...that they are not devisable.[1]

It must not be supposed, however, that, apart from seisin, the idea of an estate was ever directly connected with that of ownership of the land, as we know the phrase. In Glanvill's day seisin, possession and ownership were much the same thing; but the common law has never had a conception of ownership apart from seisin. In so far as seisin at any time fell short of what is now considered ownership, so far did the ancient con-ception of ownership vary from that of to-day. Even if our medieval lawyers had a hazy idea of ownership in its modern sense, they were fully occupied with concrete problems con-nected with seisin and possession, and had no time to speculate upon the meaning of true ownership, or how far it corresponded with their conception of an estate.

As interests of less and less duration came to be regarded as estates, the connection which might once have been maintained disappeared. Short terms of years could hardly be said to convey ownership of the land. The phrase, "ownership of an estate" soon made its appearance, but this was using owner-

[1] Preston, *Estates*, 1, 20 (3rd ed.).

CONCEPTION OF AN "ESTATE" 13

ship in a wider sense. All that was owned was the estate, an abstract thing, and if it be an estate by sufferance, it is ridiculous to suggest that it implies ownership of the land. The holding of certain estates, such as a fee, certainly implies this ownership. It depends on the latitude of definition which is given to "ownership of land", as to what estates will come within that term. The idea of "estate" is limitation in time. The idea of ownership is spacial, the amount, and not the duration, of the enjoyment.

In the Stuart period two popular meanings of the word "estate" are found coexistent with the primary technical meaning as an interest in land limited in point of time, and all three meanings have continued side by side till the present day. As we have seen, under Littleton a devise of all one's "estate" in the land would pass all interest in that land the testator then possessed. This particular extension in connection with wills is still retained. From this a person's estate came to mean all his valuable rights and interests, in land or goods, as the context might demand. The word "estate" was then used particularly in this sense to include all a person's property on his decease, which was then divided further into real "estate" and personal "estate". The former comprised those rights and interests of the testator recoverable by real action, viz. real property, the test of which soon became that of descendibility to the heir on intestacy, and not that of specific recovery. The latter consisted of those rights and interests enforceable by personal action only, subsequently distinguished rather by descent to the next of kin upon intestacy. This meaning of the word "estate" soon became generally accepted as a phrase with an almost technical meaning, but it is so different from the original primary meaning, as to be in general easily distinguishable by reference to the context.

The other lay meaning of the word "estate" which appeared about this time was where a person was in possession of, or receipt of, the rents and profits from a large area of land in one particular district. He was then said to have an estate. If he had large areas in several districts, he was said to have a number of estates, the question as to whether his interest was in fee,

14 INTRODUCTION: THE COMMON LAW

for life, or merely leasehold, being immaterial. The meaning is usually found in connection with lands which have been in the same family for a long space of time, commonly known as the family "estate". This interpretation of the word "estate" has no legal significance whatever, being a mere term of popular phraseology. The meaning we are concerned with here is the primary one developed from the Latin *status*, namely an interest limited in point of time.

Blackstone, in his enumeration of estates, speaks of an estate by sufferance.[1] The conception of a tenancy by sufferance undoubtedly existed at the beginning of the seventeenth century,[2] but at first it does not appear to have been referred to as an estate. Since Blackstone's day the expression "estate by sufferance", has been in common use, although sometimes looked upon with disfavour as an extension historically inaccurate, divorcing the conception of estate altogether from that of proprietary rights. This will be dealt with later.[3] Although he and other writers seem quite clear as to what was and what was not to be regarded as an estate, his definition is confusing. He says, "An estate in lands, tenements, and hereditaments, signifieth such interest as the tenant hath therein", and quotes Littleton, "so that if a man grants all his estate in Dale to *A*. and his heirs, everything that he can possibly grant shall pass thereby".[4] He continues:

It is called in latin *status*; it signifying the condition, or circumstance, in which the owner stands with regard to his property. And, to ascertain this with accuracy, estates may be considered in a threefold view: first, with regard to the *quantity of interest* which the tenant has in the tenement; secondly, with regard to the *time* at which that quantity of interest is to be enjoyed: and thirdly, with regard to the number and *connections* of the tenants.[5]

This definition seems too wide, savouring of a confusion of the true technical meaning with the popular conception as found in Littleton, concerning a devise of all one's "estate" in the land. An estate, in the strict technical sense, does not include all interests in land. For instance, a right of entry belonging to a disseisee is undoubtedly an interest in land, it

---

[1] II *Comm.* 140.

[2] *Powsely* v. *Blackman*, (1620) Cro. Jac. 659; Co. Litt. 57 b.

[3] See ch. v.   [4] Co. Litt. 345 a.   [5] II *Comm.* 103.

CONCEPTION OF AN "ESTATE"

descends to his heirs, etc., but it has never been considered to be an estate. Again, this definition does not allow for the fact that it has always been possible for one person to have two legal estates in the same piece of land without any merger taking place, as witness an estate following an estate tail.

Blackstone notices the historical meaning of the word "estate", its connection with tenure, and its connection with time of enjoyment, but gives us no clear idea of the true conception of the time; unless indeed his vagueness and his commixture of the technical with the popular meaning suggest that the lawyers of the time, confused by their discovery of the origin of the term in the Latin *status*, and also by the popular derivative meanings which had then lately grown up, were not very clear as to what exactly was meant by the word "estate", when the matter came to definition, although they were quite clear in their own minds as to what definite interests were to be regarded as estates, and what others, such as rights of entry, were something short of the conception thereby conveyed.

Preston, in his treatise on Estates, 1820, quotes with approval Blackstone's definition, but speaks of a right of entry in opposition to an estate, and adds further qualifications to Blackstone's definition, thereby excluding rights of entry and other interests.[1] Blackstone and the text-writers of the succeeding period, whose works are largely founded on his, seem to have used the term in two different meanings without explaining the double user, and possibly without thoroughly realizing that they were doing so. In one sense they give a legal recognition to the popular conception by allowing the term "estate" in certain circumstances to imply all one's interest in the land; and in the other sense they retained the strict legal notion, still connected in some degree with tenure, the "estate" out of which divers other "estates" might be created, etc. Happily the meaning in which the word was used is nearly always apparent from the context.

The common law had become stereotyped by the time of Blackstone. Hence there could be no further extension or application of the theory of estates at common law, save some

[1] Preston, *Estates*, I, 20 (3rd ed.); see also Tomlin's *Law Dictionary* (1835).

INTRODUCTION

theoretical change which would leave the practical working of the law in general unaltered. The century succeeding Blackstone was essentially one of jurisprudence, based upon historical research, yet enriched by the comparatively enlightened ideas of the "age of freedom". In some few instances the historical school of jurisprudence effected, or tried to effect, a change by rejecting some of the then established legal conceptions and re-establishing those of a prior generation; and in other cases they fell into the error of interpreting fixed laws, established in past centuries, in the terms of ideas which did not exist when those laws were established. Happily they did not make any changes in the common law theory of estates. The two ideas underlying the notion of an estate have remained:—the enjoyment of the "thing" in which the estate existed, usually the land itself, and the limitation of that enjoyment. This is how the conception of the common law estate stands to-day.

CHAPTER II

THE FOUNDATION OF THE EQUITY OF REDEMPTION

GLANVILL, Chief Justiciar of England under Henry II, speaks of two kinds of landed security; the *vivum vadium*, where the possession was transferred to the creditor on agreement that the rents and profits should be used by him in reduction of the debt, and the *mortuum vadium*, where the rents and profits were to be taken merely in lieu of interest. This latter was regarded as sinful, being a sort of usury. In both cases possession and not ownership passed to the gagee. The gagor remained seised of the freehold during the term of the loan, had the right to the action of Novel Disseisin against a stranger who ejected the gagee, and could even eject the gagee himself and leave him with no remedy. Glanvill explains this by saying that the creditor's right is not to the land, but to the debt itself, and that if ejected he should bring an action of debt.[1]

Sometimes there was an agreement that if the debtor did not pay by a fixed date, the creditor should hold the gage for ever. Even if there were no such agreement, whether there was a term fixed for the loan or not, the creditor could at any time obtain a judgment ordering the debtor to pay at or before some fixed and reasonable time, declaring that otherwise the gage shall belong to the creditor absolutely;[2] a decree much in the same form as the Chancellor's order to foreclose the mortgagor's equity of redemption which appeared in the seventeenth century. The King's Courts took no cognizance of an agreement to pledge or mortgage not perfected by delivery of possession, but left the ecclesiastical courts to deal with such matters if they so desired. As late as Edward IV, the latter still claimed

---

[1] Glanv. x, 11, XIII, 28–9; P. and M. *Hist.* II, 120, 121.

[2] Glanv. x, 6–8, 11, 12; Britton points out "And if the Plaintiffs say that equity ought to assist them on account of the smallness of the debt [i.e. on default of payment at the day] that shall not avail them, since every freeman may dispose of his property at will without doing any wrong to his heirs". Britton, II, 128. For a detailed account of the early English land gage see Hazeltine, "Gage of Land", *Select Essays in Anglo-American Legal History*, vol. III.

TER

2

18 THE FOUNDATION OF THE

jurisdiction over matters connected with breach of faith concurrently with the Court of Chancery.[1]

In Bracton's day the usual gage of land was a term of years conveyed to the creditor, with a proviso that, in default of payment at the day fixed, the creditor should hold the land in fee.[2] This practice of giving another the possession of land for a fixed period of years as security for payment at a fixed date, but without conveying the seisin or ownership until default, and thereby losing no status until such default, appears to have been the origin of leasehold interests in land; and, since they were but a security for money, a species of investment, they were deemed personal property, descending to the deceased's personal representatives and not to his heir.

At some time the practice arose of enfeoffing the creditor in fee at once, with a proviso for re-entry on payment at the day. The mortgage took the form which it has, in essence, ever since retained, that of a conditional conveyance to the lender, the condition being one of defeasance; the grant of the land was to determine on the repayment of money at the day fixed, the borrower being then entitled to re-enter. This also seems to have been called *mortuum vadium*, or its French equivalent, *mortgage*. Littleton's explanation of the term is quite different from Glanvill's, and illustrates the change which had taken place. Glanvill considers the gage dead when the profits are not to work off the debt as well as the interest and looks down on it as a form of usury;[3] whereas to Littleton the gage is dead because if the debtor does not pay at the day fixed the land will be lost to him for ever.[4] A variation of this appeared shortly after, where the conveyance was made absolute, but with a covenant, called a proviso for reconveyance, that the creditor should reconvey the premises on due payment, instead of a true condition of defeasance.[5] This proviso for reconveyance was a matter of obligation on the part of the lender, which could only be enforced at common law by means of an action on the

---

[1] Y.B. 8 Ed. IV, 4.

[2] Bract. 268 b; Co. Litt. §§ 216–18; Madox, *Form. Angl.*, Nos. 560–2, 569, 579 589; P. and M. *Hist.* II, 25, 117 *et seq.*; Y.B. 21–2 Edw. I, 125.

[3] Glanv. x, 6–8.   [4] Co. Litt. 209 a; Litt. §§ 332, 337.

[5] See Bills in Calendars of Proceedings (Elizabeth) praying reconveyance.

EQUITY OF REDEMPTION

covenant for damages; for the mortgagor had parted with all his estate, and an entry by him under the proviso for reconveyance was necessary before he again obtained an estate and a right to defend it by a real action.

Immediately on the feoffment the feoffee had the legal estate vested in him subject to the condition or proviso for reconveyance. If the condition were broken, his estate was indefeasible, and his position was as if he had been the absolute owner from the time of feoffment. Until such breach, possession was not usually parted with by the feoffor, at any rate not after the end of the sixteenth century. To secure this, a proviso was often inserted that the feoffor should retain possession until breach, at the same time covenanting for further assurance.[1]

The conveyance upon condition or with proviso for reconveyance has been in general use to the present day. The first was a proper condition, and the mortgagee was said to have an estate subject to a condition. He had a vested interest liable to be divested on the performance of the condition. On tender by the mortgagor in the due and proper manner, the latter did not at once obtain the legal estate, but had at law a right of entry, on the exercise of which he came in of his old estate. This right of entry was neither alienable nor devisable, but it was descendible to the heir or the next of kin as the case might be.[2] The second was not properly a condition,[3] but a covenant in the nature of a condition, again neither alienable nor devisable.[4] A condition or proviso for reconveyance could not at common law be reserved to a stranger that is, no one except the person by whom the conveyance or mortgage is made, or his representatives, could take advantage of it.[5]

Coventry points out that the mortgagor before forfeiture had but a bare possibility of an estate:

Of a mortgage condition, it is easy to find a possibility, but it is difficult to ascertain the interest to which that possibility is to be

---

[1] *Powsely v. Blackman*, (1620) Cro. Jac. 659.
[2] Dyer, 181: Co. Litt. 209 b.
[3] 2 Pres. *Conv.* 207.   [4] 2 Pres. *Abst.* 186.
[5] Litt. § 328; Co. Litt. 203 b; Litt. § 247; Co. Litt. 214 b; Shep. *Touch.* 116, 146.

20   THE FOUNDATION OF THE

annexed; for there is a considerable difference between a *right* or *scintilla juris*, and an *interest*....He will have in his own hands a species of pre-emption or right of purchasing the estate above others at a stipulated and reduced price, which is widely different....He cannot be said to have an estate on condition, not even a condition precedent....He has not any interest in the lands till the day arrives and the payment is made;[1] he has indeed a possibility (if a thing under his own control can be said to be in the nature of a legal possibility) of acquiring the estate; but he has not any interest in the lands to which that possibility may be annexed.[2]

Glanvill explains the term *mortuum vadium* as a feoffment to the creditor and his heirs, to be held of him until the debtor pays a given sum, he meanwhile receiving the rents and profits for himself, so that the estate was unprofitable or dead to the debtor until he paid.[3] Littleton makes no reference to this explanation, so it seems the original *mortuum vadium* had long before that date become totally obsolete. He describes a mortgage as a feoffment upon condition that if the feoffor pay to the feoffee a certain sum upon a certain day, then the former may re-enter upon the land conveyed. He says that it is called mortgage, because, if the debtor does not pay, then the land is lost and becomes dead to him for ever.[4] Littleton's land gage seems to have been more a form of Glanvill's *vivum vadium*, for the rents and profits were to be used in reduction of the debt after payment of the interest. The Glanvillian *vivum vadium* existed in a truer form in the Welsh mortgage, where there was no date for the repayment of the loan, but the rents and profits were to be used for its reduction after the interest had been paid.

The common law required a strict performance of conditions, though in some cases it was satisfied with the performance of the intention of those conditions which were to preserve an estate, as opposed to conditions to destroy one.[5] A mortgage condition was viewed as a condition to preserve the mortgagor's

---

[1] *Moor* v. *Hawkins*, 2 Eden, 342; *Roe* v. *Jones*, 3 T.R. 88.
[2] Powell, *Mortgages*, p. 270 n. (3rd ed.).
[3] See also Y.BB. 20–21 Ed. I, 422; 30–31 Ed. I, 208–12; Brac. 458.
[4] Litt. § 332.
[5] Shep. *Touch.* 139, 143 (Preston's ed.); Co. Litt. 205 a–206 a; Litt. §§ 332, 337; Y.BB. 22 Hen. VI, 57, pl. 7; 7 Ed. IV, 3, 4, pl. 7, 10.

EQUITY OF REDEMPTION

estate rather than a defeasance of that of the mortgagee; for the mortgagor, on performance, was considered to be seised as of his former estate, paramount to all charges connected with the mortgagee, whether in the *per* or in the *post*, such as a purchaser, a lord claiming by escheat or a husband claiming curtesy. The "intention" which the Court of Common Law followed was the literal intention of the condition, which was forfeiture of the land in case of non-payment at the day named. Such was the situation at common law, and it is difficult to conceive on what ground the Courts of Common Law could have given relief, even had they been so inclined. The mortgagee, by default of the mortgagor, had become the absolute owner of the estate in pursuance of the condition. The mortgagor had then no remedy. The land was lost to him for ever.

It appears that the Court of Chancery first took cognizance of mortgages in the reigns of Henry VI and Edward IV. Where property was delivered or conveyed as a security, and the debt was duly paid at the day, or if no day was fixed, when it had been satisfied out of the rents and profits, the Chancellor compelled a redelivery or reconveyance of the property in accordance with the proviso for reconveyance, express or implied, a more potent remedy than that of the ancient common law with its action for damages.

It is doubtful on what grounds this equitable jurisdiction was first assumed. In the first known case of a bill praying the Chancellor to decree a reconveyance (1456) there were several peculiar circumstances. The interest obtained by way of profits had been enormous, and the mortgagor was then put in a debtor's prison on a collateral bond before the day of payment had arrived. The decree was that, on payment of the sum borrowed, (there is no mention of interest), the mortgagee should deliver the borrower from prison, discharge him from the bond and re-enfeoff him of the mortgaged premises.[1]

Relief was probably given in this case on the general grounds of conscience, by reason of such unfair circumstances, amounting to gross fraud and oppression on the part of the mortgagee. It was probably the more readily given owing to the unjust

[1] *Bodenham v. Halle*, (S.S.) x, 137.

22 THE FOUNDATION OF THE

imprisonment of the debtor; since at that time the Chancellor's jurisdiction was mostly concerned with unjust imprisonments and various offences against the person, and not with uses, as is so often stated, there being comparatively few bills relating to uses and trusts to be found in the calendars before the period we are now considering.[1]

A few years later we find a bill praying for an order for reconveyance, alleging merely that the lands in question have been mortgaged, and that the feoffee has been satisfied out of the rents and profits; but the case was dismissed as not proven.[2] This suggests that some sort of general jurisdiction to order redelivery had been acquired at that date. There is a reference to some recognized equitable jurisdiction over satisfied mortgages in the Year Book of 9 Ed. IV. In an answer to an action of debt, the defendant pleaded that he had enfeoffed the lender of certain lands, there being a parol agreement that the lands should be redeemable at any time; and that, since the condition was not by deed, he could not obtain the lands again, and so should not be liable for the debt. In reply it was pointed out "although there is no remedy in our law, he may have subpoena in chancery if he pays the money".[3] St German mentions a similar jurisdiction of the Chancellor where a bond under seal was satisfied and no acquittance taken, "If such default happen in any person whereby he is without remedy at the common law, yet he may be holpen by a *subpoena*".[4] Hence it may well be that the relief of satisfied mortgages was a specific form of a like relief of bonds, for undoubtedly the two were scarcely differentiated by the lawyers of that day.

There must, then, have been at least a general custom for the Chancellor to decree reconveyance in special circumstances, a custom already so wide as to be generally recognized in such a case as the absence of any express proviso for redemption. The reports of cases in Chancery at this time are exceedingly scanty in comparison with the amount of work done by that Court. In view of the preceding cases and the fact that later

---

[1] Preface to Calendars, I. See I Cal. XI, etc.
[2] I Cal. LXVII.
[3] Y.B. 9 Ed. IV, 25, 34; C. P. Coop., App. 536.
[4] *Doctor and Student*, Dial. I, ch. XII; see also Y.B. 7 Hen. VII, 10, pl. 2.

EQUITY OF REDEMPTION

we find no special circumstances necessary, it seems probable that a general jurisdiction to decree a reconveyance without having regard to any actual circumstances had already been established.

Lord Hale twice mentions a bill presented to the King and Lords in Parliament, "To be relieved touching a mortgage which he supposed was satisfied, and to have restitution of his lands". This was in the time of Richard II. He states the judgment thus, "The said petition was not a petition of parliament, for the matter ought to be discussed at common law".[1] This is the only suggestion yet found of relief of mortgagors before Henry VI, and it would seem to imply that the Chancellor had not then established his jurisdiction.

The Chancellor was probably led to decree reconveyance and to relieve against satisfied bonds on the ground of fairness and conscience, treating each case as one of hardship, until soon a custom arose of decreeing a reconveyance whenever a mortgage was satisfied out of the rents and profits, or by payment at the day named, and the mortgagee would not return the land to the mortgagor according to the agreement of the parties. Probably he first assumed jurisdiction on grounds of conscience, but was led to establish a custom of decreeing reconveyance with the idea of preventing a breach of faith on the part of the mortgagee. This tendency to extend the doctrine of breach of faith had already greatly assisted the enforcement of the use, and was also continued in the law of contract, where the Chancellors were about to feel their way in particular cases along the path which eventually led to the remedy of specific performance of contracts generally, especially those in connection with land. Perhaps also the notion of preventing an unjust enrichment at another's expense, an offshoot of the breach of faith, to be found later in the doctrine of quasi-contract, may have had some connection with this jurisdiction, either at the outset, or afterwards when the latter had become definitely established as a general custom, and the cases in which a decree for reconveyance was sought were numerous.[2]

---

[1] *Hist. of the Com. Law*, ch. 3; *Roscarrick* v. *Barton*, 1 Ch. Ca. 219. The payment alleged was before the day for payment, Rot. Parl. III, 10, p. 258.

[2] See Cal. of Proceedings (Elizabeth).

24 THE FOUNDATION OF THE

The first cases where the Chancellor gave relief to a mortgagor who had failed to pay on the stated day, (a relief which developed later into the mortgagor's equity of redemption), occurred in the reign of Elizabeth. There is no reason to suppose, as is sometimes done, that such relief dates from the time of Edward IV. The relief given by the Chancellor at the earlier date was but a decree for redelivery when the mortgage had been satisfied at or before the day, or perhaps more usually where there was no date fixed for payment at all. This had little to do with the relief given in special circumstances to a mortgagor who had failed to perform his condition, and so incurred forfeiture; save that, since the Chancellor had already established a cognizance of mortgages, his assumption of jurisdiction over them in another direction was a comparatively easy step. It could therefore be taken without so much notice and opposition from the Courts of Common Law as might otherwise have been expected.

This new species of relief seems to have arisen out of the relief which the Chancellors began to give against forfeitures of bonds of all kinds. There is a case in Edward IV's reign of relief being given where a bond had been fraudulently obtained; but the relief was probably given on the general ground of fraud.[1] Sir George Cary quotes two more cases on this point from the same reign, but in one the bond was joint and several, and the obligee extended the time to one debtor, and then sued the other at law; and in the other case the bond was paid without making acquittance.[2] Both cases savoured of fraud, and hence the relief given was probably on that ground. No further cases are to be found until the reigns of Mary and Elizabeth, but there is little knowledge of the case law of the Court of Chancery during the interval, and hence it may have been the practice to relieve bonds in particular circumstances before the latter date.

Innumerable cases of bills for relief of bonds are to be found in the Calendars of Proceedings in Chancery in Elizabeth's reign, but few in the Reports. Monro, in *Acta Cancellariae*, reports cases in 1572 and 1593, the latter being a forfeiture owing

[1] 1 Cal. XLV; see also 1 Cal. II, XI.   [2] Cary, 1, 2, 23.

EQUITY OF REDEMPTION

to failure in payment of rent under a lease, due to the deceitful practices of the lessor.[1] Cary, writing in the first decade of the seventeenth century, gives us a notion as to how far the relief of bonds had been extended by the end of the reign. He says:

If a man be bound in a penalty to pay money at a day and place, by obligation, and intending to pay the same, is robbed by the way; or hath intreated by some other respite at the hands of the obligee, or cometh short of the place by any misfortune; and so failing of the payment, doth nevertheless provide and tender the money in short time after; in these, and many such like cases, the Chancery will compel the obligee to take his principal, with some reasonable consideration of his damages, for if this was not, men would do that by covenant which they now do by bond.

Later he continues, stating a further ground of relief, "If the obligee have received the most part of the money, payable upon the obligation at the peremptory time and place, and will nevertheless extend the whole forfeiture immediately, refusing soon after the default to accept the residue tendered unto him, the obligor may find aid in Chancery". He then says, "The like favour is extendable against them that will take advantage upon any strict condition, for undoing the estate of another in lands, upon a small or trifling default".[2]

In view of the appearance in the Reports about this time of cases where forfeited mortgages were relieved in Chancery, it would seem that Cary was certainly speaking of mortgages; for, as we have seen, a mortgage was then regarded as a feoffment upon a strict condition. This is the only early summary of the matter to be found. It appears that he considered it the established practice of the Court to relieve bonds where the money was not paid at the day in all cases of hardship, when the delay was due to accident, or the fault or fraud of the obligee, and some like cases of misfortune and unfairness; and that the like favour was extended to conditions, which would seem to apply in particular to mortgages, though he does not actually mention them. He gives us no hint of any notion of relief being

---

[1] *Hide* v. *Chowne*, Mon. 395; *Browne* v. *Wentworth*, Mon. 638.
[2] Cary, 1, 2.

26 THE FOUNDATION OF THE

given to forfeited bonds or mortgages without special circumstances of hardship being averred and proved.

During the sixteenth century there seem to be only two reported cases as to relief of mortgages after forfeiture. Tothill reports such a case in 1594, but gives no ground for the relief,[1] and a bill for relief against a mortgage is reported in Choyce Cases as being refused in 1582, owing to the defendant's having been in possession forty years.[2] Both these cases have been questioned by modern text-writers, though there seems little reason why they should be incorrect, seeing that Monro reports such a case in 1601, the delay in payment having been due to the fault of the mortgagee;[3] and again in 1608, because, as Sir John Tyndal said in giving judgment, "I find him a very poor man, and am very creditably informed that the defendants be hard-dealing men", but this time the decree was *nisi causa*.[4]

Tothill reports a case in 1612 where "the mortgagor was relieved though in infant's hands and a purchase", thus extending the relief against those claiming through the mortgagee;[5] and he reports a case about 1616 where the mortgagee was made to account for profits received and the use thereof.[6] He reports further cases about this date showing that relief was constantly being afforded to mortgagors where it seemed to the Court to be equitable, though he omits to give the grounds upon which the decisions themselves were based.[7]

Thus the relief afforded to mortgagors who had failed to perform the condition and suffered forfeiture to take place in consequence followed upon the same lines as the relief given in the case of bonds, though a trifle later in date, and in cases at first not so numerous. The original relief was given in cases of hardship, which gradually widened into customary rules as to what cases of hardship were relievable. These rules were ever growing in number as fresh types of cases found favour in the eyes of the Chancellor; until finally, both in bonds and in mortgages, as the list of cases increased where relief was given

---

[1] *Langford* v. *Barnard*, Tot. 134. [2] *Sedgwick* v. *Evan*, Choyce Cas. 167.
[3] *Courtman* v. *Convers*, Mon. 764. [4] *Wilkey* v. *Dagge*, Mon. 107.
[5] *Hanmer* v. *Lochard*, Tot. 132. [6] *Holman* v. *Vaux*, Tot. 133.
[7] *Ibid.* 130–3.

EQUITY OF REDEMPTION

as of course, the Chancellor's demand for special circumstances showing hardship were discarded, and relief was given as of course in all cases save where it was held that such relief was inequitable. The relief originally given in exceptional circumstances had become the rule, and the cases where no relief would be afforded had become rare exceptions.

Some fifteen years later we find that this relief given by the Chancellors has been extended to forfeitures of mortgages in general, irrespective of fraud or other special circumstances as the ground of relief.[1] What is more, the relief has soon not only become general in the sense that it can be given apart from special circumstances, but it has come to be looked upon as a definite rule of the Court that such relief shall always be given. Very soon the mortgagor considers that he has a right to redeem in Chancery, although the day is passed for such redemption at law. He no longer asks for relief as of special favour, but asks that the usual clemency shall be shown him. Two limitations only are imposed by the Chancellors on this new custom of granting general relief to all mortgagors upon condition forfeited. First, the mortgagor must come and tender the principal, interest and costs within a reasonable time after the forfeiture;[2] and secondly, should the mortgagee require his money, he can go to the Court and obtain a decree ordering the debtor to pay by a fixed date or be forever foreclosed of his power of redemption.[3]

Exactly when this change came about is uncertain. We cannot say definitely that there was no general relief of forfeited mortgages in 1616, for Tothill relates no special circumstances in his reports. His reports being a mere index, the failure to mention special circumstances need not imply that they did not exist, and would be of little value in the face of any definite authority to the contrary.

There is no mention of any redemption in Chancery to be found in the writings of Coke, but as he was a common lawyer this is not so significant as might be otherwise supposed; yet,

---

[1] *Emmanuel Collego* v. *Evans*, (1625) 1 Ch. Rep. 18, etc.

[2] *Bromley* v. *Dorell*, Tot. 134; *Thetford* v. *Rowe, ibid.*; *Hales* v. *Hales*, 1 Ch. Rep. 105.

[3] *How* v. *Vigures*, 1 Ch. Rep. 32.

28 THE FOUNDATION OF THE

had the Chancellor established much of a general jurisdiction over mortgages in his day, we should surely find some protest referring specifically to mortgages from such a firm opponent of the increasing power of Chancery.

In 1624 it was not yet so definite as to be recognized by statute; for in that year an act was passed enabling commissioners in bankruptcy, in the case of lands, etc., granted by the bankrupt, "upon condition, or power of redemption at a day to come, by payment of money or otherwise", to take advantage of such condition or power, no mention being made of any redemption after the day.[1]

In 1625 the Court held that, "though the Money not paid at the Day, but afterwards, the said Lease ought to be void in Equity, as well as on legal Payment it had been void in Law against them".[2] No special circumstances appear in the report as ground for this general statement. This is the first failure to mention the circumstances as a reason for the relief in a report of considerable length, and from this time onwards no special circumstances seem to have been required.

The first decree of foreclosure reported seems to be in 1629.[3] Here we have the mortgagee filing a bill for the extinction of the debtor's power of redemption, unless he pay at a short day named. This shows that the power of redemption had been greatly extended, and had already at that date come to be regarded as a probability sufficient for the creditor to go to the trouble of filing a bill in Chancery for a decree allowing him to take advantage of the forfeiture at law. Shortly after, several conflicting decisions are found as to whether, on the death of the mortgagee after the day, but before redemption, the money shall be paid to his heirs or personal representatives; and before long we find the Court making a decree as to who shall have the "benefit of the said redemption".[4]

---

[1] 21 Jac. I, c. 19, § 13.

[2] *Emmanuel College* v. *Evans*, 1 Ch. Rep. 18.

[3] *How* v. *Vigures*, 1 Ch. Rep. 32. *Coll* v. *Wood*, Reg. L. B. 1604, fol. 462, seems very like a decree of foreclosure in event of the money not being paid at a given day; but the mortgagee is stated to have "consented" to give up the land on payment of principal, interest and costs. See Spence, 1, 603.

[4] *Porter* v. *Emery*, (1637) 1 Ch. Rep. 97.

EQUITY OF REDEMPTION

Finally, in 1639, the Court boldly states that it "will relieve a mortgage to the tenth generation, though the purchaser had no notice, because it is supposed that he cannot purchase, but it must be derived from the mortgage, and in some cases, where the mortgagee will suddenly bestow unnecessary costs upon the mortgaged lands, of purpose to clogg the lands, to prevent the mortgagor's redemption".[1] The last words of this dictum show how definite the right of the mortgagor to redeem had already become. Attempts to hamper the exercise of the right were already becoming troublesome, and we observe the beginnings of the idea of protecting the mortgagor against such devices on the part of the mortgagee, a protection which soon developed into the rule that there shall be no clog on the Equity of Redemption.

Probably redemption in Chancery after the day as a general right evolved gradually at first. Then came a sudden jump when the Chancellor for the first time announced that it was not necessary to look for special circumstances, or when it was first observed by the practitioners of the Court that he had ceased to do so; followed by another gradual movement while the Court settled down to the new situation. That the Court took some time to settle down may be seen from the case of *Gird* v. *Togood*, 1643,[2] where, on a bill of the executor of the mortgagor to redeem a mortgage long since forfeited, the lands were confirmed to the mortgagee as against the executor, but he was to pay some money to the latter owing to the lands having increased in value; a peculiar form of compromise for the Court to adopt, which shows that the Chancellor did not yet consider himself bound by the custom of the Court to allow redemption in every case on payment of principal, interest and costs, but still used his own judgment as to what was equitable in particular cases.

That the general public considered this increased jurisdiction of the Court of Chancery an oppressive assumption of power seems certain, seeing the general disapproval with which the proceedings of all prerogative Courts were regarded at that time. Though the rulers of the Commonwealth found themselves unable to dispense with the Court of Chancery, they attempted

---

[1] *Bacon* v. *Bacon*, Tot. 133.   [2] Nelson, 34.

30 THE FOUNDATION OF THE

to restrict what was almost certainly regarded as an unwarranted interference with deliberate agreement, and in 1653 a bill was brought in, limiting redemption of mortgages to one year after the entry of the mortgagee for condition broken, requiring double interest to be paid on such redemption, and making the mortgagee only responsible for net profits actually made by him while in possession, and not those that he ought to have made; rules which, considering the deliberate agreement for forfeiture on non-payment of the money, would seem a very fair way of dealing with the matter. This bill was passed by Cromwell the next year as an Ordinance, was repeatedly violated in practice by the Commissioners in Chancery, and thrown over by the legislature of the Restoration.[1] It shows us how complete the mortgagor's power to redeem after the day had become by the middle of the seventeenth century. How different that general rule of redemption was from the custom of the preceding reign, where, in order to obtain relief, the suppliant had to show that the forfeiture was due to accident or the case was one of great hardship.

The date of the change from the narrow to the broad ground of relief may be put, therefore, between the years 1615 and 1630; for in 1629 we have the first case of foreclosure, and we know from Tothill that the number of cases where the Chancellor granted relief of forfeited mortgages was increasing considerably about 1616.

How was it that the Chancellors came to extend the relief afforded to mortgagors, and by what process of legal reasoning did they come to interfere with the working of the forfeited conditions, and so extend their jurisdiction at the expense of the common law? The Court of Chancery was always ready to extend its jurisdiction wherever it found a reasonable opportunity, owing to the increase of the business and importance of the Court which thereby accrued. In 1616, King James had decided the long-standing dispute between Lord Ellesmere and Coke as to whether the Chancellor's subpoena was to override the decisions of the common law, and had determined the matter in favour of Chancery; and that Court, giving vent to

---

[1] Spence, *Mortgages*, vol. 1, 602 *et seq.*

EQUITY OF REDEMPTION

31

its newly found supremacy, was soon extending its jurisdiction rapidly in many directions.

We have seen that previously the Court had obtained a certain jurisdiction over satisfied mortgages. This continued[1] along with the limited jurisdiction over forfeited bonds and mortgages which sprang up where special circumstances, such as equity could take cognizance of, could be found as a ground for relief, viz. fraud, accident, or trust.[2] The Court seems to have established a general jurisdiction to relieve against forfeitures of bonds for failure to pay a sum of money at a day named much about the same time as its general jurisdiction to relieve forfeited mortgages. Probably the mortgage and the money bond were then still regarded as much the same thing for the purposes of such relief.

In the Orders in Chancery made by Lord Ellesmere we have the following: "Bills to staie payment of debts which are due by statute recognizance obligacion or bill are not to be allowed unlesse it be in speciall cases where there is willfull default or grosse negligence And the like for condicions broken upon leasses mortgages...."[3] Again, in 1621, Norburie, writing to Lord Keeper Williams on his appointment to the Great Seal, states that Lord Ellesmere, (who was succeeded by Sir F. Bacon, 1617), "would not relieve any that forfeited a bond, unless it were in case of extremity, or that he could make appear that by some accidental means he was occasioned thereunto.... Whereas of late much lenity has been used to all debtors, so that many, after four or five years suit and charges in this court, were glad to go away with their principal without costs or damages ".[4] Indeed, this passage coincides so completely with the probable date of the extension of the right of redemption, that it may well be that the mortgage was treated merely as a particular species of bond in spite of some distinctions between the two having been already noted by some judges of the common law.[5]

---

[1] *Keebel* v. *Powell*, (1626) Tot. 135; *Sibson* v. *Fletcher*, (1632) 1 Ch. R. 59; *Hales* v. *Hales*, (1637) 1 Ch. R. 105.

[2] Coke, 4 *Inst.* 84.

[3] Sanders, *Chancery Orders*, 86.

[4] Hargrave's *Law Tracts*, 431.

[5] Co. Litt. § 334; *Powsely* v. *Blackman*, (1620) Cro. Jac. 659.

THE FOUNDATION OF THE

At any rate, the leniency shown from this period onwards to holders of forfeited bonds must have had a large influence on the extension of the like relief to cases of forfeited mortgages.

As the time when this change took place can be so narrowly defined, it is probable that it was largely due to the deliberate or careless work of one particular Chancellor. Hence we may find the true cause of the extension in the history and character of the Keepers of the Great Seal at this time.

Norburie's remarks just quoted seem to strengthen this idea. We know that Sir Francis Bacon was a politician. We know also that he was a clever lawyer and that while Chancellor he greatly strengthened the Court of Chancery by a wise and far-sighted reform of its procedure. He is usually spoken of as a man possessing a very keen regard for his own advancement. Norburie's words suggest that Bacon had greatly extended the relief given to debtors under forfeited bonds. it is extremely unlikely that such an astute lawyer and politician would have failed to take advantage of the opportunity afforded him by the newly established ascendancy of Chancery to give the like extended relief in the case of mortgages, and so add to his jurisdiction.

Bacon was a much stronger man than his successor, Lord Keeper Williams, who held the Great Seal until 1625. With his interest in his own advancement and his keen perception of the movements of politics, Bacon was much the more likely man of the two to have initiated a conscious movement for extension. Even if his short period of office did not enable him to make the change complete, his successor would naturally follow in his footsteps and keep what increase of jurisdiction he had won for the Chancery, and so increase the force of custom. Norburie states that Ellesmere kept the relief afforded to obligors of bonds within narrow limits. This being so, it is unlikely that he behaved otherwise in the similar case of the forfeited mortgage. The character of Bishop Williams, as we know it, does not lead us to expect him to take bold steps in the face of fierce opposition from the judges of the common law, depending upon what seems to us to-day an exaggerated and fictitious con-

EQUITY OF REDEMPTION

33

ception of conscience, or else upon no grounds at all.[1] If Bishop Williams were the founder of the equity of redemption, it is more likely to have been founded by accident than by intent; but one cannot imagine Sir Francis Bacon, the lawyer politician, establishing so great a gain of jurisdiction for the Court of Chancery by accident.[2]

Although the extension of general relief to the obligor under a bond and the similar extension of general relief to mortgagors coincide, the evolution of the mortgage does not follow further that of the bond. The Courts of Common Law recaptured their jurisdiction over ordinary common money bonds by adopting rules of relief similar to those of the Court of Chancery (in which jurisdiction they were finally confirmed by the Statute 4 and 5 Anne, c. 16), whereas for some reason they do not seem to have made any attempt to do the same as regards mortgages. Already, under James I, they were refusing to enforce the penalties of bonds which had become impossible of performance through no fault of the obligor. Hence it seems that in the case of bonds the Courts of Common Law were travelling much the same road as the Court of Chancery had done, but that they took half a century longer to reach the same destination.

Coke shows us what he considered was the difference between a mortgage and an ordinary recognisance or bond, and gives us a clue to what was probably the reason why the common law did not attempt to recover its power over mortgages in the same way; namely, because in a mortgage the ownership in the thing pledged had already been transferred, whereas in a bond the sum forfeited had not yet been paid over to the obligee. This seems to have been the ground on which the common law refused to enforce bonds accidently forfeited. He says:

If a Man be bound by Recognisance or Bond, with Condition that he shall appear the next Term in such a Court, and before the Day the Conusee or Obligor dieth, the Recognisance or Obligation is saved;

---

[1] Williams had to be coached in his law by Sir Harry Finch and appears to have let it be widely known that his appointment was only temporary. Hacket, 1, 56, 60.

[2] Shylock's "pound of flesh" in *The Merchant of Venice* is undoubtedly a satire on the strict enforcement of bonds at common law. Bacon's interest in Shakespeare is now generally accepted.

TER

3

34 THE FOUNDATION OF THE

and the Reason of the Diversity is, because the State of the Land is executed and settled in the feoffee, and cannot be redeemed back again but by matter subsequent, viz. the Performance of the Condition. But the Bond or Recognisance is a Thing in Action, and Executory, whereof no Advantage can be taken until there be a Default in the Obligor; and therefor in all cases where a Condition...becomes impossible by Act of God, or of the Law, or of the Obligee, etc. there the Obligation, etc. is saved.[1]

Some text-writers[2] assume that general relief from forfeiture was brought about through the extension of the custom of relieving sureties against a default of the principal, "if so be he will offer the principal debt and damages".[3] This custom of relieving sureties seems to have been established by the end of the sixteenth century; for Cary, in his reports strongly condemns it as inequitable.[4]

Though their surmise may be correct, there is no conclusive evidence on which they base their assumption, and their statements must be taken with some reservation. Indeed Cary himself continues:

But the case of the purchaser (*bona fide*) of land subject to a statute or recognisance, is better than that of such a surety; and so is the case also of the heir of the recognisor or obligor; for though the land be charged in their hand with the debt, yet equity ought to relieve them touching any penalty, unless they be found in Mora.[5]

This seems to establish that one of the special circumstances in which the relief was given to the obligors of bonds forfeited was where the heir of the obligor suffered forfeiture through no fault of his own, which seems to have been generalized early into a rule of relief in all similar cases except where he delayed payment. Such is the impression created by the wording of the report. The heir of the obligor is emphatically stated to be in a better position than the surety, and that at a comparatively early date in the growth of the generalization of the relief of bonds; so that it does not seem probable that the growth of the latter was more than slightly assisted by the indulgence shown to sureties.

[1] Co. Litt. § 334.
[2] E.g., Ashburner, *Equity*, p. 47.
[3] Cary, 12.
[4] *Ibid.*
[5] Cary, 13.

EQUITY OF REDEMPTION

Though it is easy to see the reason why the Chancellors sought to extend their jurisdiction and to realize that forfeitures offered a convenient field for such extension; yet on what theoretical grounds, if any, they based the extension, we can only attempt to guess vaguely, as there is little help to be found in the early reports.

The Courts of Chancery at this time acted on two general principles: firstly, custom, the respect held for the decisions of previous Chancellors in similar circumstances and the rules which they followed, (at this date merely persuasive and not conclusive authority), which secured the Court in the jurisdiction already obtained; and secondly, conscience, the desire of the Chancellor to do justice in each particular case where the common law worked hardship, which afforded many suitable excuses for extending his power. This seems to have been vaguely recognized as early even as 1467, for when in that year the Great Seal was delivered to Bishop Robert Kirkham the King commanded "that all manere of maters, to be examyned and discussed in the Court of Chauncery, should be directed and determined accordyng to *Equite* and *Conscience*, and to the old cours and laudable custume of the same Court".[1]

Thus, we find Lambarde discussing the question

whether it be meete that the Chancellour should appoint unto himselfe, and publish to others any certaine *Rules* and *Limits* of *Equity*, or no....For on the one part it is thought as hard a thing to prescribe to *Equity* any certain bounds, as it is to make any one generall Law to bee a meet measure of *Justice* in all particular cases. And on the other side it is said, that if it bee not knowne beforehand in what cases the Chancellour will reach forth his helpe, and where not, then neither shall the Subject be assured how, or when he may possess his owne in peace, nor the practizer in law be able to informe his Client what may become of his Action.[2]

The early cases where relief was given against the penalty of a bond or the forfeiture of a mortgage were undoubtedly cases of conscience. The Chancellor gave his assistance owing to the hardship of the case. Thus there grew up a definite series of

---

[1] Hardy, *Introduction to Close Rolls.*

[2] *Archeion,* 83. For further details as to growth of precedent in the Court of Chancery, see Ashburner, *Equity,* pp. 45 *et seq.*

3-2

36   THE FOUNDATION OF THE

precedents for relief of forfeitures, ever widening as new circumstances were brought before the Court.

Now a series of precedents has a two-fold effect. Firstly, it tends to bind down a Court which professes to follow its own custom, and render it difficult to determine a case purely on the grounds of hardship to the individual. Secondly, as a case is only cited as a precedent because it is supposed to lay down some general principle, in citing it for that purpose, it is convenient to cite it in as abstract a form as possible, and special circumstances, on which the decision may have hinged, are apt to be omitted. The precedent becomes authority for a wider proposition, and so the class of cases in which the court gives relief is insensibly enlarged until an entirely new head of jurisdiction arises. This seems to have been exactly what happened in the case of legacies. At the end of the fifteenth century and the beginning of the sixteenth century it was generally admitted in Chancery that suits for personal legacies were exclusively within the jurisdiction of the Ecclesiastical Courts.[1] About the same time as relief was given in special circumstances to forfeited mortgages and bonds, the Chancellor began to take cognizance of legacies also, where they were payable at a distant date,[2] or where the original executor was dead,[3] for in these cases the Ecclesiastical Courts provided no satisfactory remedy. This was extended gradually till by the middle of the seventeenth century the Court had established a jurisdiction over legacies in general, concurrent with the Ecclesiastical Courts, and eventually superseded them entirely.

It is usually put forward that the chief ground on which the extension of the Chancellors' jurisdiction was based was that a mortgage, and likewise a bond, was to be regarded as only a security for a loan, and that when the borrower had paid the lender his principal, interest and costs, it was all the latter could in fairness and reason expect for his money. Hence, even though a forfeiture had occurred owing to delay in payment, yet the

---

[1] *Nelson* v. *Nelson*, (1591) Mon. 10; *Smith* v. *Doughtie*, (1609) Mon. 117; *Cliffe* v. *Cliffe*, (1575) Mon. 425, *contra*.

[2] *Wickham* v. *Dighton*, (1607–8) Mon. 94, 109; see also *Awlry* v. *George*, (1600) Mon. 757, and *Browne* v. *Richards*, (1600) Mon. 761.

[3] *Gwinne* v. *Hobbes*, (1616) Mon. 239; *Hale* v. *Sparry*, (1614) Mon. 199.

EQUITY OF REDEMPTION

Court, on tender by the debtor of the sum due and damages, acted on the conscience of the borrower and ordered him to accept it in lieu of the forfeiture, as being all to which he was in conscience entitled.

The authority for this view is the case of *Emmanuel College* v. *Evans*, 1625, where it is reported that the Court "conceived the said Lease being but a security, and that Money paid, the said Lease had been void".[1] It must be noted, however, that those words were written over sixty years later, when it was one of the central principles of the Court of Chancery relating to mortgages to regard them in equity as a mere security for money. Hence it is quite possible that the reporter was guilty of an anachronism, in supplying a reason for the decision in question in terms of the ideas of a later period.

The familiar statement that it was equity which first took the view that a mortgage was to be looked upon as a mere security is clearly erroneous. This fact was recognized in the reign of Edward II[2], and Littleton expressly notices this conception of the mortgage. He gives as his reasons why the money to be paid at the day named should be paid to the executors of a deceased mortgagee rather than to his heir, even if the latter "entreth into the Land as he ought"; "because the Money at the Beginning trenched to the Feoffee in manner as a Duty, and shall be intended that the Estate was made by reason of the lending of the Money by the Feoffee, or for some other Duty".[3] He gives the same reason why the heir of the mortgagor, as well as the mortgagor himself, has a right to enter upon the land on tender of the money to the mortgagee at the due and proper time: namely that "the Intent was but that the Money should be paid at the Day assessed, etc. and the Feoffee hath no more Loss if it be paid by the Heir". He then notes, if a stranger, "Who hath not any Interest, etc., will tender the aforesaid Money to the Feoffee at the Day appointed, the Feoffee is not bound to receive it".[4] The probability of the Chancellor's using this conception of the mortgage to assist his assumption of juris-

---

[1] I Ch. Rep. 20.
[2] Eyre of Kent (S.S.), III, 85, *per* Spigurnel, J.
[3] Co. Litt. § 339.   [4] *Ibid.* § 334.

38   THE FOUNDATION OF THE

diction over mortgages is increased by this previous use of it in the works of so well respected a lawyer as Littleton.

In 1611 there is a case which shows that at least for some purposes the common law regarded a pledge of chattels in exactly the same light. A strong Court held that the property pledged must be returned on tender of the money after the death of the pledgee, but not after the death of the pledgor. The judges are reported as saying, "Pledging doth not make an absolute property, but it is a delivery only until he pays, etc. so it is a debt to the one, and a retainer of the thing to the other:... for the pledge delivered is but as security for his money lent, so as he who borrows the money is to have again his pledge when he repays it". They then point out the difference between a mortgage and a pledge in much the same terms as Coke distinguishes the mortgage and the bond. "There is difference between a mortgage of land and pledging of goods; for the mortgagee hath an absolute interest in the land, but the other hath but a special property in the goods, to detain them for his security".[1]

At that time a debt was regarded as a definite thing, a "chose", a "chose", in action, it is true, but nevertheless, a "chose". Perhaps the Chancellor was assisted in extending his relief to mortgagors generally because, whereas the debt was a definite "thing", the mortgage could be regarded as a transaction collateral to the "thing", i.e. a mere security. The debt was the principal matter with which the parties were concerned, and hence, provided the mortgagee got his debt paid with interest and costs, he could not with fairness take advantage of the forfeiture under the collateral mortgage transaction.

But for the single instance of *Emmanuel College* v. *Evans*, we do not hear, either in argument or judgment, of the mortgage being a mere security for a debt as a reason for equitable relief being afforded to the mortgagor, until some time after the Restoration. Then it seems to have been used to determine several points of importance, the chief of which being its use by Nottingham in *Thornbrough* v. *Baker*, 1676, to decide finally that the interest of the mortgagee was personalty and hence

[1] *Ratcliffe* v. *Davies*, Cro. Jac. 245; Yelv. 178.

EQUITY OF REDEMPTION

39

descended to his executors instead of to his heirs.[1] The Chancery Reports of the intervening period are still so scanty and lacking in detail that we cannot thereby assume that the Chancellor took over this theory from the common law after the mortgagor's power of redemption was firmly established.

In *Thornbrough* v. *Baker*, Nottingham is reported as citing the common-law rule as to payment to the heir or executor at the day, the mortgage being but a security, in language which at once gives the impression that he was quoting Littleton, although he may not have been conscious of doing so. He speaks of this rule as one of "natural justice and equity", fit to be applied in equity by analogy with the common law. This may be taken as implying the probability of some use having been made in equity of this conception of the mortgage before the time of Nottingham. Certainly from Nottingham's time onwards to the present day it has been a leading principle of the Court of Chancery; but in view of the fact that there is such little evidence to support the contention, it seems very uncertain whether or not it was used fifty years earlier as the ground upon which the extension of the Chancellor's notion of conscience in the matter of mortgages was based. Even if it were so used, it can only be conjectured how far that use was merely in order to give a cloak of legal reasoning for a new assumption of jurisdiction, either before or after the event, and how far it was used as a *bona fide* reason and ground of conscience. It seems fairly clear, however, that at whatever date the notion of the mortgage as a mere security found its way into Chancery, it was borrowed from the common law as laid down by Littleton.

Something of the considerations which affected the Court of Equity, in their limitation or extension of the equity of redemption to various classes of conditions forfeited and agreements of like nature, can be gathered from the way in which equity dealt with forfeitures in general. When a forfeiture in the nature of a punishment for doing or failing to do some forbidden act arose out of the ancient law of property, as where a copyholder leases for more than a year, or a tenant for life makes a tortious

---

[1] 3 Swan, 628; 1 Ch. Ca. 284, *post*, p. 59.

40   THE FOUNDATION OF THE

alienation, the danger of forfeiture on the doing of that act was regarded as a recognized incident of the estate of the holder, and the Court of Chancery has never attempted to relieve against it;[1] but in matters of agreement creating penalties for non-performance in the shape of forfeiture, equity would relieve against them, wherever it was possible to assess the damage to the other party with accuracy.[2]

One of the cases where equity has always assumed this possible is where the agreement was for the payment of a sum of money.[3] In such cases, time was not regarded as the essence of the agreement, as it was in the case of a special condition. The payee, on payment of principal, interest and costs, even after the day named for payment, had all he really expected to get, unless he was attempting to take an unfair advantage of the need of the other party which had caused the latter to agree to the clause of forfeiture; whereas, in the case of a special condition, if a particular time for the performance had been agreed upon, equity could not as a general rule accurately compensate for the extension of that time. Thus a lessee who forfeited his lease for mere failure to pay rent on the precise day fixed could obtain relief in equity; but no relief was given against forfeiture for breaches of other covenants, as it was impossible to assess the damage exactly.

This would suggest that a vague conception of the mortgage as a security may have played some part in the extension of relief. The mortgage, viewed as a forfeited condition, arose out of the law of property; but, viewed as a debt with security attached, would be relievable as an agreement for a sum of money. But at the time of the extension of relief this general rule for dealing with forfeitures did not exist. It was a principle observed from the general practice of the Court long afterwards. A more likely reason for granting relief only in cases of agreement concerning money payment, etc., was the subconscious one that, had the Chancellor meddled with the property law

---

[1] *Peachey* v. *Duke of Somerset*, (1720) 1 Str. 446, 453; *In re Dixon*, (1900) 2 Ch. 561, 577; *In re Wright*, (1907) 1 Ch. 231.

[2] *In re Newman*, (1876) 4 Ch. D. 724.

[3] *Davis* v. *Thomas*, (1830) 1 Russ. and My. 506; *In re Dixon*, *supra*.

EQUITY OF REDEMPTION

as such by granting relief, he would have found the opposition of the common law too strong for him.

It is often said that the establishment of the equity of redemption was due to the fact that a mortgage was a matter of contract; and that in agreements for the payment of money time was not regarded in equity as of the essence of the contract, and so the Chancellor was willing to extend the period of payment. This is an anachronism. It is putting into the mind of the Chancellor theories which were not current for at least another half century, theories which were not the cause of the interference of the Court of Chancery in early cases of forfeiture, but which were rather the result of an attempt by a later generation to justify that interference and further activities of a like nature.

The fact that, even though the money was not paid at the time stipulated, the mortgagee got all that he had really bargained for, or ought in fairness to expect, was perhaps in the mind of the Chancellors when they first granted relief to the mortgagor in special circumstances, or later when they dispensed a more general relief; for they were administering a sort of equitable conscience, and some such considerations as these, connected with the fairness of their decisions, must have passed through their minds before they dared to interfere with the course of the common law.

In the particular case in hand it might have been noticed that an extension of time would still give the mortgagee all that he could in fairness ask, and the case may have happened to be one concerning the payment of money; but a principle that, in general, where there was an agreement for the payment of money, the time when the money was to be paid was not of the essence of the contract, was not established till a much later date. There was, as yet, no relief given in equity extending the time of payment in agreements which involved the payment of money at a fixed date, other than mortgages and specialty bonds, for the rules of the common law concerning simple contract were as yet in their infancy, and it was not until some time later that the Chancellor deemed it advisable to grant such relief.

All the Chancellor was really concerned with was fairness.

42 FOUNDATION OF EQUITY OF REDEMPTION

He must do justice to the particular case before him. Why he suddenly decided to grant relief to all mortgagors who asked for it is not known, save that the effect upon his pocket and his position must have been a strong inducement to do so. Why the theory as to time not being of the essence of the contract, a theory which does not appear as such for another half century and more, is suggested as the ground upon which he based the justice of his interference, we do not know. We have before us a case where the reason for the mortgagor's general power to redeem in equity is reported as being that a mortgage is but a security, and this theory had been in use for some purposes a long time previously at common law. Hence it is possible that the Chancellor adopted this principle of the common law as a ground for granting general relief against forfeitures; but to base the original granting of such relief upon grounds which, though they certainly existed in each particular case, had not yet been formulated as a principle of law, and were not to be so formulated for many years, is to be guilty of an anachronism. No, the Chancellor, relying on conscience as his main principle of law, possibly using the notion that the mortgage was but a security as a subsidiary rule to support that conscience, was, we submit, chiefly actuated by the desire of extending his jurisdiction.

CHAPTER III

HALE AND NOTTINGHAM:
THE EQUITY OF REDEMPTION AS A THING,
AN INTEREST IN LAND

WHEN the Court of Chancery, somewhere about the time of Richard II,[1] adopted the writ of subpoena, under which the feoffee to uses was soon made liable to be summoned into Chancery and compelled to perform his duty to the *cestui que use*, this subpoena lay only against the feoffee personally, for the confidence was declared to be personal and not to accompany the devolution of property.[2] Soon both heir and assign were held liable to the subpoena at the plea of *cestui que use*,[3] while at the other end of the scale a purchaser for valuable consideration without notice was held exempt from the use or trust.[4]

The principle upon which the interest of the *cestui que use* depended was what was called privity. Thus, on his death the right to use the subpoena descended to the heir, on the ground that the latter took by substitution and now had the same rights against the trustee as the deceased had before him. The wife, husband, or judgment creditor, had not the same privilege, for their respective estates were founded, not on privity with his person, but on the course of the law. Likewise a use was not an asset, nor subject to forfeiture for treason or felony, nor did it escheat to the lord on failure of the heirs of the *cestui que use*. Again, there was no remedy against a creditor of the feoffee to uses or trustee, nor his doweress, nor a tenant by the curtesy, nor the lord who was in by escheat.[5]

Before the Statute of Uses, to have complete ownership a person must have united the seisin in possession of the land

---

[1] See *Select Essays in Anglo-American Legal History*, II, 705 *et seq.*; Stat. 20 Ed. III, c. 5; 1 Pro. Priv. Counc. 21 Ric. II; *Scaldewell* v. *Stormesworth*, 1 Cal. Ch. 5; 1 Royal Letters Hen. IV, (Rolls ed.) 523; Palgrave, *King's Council*, pp. 131, 132, n. x.   [2] Y.B. 8 Ed. IV, 6.

[3] Y.B. 22 Ed. IV, 6; against the heir by Fortescue, C.J., *temp.* Hen. VI, Bac. *Abr. Uses and Trusts*, B, 312; Keilw. 45 b; Cary, 13.

[4] Y.B. 14 Hen. VIII, 4, 7, 8; Bac. *Abr. Uses and Trusts*, B, 312.

[5] Y.B. 5 Ed. IV, 18, pl. 7 b.

44 HALE AND NOTTINGHAM

and the use of the profits. If he had not possession as well as the use he would be liable to all the charges, such as dower, to which the land might become subject by reason of the possession of the feoffee to uses. The possession and the use were, even at common law, recognized as distinct interests, though the *cestui que use* was left to seek his remedy in Chancery.[1] The *cestui que use* was regarded as having a mere action in equity against the feoffee to uses and those in privity, and not as having an interest in land. Yet, as we have seen,[2] the use was at a very early period considered itself a thing in which there might be "estates".

Although the Statute of Uses, 1535, followed by *Jane Tyrell's Case*, 1557, which decided that there could still be no use upon a use,[3] converted the majority of uses into legal estates, thereby checking the jurisdiction of the Chancellor, the Court of Chancery continued to enforce those active trusts and trusts of terms of years which did not fall within the Statute. The nature of these trusts or uses was still much the same. In Elizabeth's reign a trust or use was said to be "a thing in privity, and in the nature of an action", and therefore, a use in a term of years did not vest in the husband by survivorship, since he had not reduced it into possession;[4] and again, it was called "a matter of privity, and in the nature of a chose in action"; and therefore it was held not assignable.[5] There were estates in this "thing", the trust, just as there were in the use.

Much about the same time as the Chancellors were widening their jurisdiction over mortgages and establishing a general right of redemption, they began in special circumstances to enforce the use upon a use.[6] Previous to this they had enforced

---

[1] Litt. §§ 462–3; Co. Litt. 272 b; *Porey* v. *Juxon*, Nels. 135; *Megod's Case*, Godb. 64.   [2] *Ante*, p. 7.

[3] 2 Dyer, 155; 1 And. 37 (pl. 96), 313; 2 And. 136; Bro. *Ab. Ff. al Uses*, 40, 54; Gilb. *Uses*, 161.

[4] *Witham's Case* (32 Eliz.), 4 *Inst.* 87; S. C. Popham, 106.

[5] *Finch's Case* (39 and 40 Eliz.), 4 *Inst.* 86; 2 Leon. 134; 3 Dyer, 369.

[6] *Case of Sutton's Hospital*, (1613) 10 Co. R. 34 a; *Sambach* v. *Dalston*, (*circa* 1634) Tot. 188; perhaps also *R.* v. *Daccombe*, Cro. Jac. 512, and *Foord* v. *Hoskins*, (1615) 2 Bulst. 337. It appears from *Finch's Case*, *supra*, *Reynell* v. *Peacock*, (1620) 2 Rolle, 105, and *Holloway* v. *Pollard*, (1605) Moore, 761, that the secret trust was enforced no earlier. See also *Select Essays in Anglo-American Legal History*, II, 747 *et seq.*

EQUITY OF REDEMPTION AS A THING   45

such a use in cases of gross fraud,[1] but now this jurisdiction was widely extended. The Civil War and the Commonwealth have obscured its subsequent growth. Probably the position during that period was uncertain, as in the case of the mortgage; but, with the abolition of the chief incidents of tenure on the accession of Charles II, the main reason holding back the Courts of Chancery, the loss to the King's feudal revenue occasioned by an extension of trusts, was removed. Within ten years the matter was past discussion and the second use enforced as a matter of course.[2] This at once increased the volume of trusts and soon caused a rapid development of the principles relating thereto.

In 1630 it was still held that, as a Court of Equity had no jurisdiction where there was no "fraud or covin" to be found and as a feme was dowable "by act and rule of law", the widow of a trustee was not bound by the trust.[3] However, three years previously, the Chancellor, assisted by all the judges, declared "that howbeit a Grant of future Possibility is not good in Law, yet a Possibility of a Trust in Equity might be assigned".[4] The old stringent rules, such as those connected with privity, which had been applied to uses were being found inconvenient when applied to the mass of trusts which grew up on the appearance of the second use. Though these were gradually swept away during the next half century, the Court adhered largely to the general principle that the new trust was of the same nature as the old use had been before the Statute; and that the same rules would still apply to the trust, so long as those rules appeared equitable. The doctrines applied to the use continued to be regarded as important guiding principles

---

[1] *Chudleigh's Case*, (1574). Bacon, *Works* (ed. Spedding), VII, 636; Cary, 14; see *Finch's Case*, (39 and 40 Eliz.), 4 Inst. 86; 2 Leon. 134; 3 Dyer, 369.
[2] The matter was debated as late as 1668, *Ash* v. *Gallen*, 1 Ch. Ca. 114; also *Compleat Attorney*, (1666) 188, 265; see also Cary, 19; 1 And. 294; 1 Coke, 139 b, 140 a. In 1670 the Lord Keeper told the House of Lords that "the trust is now the same as uses were before". *Hist. MSS. Com.* 7 *Rep.* App. Parl. 1, 3, n. 16.
[3] *Abington's Case*, Cro. Jac. 513; Hob. 214.
[4] *Warmstrey* v. *Tanfield*, 1 Ch. Rep. 29; see also *Goring* v. *Bickerstaff*, (1662) 1 Ch. Ca. 8; *Courthope* v. *Heyman*, (1642) Cart. 25, per Lord Bridgeman; *Cornbury* v. *Middleton*, (1671) 1 Ch. Ca. 208.

HALE AND NOTTINGHAM

for another century at least, and still remain of considerable authority whenever a complicated question concerning trusts arises to-day.

Even after the Restoration some of the old stringent rules were still enforced. For instance, it was still held that the trust of a fee descended to the heir free from debts,[1] that a widow should not have dower of a trust,[2] and that the heir took the estate free from judgment creditors.[3] But the narrow doctrine of privity was being steadily relaxed. In 23 Car. I it was said, "A trust is not a thing in action, but may be an inheritance or a chatell, as the case falls out", and *Witham's Case*, that the husband was not entitled to survivorship of a trust for a term of years, was held to be overruled.[4] This is the first sign we have of a new era in the conception of the trust. It is no longer a mere "action" against the trustee and his privies, but is henceforth to be treated as an actual "interest" in land in equity, a species of property in the land. As such, it soon draws to it many of the rights and incidents which accompany the idea of landed property at law. Soon grows up a rival principle to that of the analogy of the use as it was before the Statute; namely, the analogy of the common-law estate in land, or, as the doctrine is usually more widely stated, "Equity follows the law".

The new conception of the trust as an equitable interest in land was first firmly established by Lord Nottingham, Chancellor from 1673 to 1682, whose bold judicial legislation based on broad general principles has earned for him the title of the "Father of Equity".[5] To do this he discarded the analogy of the use wherever that analogy appeared to produce inconvenient results, and followed instead the general principles applicable to the legal estate. Thus it was laid down by Lord Hale,[6] and afterwards determined by Nottingham as the constant practice of the court,[7] that a tenant in dower should be bound by a trust

---

[1] *Bennett* v. *Box*, (1662–3) 1 Ch. Ca. 12.
[2] *Colt* v. *Colt*, (1664–5) 1 Ch. Rep. 254.
[3] *Prat* v. *Colt*, (1669) 1 Ch. Ca. 128.
[4] *R.* v. *Holland*, (1648) Styl, 21; Al. 15.
[5] *Brydges* v. *Brydges*, 3 Ves. 127; *Kemp* v. *Kemp*, 5 Ves. 858.
[6] *A.-G.* v. *Pawlett*, Hard. 469.   [7] *Noel* v. *Jevons*, (1678) 2 Freem. 43.

EQUITY OF REDEMPTION AS A THING   47

as claiming in the *per*, by the assignment of the heir. This was shortly afterwards extended to freebench.[1]

A further step in the protection of the interest of the *cestui que trust* was taken when Nottingham clearly enunciated the principle that it was to be preferred as against the creditors of the trustee.[2] This was finally established beyond dispute by Lord Cowper in 1715.[3] The safety of the beneficiary as regards creditors was eventually made complete in 1725 by a ruling that even the bankruptcy of the trustee did not affect the interest of the *cestui que trust*.[4] Similarly, the benefit of a trust was extended to those who came in the *post* as well as those in privity. Nottingham further held that a judgment creditor might prosecute an equitable *Fi. Fa.* against the *cestui que trust*.[5] The Statute of Frauds made trust estates liable to creditors both of living and deceased beneficiaries; and a trust was declared assets in the hands of the heir;[6] and though the latter was after-wards disputed[7] Nottingham's views on this point also eventually prevailed. Curtesy was also permitted of a trust estate;[8] but the widow of the *cestui que trust* never made good her right to dower.[9]

Lord Mansfield, after an account of the early history of the trust, concludes:

In my opinion, trusts were not on a true foundation till Lord Nottingham held the great seal. By steadily pursuing, from plain principles, trusts in all their consequences, and by some assistance from the legislature, a noble, rational, and uniform system of law has been since raised. Trusts are made to answer the exigencies of families, and all purposes, without producing one inconvenience, fraud, or private mischief, which the statute of Henry VIII meant to avoid.[10]

---

[1] *Bevant* v. *Pope*, 2 Freem. 71.
[2] *Burgh* v. *Francis*, (1673) 1 Eq. Ca. Abr. 320.
[3] *Finch* v. *Earl of Winchelsea*, (1715) 1 P. Wms. 277.
[4] *Bennet* v. *Davis*, (1725) 2 P. Wms. 316.
[5] *Pitt* v. *Hunt*, (1681) 2 Ch. Ca. 73; *Anon. Case*, cited *Balch* v. *Westall*, 1 P. Wms. 445.
[6] *Grey* v. *Colvile*, (1678) 2 Ch. Rep. 143.
[7] *Creed* v. *Colville*, (1683) 1 Vern. 172.
[8] *Colt* v. *Colt*, (1664) 1 Ch. R. 254.
[9] See Hardwicke, *Casborne* v. *Scarfe*, 1 Atk. 605; *Burgess* v. *Wheate*.
[10] *Burgess* v. *Wheate*, (1757–59) 1 Eden, 223.

HALE AND NOTTINGHAM

The relief against forfeiture given to a mortgagor on tender of principal, interest, and costs became established early in the reign of Charles I as a definite right or power which could only be extinguished by lapse of time or decree of the Court. It then became necessary to determine the nature of this power, how far it was alienable, inheritable, liable for the debts of the holder, etc.

The development of the trust estate, though largely in abeyance for the best part of a century after the Statute of Uses, was nevertheless in a much more advanced position than that of the newly created equity of redemption. The old rules relating to uses before the Statute were likewise applied to the new growth of trusts, though some of the more technical of them were soon afterwards rejected. The amount of litigation connected with trusts was also far greater than that connected with relief given to the mortgagor. Hence the Court of Chancery, in working out the nature of the "equity of redemption", as this power came to be called, naturally used those ideas of justice which were already to hand, and applied the rules and principles which they had already applied to the interest of the *cestui que trust*; and, as the expansion of these two creations of equity continued, evolved equitable principles and doctrines which were applied in common to both.

From now onwards, the evolution of the equity of redemption and the trust are very closely connected. The rules applied to the one are being constantly used in support of the application of similar rules to the other, and the differences in the nature of the two constantly emphasized to prevent the analogy between them being carried beyond its rational limits.

The Reports of proceedings in Chancery during the Civil War and the greater part of the Commonwealth are still very scanty, and it is difficult to ascertain what advance was made with the equity of redemption; but, until the time of Hale and Nottingham, there seems to have been little real progress. From the Restoration onwards the relations of the parties after the day for payment was passed, both *inter se* and in regard to strangers, were being steadily worked out, together with a number of theories as to the nature of their respective interests

EQUITY OF REDEMPTION AS A THING   49

and the general rules applicable thereto. The right of redemption had by then been consolidated by a thirty years' custom of the Court. Yet we find many decisions of an elementary character reported shortly after the Restoration as to the classes of persons entitled to that right. This shows that, in regard to the extent of that right, custom was not yet sufficiently established to prevent dispute. Some of these elementary matters may not have been dealt with previously. On this point we cannot be certain owing to the brevity and scarcity of the earlier Reports. After 1660 there is no lack of reported cases dealing with the redemption of mortgages in equity. A great number of decisions are found; but the reasons for these decisions and the rules upon which they were based are still reported but briefly, and have often to be conjectured with the aid of conclusions drawn from what are observed to be the general tendencies of the times.

Apart from the improvement in the Reports, there was undoubtedly a great increase in the amount of litigation as to the nature of this new power of redemption. This enabled progressive Chancellors to establish in a short time a number of customary rules concerning this new creature of the Court. It also enabled them quietly to extend their jurisdiction, and to encroach yet further on the common law. Soon practically all questions connected with mortgages were dealt with by the Court of Chancery to the exclusion of its rival. For instance, a jurisdiction was established over such transactions as Welsh mortgages, which were properly cognizable at common law, there being no legal forfeiture, since no day was fixed for payment, and hence no need for a power of redemption in equity, nor any real cause for interference by the Court of Chancery.

The equity of redemption seems always to have been regarded as realty and descendible to the heirs, just as the benefit of the condition or proviso for redemption was descendible at common law. The first decree of foreclosure to be found—1629—was against the heirs of the mortgagor.[1] Shortly after, the devisee also was held entitled to redeem.[2] We have seen that the heir

---

[1] *How* v. *Vigures*, (1629) 1 Ch. R. 32.
[2] *Porter* v. *Emery*, (1637) 1 Ch. R. 97.

TER   4

HALE AND NOTTINGHAM

of the *cestui que trust* acquired a similar right against the trustee at an early date. Again, relief in equity had been granted against the heirs of, and purchasers (presumably with notice) from, the mortgagee, even before the general right of redemption had been established.[1] The right of the heir[2] and devisee[3] of the mortgagor to redeem seems to have been last disputed shortly after the Restoration. So also, a volunteer taking from the mortgagor[4] and a jointress[5] were then held entitled to redeem. The position of a second mortgagee soon came under consideration,[6] and it was held by Lord Hale that a fine with proclamations would bar both a trust and an "equitable power of redemption" when levied by a stranger, but not when levied by the trustee or mortgagee.[7]

At first it was held that, if a mortgagee were given an estate in fee, it became liable to his wife's dower, which took precedence of the right to redeem, in the same manner as the widow of the trustee was held not to be bound by the trust; because, "when she is dowable by act or rule in law, a Court of Equity shall not bar her to claim her dower; for it is against the rule of law, viz. 'where no fraud or covin is, a Court of Equity will not relieve'".[8] It had always been regarded otherwise in case of redemption at the day; for in that case the question was one of common law and not of equity. The mortgage was not yet forfeited, and, on the fulfilment of the condition, the mortgagor was in of his old estate, paramount to all encumbrances subsequent to the mortgage. This liability to dower brought mortgages for long terms of years into vogue,[9] as the wife could claim no dower out of a leasehold. Such an inconvenient rule was objected to by Hale,[10] and finally overruled by Nottingham.[11]

[1] *Hanmer* v. *Lochard*, (1612) Tot. 230.
[2] *Lapworth* v. *Smith*, (1661) 1 Ch. R. 186.
[3] *Rowell* v. *Walley*, (1662) 1 Ch. R. 219. See also 1 Ch. R. 190; 1 Ch. R. 183.
[4] *Rand* v. *Cartright*, (1664) 1 Ch. Ca. 59. See also 1 Ch. R. 183.
[5] 1 Ch. R. 221; Rep. t. Finch, 97.
[6] 3 Ch. R. 73, 78.   [7] *Wolstan* v. *Ashton*, (1670) Hard. 512.
[8] *Nash* v. *Preston*, (1632) Cro. Car. 190.
[9] Bl. *Comm.* II, 158.
[10] *A.-G.* v. *Pawlett*, (1667) Hard. 466.
[11] *Noel* v. *Jevons*, (1678) 2 Freem. 43.

EQUITY OF REDEMPTION AS A THING 51

In *A.-G.* v. *Pawlett*, 1667, Chief Baron Hale is reported at length. The report of the case is perhaps the longest concerning relief of the mortgagor to be found in that century. The question was whether a trust estate was liable to forfeiture for felony. He pays great attention to the analogy of the equity of redemption, and emphasizes the differences in the nature of the two interests, which limits the extent to which the analogy may reasonably be used.

He says:

In natural justice redemption of a mortgage lies against the King. ...The King cannot be compelled to reconvey; but that an *amoveas manum* only lies in such case. And this is all that can be done, if the trustee forfeit the estate....I conceive that a mortgage is not merely a trust; but a title in equity.[1]

Again[2]:

There is a diversity betwixt a trust and a power of redemption; for a trust is created by the contract of the party, and he may direct it as he pleaseth; and he may provide for the execution of it, and because one who comes in in the post shall not be liable to it without express mention made by the party....A tenant in dower is bound by it, because she is in the per, but not a tenant by courtesy, who is in the post. So all who come in in privity of estate, or without notice, or without a consideration. But a power of redemption is an equitable right inherent in the land, and binds all persons in the post, or otherwise. Because it is an ancient right, which the party is entitled to in equity....The law takes notice of it and makes it assignable and deviseable.

In this case we first hear of the equity of redemption as a "title in equity", an "equitable right inherent in the land", which (in general) binds all comers. By the time of the accession of Charles II the mortgagor had acquired a customary right to be relieved of a forfeited mortgage on payment of principal, interest, and costs, provided he was not dilatory in seeking that relief. Yet, although he was beginning to regard the relief to be sought in Chancery as a right, by reason of the great number of previous cases in which it had been granted, he could never be certain that the Chancellor would not make exceptions to

---

[1] Hard. 465.   [2] Hard. 469.

4-2

HALE AND NOTTINGHAM

the general rule, or that a new Chancellor might not be less friendly disposed towards relieving forfeited mortgages and bonds. Again, the Chancellor sometimes decreed reconveyance of the land on terms other than payment of principal, interest, and costs.[1] We can see how uncertain the mortgagor's position still was, when we call to mind the reactionary measure of the Commonwealth Parliament, limiting redemption to one year after legal forfeiture, and even then imposing more onerous terms. It could hardly be said that he had an interest in land until he had obtained a decree for redemption. His interest was wholly forfeited at law and he had merely the right to a relief in Chancery on uncertain terms. Further, it was uncertain against what classes of persons taking under the mortgagee this right of redemption in equity would prevail. Even when he had obtained relief, the land returned to him was subject to all the charges, such as dower, to which it had become subject while in the hands of the mortgagee. The latter's creditors, his widow, etc., took precedence of the mortgagor redeeming, and it was uncertain as to how far the mortgagee, by his dealings with the property, might not be able to put obstacles in the way of redemption.

Just as the trust had come to be regarded no longer as a chose in action, but as an inheritance,[2] so now the equity of redemption is spoken of as a title to land. It is a right which takes precedence of the mortgagee's widow and creditors. It is an interest in land which is both devisable and alienable, and no longer a mere right to bring an action for relief, the terms of which were still somewhat in doubt.

As reported, the reason for this, "Because it is an ancient right which the party is entitled to in equity", is rather obscure. As it stands, it is absurd; for Hale was speaking in contradistinction to the trust, which is by far the older right of the two. It has been explained by assuming that Hale regarded the equity of redemption as the "ancient right" in equity; that is, the same estate in equity as the mortgagor had before the mortgage was made. This seems the more plausible,

[1] *Gird* v. *Togood*, (1643) Nels. 34. *Ante*, p. 29.
[2] *R.* v. *Holland*, (1648) Styl, 21, Al. 15.

EQUITY OF REDEMPTION AS A THING 53

in that he gives it as a reason after stating that the equity of redemption bound everyone in the *post* or otherwise, for which it would seem a very good reason indeed. However, this interpretation assumes that, whereas Hale, being a common-lawyer, was probably rather conservative in his views on equity, (as witness his application of the old burdensome rules of uses to the trust), he was, on this point at least, many years in advance of contemporary thought. This conception of the interest of the mortgagor does not appear as a general principle of equity till over half a century later. The only fact which lends any credence to this view is that Hale was considering the mortgage in opposition to the trust, and was regarding it as a greater interest in land than the latter, "a right inherent in the land". Yet this interpretation is very plausible and cannot be lightly set aside.

Again, Hale expressly points out that the equity of redemption is a title to land, whereas a trust savours of contract, the incidents of which may be directed at the pleasure of the contracting parties. It is dangerous to take a few sentences from a single judgment, especially an *obiter dictum*, and from that to attempt to construct some idea of the general theories of one man, much less the general notions of the time. This becomes more dangerous when we cannot be quite certain of the accuracy of the report, and there is little other material at hand to contradict an erroneous conclusion; but, while these remarks of Hale do not necessarily imply a particular line of thought, they suggest his opinion on the subject, and hence what was possibly the general conception of the time.

Bearing this limitation in mind, Hale's comparison suggests that he regarded the equity of redemption rather as a proprietary right left to the feoffor of the land upon a conditional feoffment, "a right inherent in the land", and not in any way contractual. In this he opposes an equity of redemption to a trust, which he says "is created by the contract of the party". Although he is probably using the word "contract" in the general sense of agreement, and not in the technical, legal sense, especially as the limits of that technical sense were as yet unknown; it seems evident that the equity of redemption and the notion of contract had to him no connection whatever. The idea that the

54 HALE AND NOTTINGHAM

equity of redemption was a term of the contract between the parties implied by law had not yet come into existence, nor had the notion that the time of the condition was not to be regarded in equity as of the essence of the contract. No! Hale regarded the equity of redemption as a proprietary right, an incident of the former ownership. Later this conception was extended, and the mortgagor was held to part with no land at all in equity, but still to be in of his old estate. Then the equity of redemption will be found to be regarded not only as a title to land, a proprietary right, but also as an equitable estate.

Hale's opinion as to those against whom the equity of redemption and a trust were enforceable is also worthy of attention. The equity of redemption bound all persons in the *post*, "or otherwise". Does he mean everybody, even the *bona fide* purchaser from the mortgagee without notice? Or is he loosely reported? Or is he making a general statement without regard for its limitations?

In the first place, the purchaser from a legal mortgagee without notice, actual or constructive, is very rare; indeed, it is difficult to imagine a practical illustration to-day. There seems only one reported case where the defendant pleaded he was such a purchaser, in 1673, and it was then held to be a good defence.[1] Hale's opinion as to the trust, which, he says, does not bind those in the *post*, creditors and tenants by the curtesy of the trustee, and his placing the equity of redemption in opposition thereto, tend to show that his statement as to the equity of redemption was a mere generalization. In one case Nottingham himself conveys the impression that he thought an equity of redemption more of an interest in land than a trust. He says "an equity of redemption charges the land, not a trust".[2] It would seem then, that, in spite of the more liberal principles which he applied to the trust and which soon gave the *cestui que trust* a right against all who were in the *post*,[3] he considered

---

[1] *Harding* v. *Hardrett*, Rep. t. Finch, 9.

[2] MSS. cited *Tucker* v. *Thurston*, 17 Ves. 134; see also "For the Debt due upon this Mortgage did originally charge the land which the Debts by Bond did not", *Burgh* v. *Francis, infra.*

[3] As to creditors, see *Burgh* v. *Francis*, (1673) Rep. t. Finch, 28; *Finch* v. *Earl of Winchelsea*, (1715) 1 P. W. 277.

EQUITY OF REDEMPTION AS A THING   55

the equity of redemption as binding in general, and a trust only binding on particular individuals. Following the opinion of Hale in *A.-G.* v. *Pawlett*, he appears to have held the equity of redemption binding against the lord who took by escheat.[1]

These two quotations are both *obiter dicta*. Hence it is quite possible that they were mere generalizations, and that neither speaker really meant to imply the change of thought involved. This is especially so in that the plea of purchaser for value, etc., was held good by Nottingham in 1673. Still, these sudden generalizations from specific cases have been the way in which the English law has been built up. The equity of redemption was itself established in this way, and so also was the idea that this equity was an interest in land; and this was possibly an intentional or unintentional generalization of the same nature, which was in turn soon limited again on the analogy with the trust.

Doubtless the better position in which the mortgagor was said to be as against those in the *post* greatly influenced a similar change in the principles applied to that of the *cestui que trust*. Whatever the opinion of Hale or Nottingham, the analogy of the trust, where equity has refused to follow the land into the hands of purchasers without notice ever since the time of Henry VIII, has spread so as to cover all other equities, including that of the mortgagor. It seems certain that to-day, if a valid plea of *bona fide* purchaser from the mortgagee for value without notice could be made, it would be successful against the mortgagor.

In *A.-G.* v. *Pawlett* we find Hale reported as referring to this right of the mortgagor to redeem as his "power of redemption". The date when the term "equity of redemption" came into vogue is difficult to determine. As we have seen, in 1637 the Chancellor is reported as deciding that the "benefit of the said redemption" belonged to the plaintiff.[2] The expression "power of redemption" is to be found as early as the Bankruptcy Statute of 21 Jac. I,[3] but it is there applied to the right to redeem at law. It is possible that the term "equity of redemption" is

---

[1] *Palmer* v. *A.-G.*

[2] *Porter* v. *Emery*, (1637) 1 Ch. R. 97; see *ante*, p. 28.

[3] c. 19, § 13, *ante*, p. 28.

HALE AND NOTTINGHAM

a shortened form of some such phrase as "power in equity of redemption".

The first appearance of the phrase "equity of redemption" seems to be in the report of a case which occurred in 1654.[1] The first volume of Chancery Reports, in which the case appeared, was not published till 1693. Other reports, in which cases dated from 1659 onwards are to be found containing the phrase, were all first published at an even later date.[2] The reports in question are not *verbatim*, and it may well be that the cases in which the expression appears are all reported in the phraseology of the reign of William and Mary. Hence it cannot be concluded that the expression became common about the time of the Restoration; but only that, since it is found with great frequency in the various Chancery reports published at the end of the century, it had become recognized as the generally accepted term for the relief given to the mortgagor in equity before the accession of William of Orange.

It is possible, however, that the usage of the phrase synchronized with its appearance in the reports, for the first volume of Chancery Reports, in which it appears frequently, is generally regarded as consisting of extracts from the Registrar's Books, though usually written in the reporter's own language. The case in which the term is first mentioned, (and it is there mentioned four times), has much the appearance of such an extract, perhaps *verbatim* in parts. It is composed of a statement of claim, answer, and judgment, the whole being in the form, "That James, Earl of Dirlton, being seised in Fee....And for Non-payment the Premisses became forfeited in the said Earl of Dirlton's Lifetime, who having such Title, Trust", (it was conveyed to the trustees subsequent to the mortgage), "and Equity of Redemption in the said Premisses...".

In *Roscarrick* v. *Barton*, 1673, it was argued that an equity of redemption was a mere chose in action, and not such an inheritance as was entailed by *De Donis*, and, therefore, could not be entailed in equity; but this contention was overruled by

[1] *Duchess of Hamilton* v. *Countess of Dirlton*, 1 Ch. R. 165.

[2] Nelson reports a case (1659), *Earl of Carlisle* v. *Gower*, mentioning the "equity of redemption" twice; (last reported case in Nelson, 1692, 1st ed. probably 1717; Hardres published 1693; 1 Ch. Ca. published 1697).

EQUITY OF REDEMPTION AS A THING 57

Hale and the Lord Keeper. This was the last suggestion that the equity of redemption or the trust was only a right of action and not an interest in land. Hale, as Lord Chief Justice, appeared to have become jealous of the increasing jurisdiction of the Chancery, and viewed the extension of the equity of redemption with suspicion. In this case he said, "By the Growth of Equity on Equity, the Heart of the Common Law is eaten out,...As far as the Line is given, Man will go;...An Equity of Redemption is transferable from one to another now.... We will go no further than Precedents in the matter of Equity of Redemption, which hath too much favour already". Hence he held that a decree to foreclose a tenant in tail would bind his issue in an equity of redemption "because that is a right set up only in a Court of Equity and so may be here extinguished".[1]

The Keeper of the Great Seal from 1667 to 1673 was Sir Orlando Bridgeman, a great common lawyer and conveyancer. He was essentially a lawyer and not a statesman. Hence his respect for the principles of the common law, even when as Lord Keeper he was in a position politically antagonistic to that Court. This probably explains that deference shown to the legal estate in the doctrine of tacking, which was established in 1670 by Bridgeman, Hale, and Rainsford, B., three common-lawyers sitting in the Court of Equity.[2]

Probably the favour shown by Bridgeman to the common law also paved the way for Nottingham's formulation of the principle "Equity follows the law". Nottingham, in his bold enunciation of this rule as applicable to equitable interests generally, was really stating as a principle what had long before been applied in fact, though not in name, whenever it suited the convenience of the administrators of equity. They had to find a number of general rules upon which to work out the interests which their predecessors had created, and, in the search, what could be more ready to hand than the principles of the common law. The theory of estates and many other incidents of the use had been borrowed from the common law. After the Restoration, and

---

[1] 1 Ch. Ca. 217, 219.
[2] *March* v. *Lee*, 2 Vent. 337; 3 Ch. Rep. 62; 1 Ch. Ca. 162.

58 HALE AND NOTTINGHAM

especially under Bridgeman, the analogy of the law is given as a reason for judicial decision, though it is left to Nottingham to establish that analogy as one of the chief guiding principles of equity.

In 1661, a mortgagee in possession was successful in pleading the Statute of Limitations against the mortgagor attempting to redeem;[1] and in 1668 Lord Keeper Bridgeman said, "he would have a rule to limit what time a mortgage shall be redeemable, and conceived 20 years to be a fit time, in imitation of the Statute of Limitations of real actions".[2] Three years later, he said, "he would not relieve mortgages after 20 years, for that the statute of 21 Jac. did adjudge it reasonable to limit the time of one's entry to that number of years", for, "'tis best to square the rules of equity as near the rules of reason and law as may be".[3] Lastly in *Roscarrick* v. *Barton*, Wyld, J., another common-lawyer sitting in Equity by Bridgeman's invitation, argued in his dissenting judgment that, "a decree against a tenant for life will not bind him in remainder in case of an estate at law, and he did not see why it should be in equity".[4] This was what made Hale point out that the decree of foreclosure was the extinguishment of a right established by equity. It was, in truth, the Court's permission to the mortgagee for him to exercise his legal rights.

This rule, "Equity follows the law", was applied by Nottingham to settle a matter which had been a *vexata quaestio* almost ever since the relief of mortgagors became general; namely, whether, on the mortgagor's redeeming in equity after the decease of the mortgagee, the heirs of the latter or his personal representatives were entitled to the money. The numerous decisions on the point had of late shown a tendency to favour the right of the personal representatives. In *Thornbrough* v. *Baker*, 1676, Nottingham definitely settled the matter in their favour, giving his reasons as follows:

The Reason of the Common Law in these Cases ought, as near as may be, to be followed in Equity. Now by the Common Law, if the

[1] *Saunders* v. *Hord*, 1 Ch. Ca. 184.
[2] *Pearson* v. *Pulley*, 1 Ch. Ca. 102.
[3] *White* v. *Ewer*, 2 Vent. 340.   [4] 1 Ch. Ca. 217.

EQUITY OF REDEMPTION AS A THING 59

Condition or Defeazance of a Mortgage of Inheritance be so penned, that no Mention is made either of Heirs or Executors to whom the *Money* should be paid; in that case the *Money* ought to be paid to the Executrix, in regard that the *Money* came first out of the personal Estate, and therefore usually returns thither again; but if the Defeasance appoints the *Money* to be paid either to heirs or Executors disjunctively, there by the Common Law, if the Mortgagor pay the *Money* precisely at the Day, he may elect to pay it either to the Heirs or Executors, as he pleaseth: But when the precise Day is past, and the Mortgage forfeited, all Election is gone in Law; for in Law there is no Redemption. Then when the Case is reduced to an Equity of Redemption, that Redemption is not to be upon Payment to the Heirs or Executors of the Mortgagee, at the Election of the Mortgagor; for it were against Equity to revive that Election; for then the Mortgagor might defer the Payment as long as he pleaseth, and at last for a Composition by Payment to that Hand which will use him best; much less can the Court elect...for a Power so arbitrary might be attended with many Inconveniences throughout. Therefore to have a certain Rule in these Cases, and better cannot be chose than to come as near unto the Rule and Reason of the Common Law as may be...'tis all one in Equity, as if either Heir or Executor were named, and then Equity ought to follow the Law, and give it to the Executor; for in natural Justice and Equity, the principal Right of the Mortgagee is to the *Money*, and his Right to the Land is only as Security for the *Money*; wherefore when the Security descends to the Heir of the Mortgagee attended with an Equity of Redemption, as soon as the Mortgagor pays the *Money*, the Lands belong to him, and only the *Money* to the Mortgagee, which is meerly personal, and so accrews to the Executors or Administrators of the Mortgagee....The Land was never more than a Security; and that after Payment of the *Money*, the Law keeps a Trust for the Mortgage, which the Heir of the Mortgagee is bound to execute;...The Right to a Sum of *Money* which is a personal Duty, ought always to be certain, and not to be variable upon Circumstances. Wherefore his Lordship did not think it material whether the Administratrix in this case had assets...or that there was no personal covenant to pay the mortgage *Money*.

Finally, he says: "All Mortgages ought to be looked upon as Part of the personal Estate, unless the Mortgagee in his Lifetime, or by his last Will, do otherwise declare and dispose of the same".[1] Thus, a few years later, where a man purchased of a

---

[1] *Thornbrough* v. *Baker*, (1676) 1 Ch. Ca. 284.

HALE AND NOTTINGHAM

mortgagee, apprehending he had an absolute estate, and the mortgagor came to redeem, the money was decreed to be paid to the heir of the purchaser, and not to his executor, "for that he intended it for the benefit of his heir".[1]

Nottingham followed the common law as a general principle in the determination of many other questions relating to the trust and the equity of redemption, and the succeeding Chancellors followed his lead. On that principle he held that a trust estate was assets in equity;[2] and that, if property be mortgaged after it has been devised by will, although at law the devise lapses upon forfeiture of the legal estate, yet, as until forfeiture a mortgage is a revocation *pro tanto* only at law, a mortgage was a revocation *pro tanto* only in equity, even after forfeiture.[3] Likewise, an equity of redemption was shortly afterwards made liable in equity to answer the specialty debts of the borrower.[4]

It is sometimes suggested that the analogy of the legal estate, though under Nottingham it proved a ground of settling many principles relating to equitable interests on a firm and rational basis, led to the destruction of many opportunites for the Chancellors of the succeeding century to introduce desirable reforms and checked the growth of those already established. This is scarcely correct. Doubtless it prevented the systems of law and equity from becoming too widely separated, which seems advantageous rather than the reverse; but the Court of Chancery was a great reforming influence in the civil law all through the eighteenth century, and only ceased to be so on the application of the theory of precedent under Lord Eldon and his contemporaries. There are no Acts of Parliament of first-class importance in the civil law to be found in that century as in that immediately preceding; viz. the Statutes of Limitations, Tenures, Frauds, etc.; and it was not until equity had ceased to be an active reforming agency that the reformed

[1] *Cotton* v. *Iles*, 1 Vern. 271.   [2] *Grey* v. *Colvile*, (1678) 2 Ch. R. 143.
[3] *Perkins* v. *Walker*, (1682) 1 Vern. 97; *Thorne* v. *Thorne*, (1683) 1 Vern. 141, 182; *Hall* v. *Dench*, (1685) 1 Vern. 329, 342. In this last case the reason for the decision is reported "for the intent of the mortgagor making the mortgage could be no other than only to serve his special purpose of borrowing money to supply his present occasions". This shows the use even here of the theory of the mortgage as a mere security.
[4] *Cole* v. *Warden*, (1686) 1 Vern. 410; *Plucknet* v. *Kirk*, (1686) 1 Vern. 411.

EQUITY OF REDEMPTION AS A THING 61

legislature of 1832 took up the task. It was not so much the theory, "Equity follows the law", but the dislike to break the established practice of the courts, which deterred equity judges from making a greater number of changes in the law than they did. Where a reform was urgently desired, they soon found a mode of effecting it; and the analogy of the law received scant acknowledgment when, in the view of the period, the rule of law had become inequitable. The fact that the custom of his own court was otherwise became a much more potent check on a Chancellor proposing to vary the common law than the analogy between law and equity. Equity only followed the law where the latter was found satisfactory.

Nottingham's judgment in *Thornbrough* v. *Baker* also brings forward one of the chief guiding principles, upon which perhaps the existence of the equity of redemption itself, and at any rate a large number of general rules applicable thereto, have ever since been based; namely, that the mortgagee's right to the land is in equity merely as a security for his money, for that was the intention of the parties at the time the conveyance was made. We have seen that this conception of the mortgage is found at common law as early as Littleton, and also that the mortgagor's power to redeem has always been considered as savouring of the land sufficiently to descend to the heir. In deciding that the mortgagee's interest was personalty, Nottingham stated the common-law rule in case of payment at the day in terms which suggest that he was quoting Littleton, and then applied the principle, "Equity follows the law". The common-law rule was based upon the notion that the mortgage is but a security, and hence the latter doctrine, which Nottingham enunciated as a principle of equity as well, was also satisfied by upholding the claim of the personal representatives.

At what date this notion of the mortgage as a security was first conceived and acted upon in equity to assist in the development of the equity of redemption is uncertain. We have seen that the establishment of the general right of redemption after the day may have been based to a large extent upon this idea.[1] *Thornbrough* v. *Baker* was almost certainly not the

[1] *Ante*, pp. 37–39.

HALE AND NOTTINGHAM

first case in which this conception of the mortgage transaction was consciously brought into operation by the Chancellor. Something of the same kind is to be found in 1667, where it was argued in favour of an equity of redemption in fee being made assets in equity, that, "this is a stronger Case", (than that of a trust), "for here the Lands were once in the Obligor, and never absolutely put out of him, but conditionally by way of Pledge for Money".[1]

From Nottingham's time onwards, the theory that in equity a mortgage was to be regarded primarily as a security was constantly employed as a leading principle upon which the decision of new or doubtful questions might be based; for instance, it was held that since the mortgagee's estate was personalty, his interest, being but a security, did not pass by a devise of all his lands,[2] even though the mortgagor was afterwards foreclosed.[3] Again, the test of a mortgage, that is, the test as to whether there was a right of redemption in equity if there were none left at law, was held to be whether the conveyance had originally been made as a security.[4] It was further laid down by Nottingham that, once a conveyance had been so made as a security, it was redeemable in equity until the right was extinguished by foreclosure or lapse of time, and it would remain so in spite of any agreement to the contrary, even where the parties on or before the execution of the deed had agreed to limit the right of redemption to a certain period, or to hamper or clog it in any way.[5] These doctrines were propounded as the maxims, "Once a mortgage always a mortgage", "There shall be no clog on equity of redemption", and later extended to "The land shall be returned to the mortgagor exactly as he parted with it". Even parol evidence was admitted in some cases, as in fraud, accident, or mistake, to show that a conveyance, absolute on its face, was intended between the parties to be a security for money, and hence redeemable in equity.[6]

---

[1] *Trevor* v. *Perryor*, 1 Ch. Ca. 148.

[2] *Littleton's Case*, (1680) 1 Vern. 4; 2 Vent. 351.

[3] *Strode* v. *Russell*, (1708) 2 Vern. 621.   [4] *Newcomb* v. *Bonham, infra.*

[5] *Newcomb* v. *Bonham*, 2 Ch. Ca. 58, 1 Vern. 7; *Howard* v. *Harris*, 1 Vern. 33, 190; *Clench* v. *Witherby*, (1678) Rep. t. Finch, 376. *Jason's Case*, (1681) Freem. 81, 2 Freem. 69.

[6] *Maxwell* v. *Montacute*, (1719) Prec. Ch. 256; *England* v. *Codrington*, 1 Ed. 169; *Vernon* v. *Bethel*, 2 Ed. 110.

EQUITY OF REDEMPTION AS A THING   63

The report of the case of *Newcomb* v. *Bonham*, 1681, illustrates these doctrines in their early stages of development. "But a Redemption was decreed by the Lord *Chancellor*, and the Personal Estate to be applied to the Heir towards the Satisfaction of the Mortgage, because it was a Security, and being so, could not be extinguished by any Covenant made at the Time of the Mortgage".[1] The decision was afterwards reversed by Lord North, but on other grounds.[2]

Many further results appeared from the conception of the mortgage as a security. Lord Nottingham also held that, on the death of the mortgagee, the mortgage money was assets in equity, and, as such, was to be applied for payment of debts.[3] He further held that, as the mortgage was but a secured debt, the covenant for payment was in the nature of a bond, and hence, on the death of the mortgagor, in accordance with the ordinary rules as to the administration of estates, his personal estate must be applied to discharge the debt in exoneration of the mortgaged property; and this whether such property was devised by will or passed to the heir. A few years later, this was held to apply none the less because the mortgagee was in possession, for, "it would not have made it less a debt";[4] or because there was no covenant for payment, the mortgage being in the nature of a Welsh mortgage, which it was said created "a debt of special nature,...the remedy...being not by *mutuatus* at law, or by bill in equity, but still a plain remedy, *viz.* by ejectment to recover the possession on default of payment".[5] This last shows how the Chancellors extended their jurisdiction still more by applying the doctrines already applied to the ordinary mortgage with condition forfeited to the Welsh mortgage, where there was no legal forfeiture, and hence no real reason for an assumption of jurisdiction of a Court of Equity. In the same case, Lord Cowper says, "If the mortgagee had been in possession, it would not have been less a debt since the creditor would thereby have had his remedy in his own hands".

---

[1] 2 Ch. Ca. 58.   [2] 1 Vern. 7, 8; 214, 232.

[3] *Bridgman* v. *Tyrer*, (1675) Rep. t. Finch, 236.

[4] *Starling* v. *Drapers Co.*, (1678) Rep. t. Finch, 401; *Corsellis* v. *Corsellis*, (1677) Rep. t. Finch, 251; *Pockley* v. *Pockley*, (1681) 1 Vern. 36. This was also the opinion of Hale, *Wolstan* v. *Ashton* (1670), Hard. 512.

[5] *Howell* v. *Price*, (1715) 1 P. W. 294.

64   HALE AND NOTTINGHAM

This rule as to the exoneration of the mortgaged property on the death of the mortgagor was reversed by the Real Estate Charges Act, 1854, commonly called Locke King's Act, and the later Acts amending it,[1] so that now a mortgagor's devisee must take the land subject to the mortgage, unless a contrary intention be signified by the mortgagor in the will, or in some other document.[2] The rule established by these Acts does not affect the right of the mortgagee to obtain full payment of the mortgage debt out of the personal estate, the representatives so paying having a right to a transfer of the mortgage to hold against the devisee until redemption.

---

[1] 17 and 18 Vict. c. 113; 30 and 31 Vict. c. 69; 40 and 41 Vict. c. 34.

[2] See *Re Flack*, 37 Ch. D. 677; *In re Darby's Estate, Rendall* v. *Darby*, (1907) 2 Ch. 465.

CHAPTER IV

HARDWICKE: THE EQUITY OF REDEMPTION AS AN ESTATE IN LAND

THE analogy between the trust and the equity of redemption has already been frequently pointed out. In the search for doctrines to apply to each, as new points came to be decided, Nottingham and the Chancellors who succeeded him continued to use this analogy wherever the nature of the two interests so allowed, and any progress made by the one greatly assisted the development of the other in paths which usually led towards much the same end.

The succeeding Chancellors consolidated Nottingham's work by applying the general principles laid down by him to particular sets of facts, thereby working out in greater detail the application of the doctrines which he so definitely brought into common use. They did little else. The succeeding age is essentially the age of Nottingham. Indeed, it may well be said that the equity of redemption and other equitable interests in property were regarded much in the same light some fifty years after Nottingham's retirement, as they were when he laid down the Great Seal. So far as the general conception of their nature and the general rules applicable thereto were concerned, such progress as had been made was merely the working out of secondary rules derived from his basic principles. Some of these will be dealt with later.[1] It needed another bold and farsighted judicial legislator to finish the work Nottingham had begun, and to place the principles of the Courts of Equity in such a wise, broad and conscionable position, that they would prove durable yet fair, despite the stress of time and the growing tendency to rigidity with which they were faced.

This was found in the person of Lord Hardwicke, Chancellor from 1736 to 1757, who, having before him the foundations of modern equity as laid down by Nottingham and cemented by

[1] See Chap. VIII, A, *infra*.

66 HARDWICKE: THE EQUITY OF

the equity judges of the next half century, continued the building on new lines, using, if anything, still broader principles, based upon the old it is true, but now presented in a very different aspect. By reason of this more comprehensive treatment he was enabled to make broader and wiser decisions than the growing mass of detail, tending to obscure fundamental principles, had allowed his predecessors to undertake. He thus assured the rules of equity a fair and rational basis, ere they became so rigid as to be regarded as a definitely settled system of law.

This is especially true of the equity of redemption. A general idea of the advance involved in Hardwicke's conception of its nature can be gathered from his famous judgment in the case of *Casborne* v. *Scarfe*, 1738, where a husband was held by him to be entitled to an estate by the curtesy in the equity of redemption, although he had made no offer of redemption during the life of his wife, and hence, it was argued, had not brought her estate into his possession. The reason he gave was that the equity of redemption was an equitable estate of which the wife had an equitable seisin; and further, that it was an equitable estate in possession, and hence liable to the curtesy of the husband on the wife's decease.

In his manuscript notes of his judgment, which have fortunately been preserved to us, he says:

An equity of redemption is considered as an estate in the land; it will descend, may be granted, devised, entailed, and that equitable estate may be barred by a common recovery. This proves that it is not considered as a mere right, but as such an estate whereof, in the consideration of this court, there may be a seisin, for without such seisin, a devise could not be good.

The person having the equity of redemption is considered as the owner of the land, and the mortgagee is entitled only to retain it as a security or a pledge for a debt. For this reason a mortgage, though in fee, is considered in this court as personal assets, and shall go to the executor, notwithstanding that the legal estate vests in the heir in point of law. The husband of a feme mortgagee shall not be tenant by the curtesy of the mortgage, unless the mortgage be foreclosed, by which it ceases to be a pledge. It shall not pass by a devise of all his lands, tenements and hereditaments.[1] ...

[1] Citing 2 Vern. 625.

REDEMPTION AS AN ESTATE IN LAND 67

On the like reason, a mortgage in fee of the wife was held to be only a chose in action,[1]...hence that the nature of the interest of the person who has the equity of redemption must, in the eye of this court, be a real estate; for otherwise the ownership of the land, the real property in equity, will be sunk and vested nowhere, which is not to be admitted, and therefore if it be not in the mortgagee, it must remain in the mortgagor. This will be further proved by considering the common case of the mortgage in fee made after a devise of the land. It is, in law, a total revocation of the devise; but in the consideration of equity, it is only a revocation *pro tanto*, it amounts to the same as letting in a charge upon it. The true ground of this is, that the ownership of the land doth, in equity, remain in the mortgagor, and therefore it shall pass by his devise though made precedent to the mortgage.

It had been objected...that an equity of redemption is only a right of action in equity, to be recovered on certain terms,...it is no otherwise a right of action in equity than any interest is which a man cannot come at but by suing a subpoena;...and that is the case of every mere trust of land, which is admitted to be considered always as a real estate by this court. To say this is a mere right of action in equity...then the estate in the land in nobody, for it has been determined by this court, that the mortgage is only in the nature of a chose in action....

She had no seisin whatsoever of the legal estate, either in fact or in law. The true question upon this point is, whether there was such a seisin, or possession in the wife, of the equitable estate in the land, as in the consideration of this court, is equivalent to an actual seisin of the freehold at common law....I am of opinion that there was such a seisin....An equity of redemption,...unforeclosed, is the ownership of the land, or the real estate in equity; then there must be such a thing as a seisin of it in the notion of equity, and what other seisin could there be besides that which the defendant and his wife had in this case.[2]

The conception of the equity of redemption which is here formulated by Hardwicke, a conception which has now stood the test of nearly two centuries with little contradiction, may be summed up in the sentences, "An equity of redemption is considered as an estate in the land",—"An estate whereof, in the consideration of this court there may be a seisin", and "the ownership of the land doth, in equity, remain in the mortgagor".

[1] Citing 2 Vern. 401.　　　　[2] 2 J. and W. 194.

68   HARDWICKE: THE EQUITY OF

Let us notice Hardwicke's reasons for this new doctrine. The equity of redemption may be alienated, entailed, etc. There are "estates" in it similar to common-law "estates". In other words, various interests, limited in point of time, may be carved out of it. This thing, the equity of redemption, is an "estate in equity". The person owning the equity of redemption is the owner of the land. Why? Because the mortgagee has the land but as a security. His interest is personalty, which will not pass by a general devise, nor afford a husband curtesy. The mortgagor's interest is realty. The ownership of the land must be somewhere, therefore in equity it must be in the mortgagor. Lastly, since in equity the mortgagor has an equitable estate which is obviously of the same value in point of time as the corresponding legal estates which he had before the mortgage conveyance, he must still be in of the same estate in equity as he formerly had at law. Incidentally this explains why, in the construction of wills, a mortgage is regarded in equity as a revocation *pro tanto* only.

This new doctrine is the result of Lord Nottingham's two principles: the one, "Equity follows the law", allowing estates, or interests analogous to estates, to be limited out of the equity of redemption, and applying to those interests rules similar to those applied to the like estates at law; the other, that the mortgagee has but a chattel interest in the land for the purpose of his security, and hence the mortgagor is still the owner in the eyes of equity, much as at common law the tenant by *elegit* or statute had been denied seisin, which was still retained by the debtor. These are the principles used by Nottingham in his general settlement of equitable interests. So obvious does Hardwicke's conclusion seem, that it is difficult to understand why fifty years passed away before it came to be regarded as a fundamental equitable principle.

Probably some such notion as this had been growing in the minds of the lawyers of the preceding generation. Thus Peerre Williams reports the following argument as taking place in 1715, "that if a trustee confessed a judgment or statute, tho' at law these were liens on the estate, yet, in equity they would not affect it; because the estate in equity would not belong to the

REDEMPTION AS AN ESTATE IN LAND   69

trustee, but to the *cestui que trust*".[1] Again, in 1730, a strong Court held that

an estate, though mortgaged, continues still to be the estate of the mortgagor, subject to the payment of the pledge which is upon it; and for which reason, the mortgagee's right is only to the money due upon the land, not to the land itself; till the mortgage is fore-closed, it is not properly the mortgagee's land, or to pass as such by the devise of all his lands, if the testator had other lands to satisfy the words of the will.[2]

There is, however, hardly any mention of this doctrine in the reports until Hardwicke's famous judgment in *Casborne* v. *Scarfe*. No one appears to have been so bold as to pronounce it in such a manner as to make it a fundamental principle, upon which the equitable rules relating to mortgages should for the future be based. This was left to Hardwicke, who, by basing his reasoning upon this more advanced view of the mortgagor's equity, was able to throw over most of the unsatisfactory technicalities retained or introduced by pre-ceding Chancellors in working out the principles enunciated by Nottingham and which threatened to become fixed rules. He was thus able to take big strides in the evolution of the law of mortgages, and to place that law on a wider and hence more durable basis from which it would continue to expand on fair and rational lines, until a noble structure had been erected by the Court of Chancery, a structure which soon became one of the most important features of English land law, having a far-reaching effect upon the internal economic position of the country.

Both Nottingham's dominating principle, "Equity follows the law", and Hardwicke's conception of the mortgagor as owner of the land in equity, were general principles founded upon particular rules already established supporting the enunciation of the principle concerned. In Nottingham's case these rules had been brought into being by an unconscious use of the principle itself, not as a general working principle of law with which to support the rule to be applied, but by an experimental application of it in certain cases, because it seemed the most convenient theory to adopt. For instance, Equity followed the law long before the Statute of Uses, in allowing like estates

[1] *Finch* v. *Winchelsea*, 1 P. Wms. 278.   [2] 3 P. Wms. 62.

70   HARDWICKE: THE EQUITY OF

in the use to those allowed at common law, and it had always thereafter been consciously or unconsciously borrowing the common-law rules for the regulation of equitable interests, such as the use, the trust, and later the equity of redemption.

Having established a general principle from the particular rules already in force, the law is able to take a further step forward and work out other rules from this general principle to suit a variety of difficult situations. If these new rules are just and equitable when applied to new cases, and, where they come into conflict, more just and equitable than the old rules which do not fit in with the new principle, that principle will stand the criticism of the age and be a stepping stone in the law of the land. This is the way in which our common law and equity have been built up, by a process of trial and error. Just as the invention of a new and simple symbol in the place of a long mathematical formula simplifies the calculations to· be made, and, when all the ideas involved can be carried in the head mechanically by means of that symbol, the mind is able to make a further advance into unknown realms of mathematical speculation; so, a new and simple explanation of a number of closely related, yet complicated series of juristic ideas, put into a single commonplace legal phrase which conveys the whole, leads to a great advance in jurisprudential thought, which must result in a corresponding advance in practice.

This was certainly true of Hardwicke's new formula for the equity of redemption. It enabled the Court of Chancery to reject some subsidiary technical rules followed by the preceding Chancellors in their administration of the doctrines of Nottingham. The Court then proceeded with the settlement of the equity of redemption unhampered by these technicalities, following a new, clear, fundamental principle wide enough to cover the whole field, and thus formed a fair and rational system, ere the doctrines of equity became stereotyped; a system which would prove durable despite the changing conditions of life involved in the last two centuries.

In *Casborne* v. *Scarfe*, Hardwicke did not definitely state that he regarded the estate of the mortgagor as the same beneficial estate in equity as he had before the mortgage relationship began.

REDEMPTION AS AN ESTATE IN LAND 71

However, he declares, "the ownership doth in equity remain in the mortgagor", which, in view of his other remarks, would seem to imply also that the estate was the same estate as he had before the mortgage transaction. His words in *Sparrow* v. *Hardcastle*, 1754,[1] would also give that impression. The question concerned the revocation of a devise by a subsequent mortgage of the land. He says:

The general principle by which cases of this kind are governed is, that at the time of the devise the devisor must have a disposing capacity, and an estate in the land devised; and that the estate must remain in the same plight and condition to the time of his death.... Mortgages and securities are the only exceptions;...the true ground of those exceptions is, because a mortgage is merely a security, and though the conveyance be of a real estate, yet, in the consideration of this court, it is a chattel interest only.

Hence in the eye of the Court of Chancery the same estate must still remain in the mortgagor. This, at any rate, is the view of the matter taken by Arden, M.R., in 1800. After speaking of Hardwicke's ruling on this point, he says, "By the mortgage there is a complete revocation at law: but a Court of Equity says, he still remains possessed of the estate in equity, subject to the debt secured by the mortgage....Put the case, not of a mortgage; for it may be said, that in equity is only a chattel interest; and that he is seised of his former estate".[2]

The acceptance of this new conception of the nature of the interest of the mortgagor was made the more certain by the circumspect manner in which Hardwicke and his immediate successors refrained from stretching the doctrine involved beyond its rational limits. Its immediate effect may be seen from the case of *Ryall* v. *Rolle*, 1749, where the question was whether goods mortgaged and left in the possession of the debtor were goods in his possession "by the consent and permission of the true owner" within the bankruptcy statute of 21 Jac. In the words of Sir Thomas Parker, C.B.:

The principal difficulty upon this case arises from words of the statute, "by the consent and permission of *the true owner*", and it

[1] Amb. 224.
[2] *Harmood* v. *Oglander*, 6 Ves. 221, the decision was afterwards reversed, 8 Ves. 126, but not on this point.

72   HARDWICKE: THE EQUITY OF

is insisted that they are only applicable to absolute, and not conditional sales, because a mortgagor, having a right to redeem, is considered as the true owner. But [he points out] the words are put in opposition to false and pretended ownership, the bankrupt appearing to have the true ownership of the goods by *the possession*.[1]

He then shows that this is the same in the case of land where the mortgagor is left in possession, and hence mortgages are within the Act.

Burnet, J., a common-law judge, takes no notice of this new equitable doctrine of the mortgagor's ownership, but regards the matter from the point of view of common law only. He says:

There is no reason to make a distinction between an absolute and a conditional vendee, but by confounding the difference betwixt pawns and mortgages. There might some doubt arise, if this were the case of a pawn, but it cannot be doubted in the case of a mortgage, for it is an immediate sale to the mortgagee; and though the mortgagor may buy it again, or redeem by favour of a court of equity, yet, till then, the vendee is the absolute proprietor.[2]

Hardwicke applies the principle, "Equity follows the law", abandoning the notion of equitable ownership completely in a case such as this, where its application would defeat the object of a Statute. He says, "Equity ought to follow the law; if it does not, infinite mischief would follow. It is easy to turn a legal into an equitable interest, and if parliamentary provisions as to a legal interest were not to be followed as to equitable interests, it would defeat the act".[3] Next year Strange, M.R., likewise declined to apply the equitable rule of the mortgagor as owner in construing the Mortmain Act.[4] He says:

The design of the act was to lay a restraint on every method, whereby land might possibly come to such hands, unless by the manner therein prescribed.... But was there no other way whereby the interest in land might come to a charitable use? Yes, money due on mortgage was a charge and incumbrance on land; the payment of which depended on the pleasure and ability of the mortgagor.[5]

The question as to how far the doctrine "Equity follows the law" could be carried came to a head in the case of *Burgess*

[1] 1 Atk. 174.   [2] *Ibid.* 170.
[3] *Ibid.* 184.   [4] 9 Geo. II, c. 36.
[5] *A.-G.* v. *Meyrick*, 2 Ves. S. 47.

REDEMPTION AS AN ESTATE IN LAND 73

v. *Wheate*, 1757–9. The point to be decided was whether, on the death of the *cestui que trust* intestate and without heirs, his lands held in fee would escheat to the lord; and this question in the case was before the Court for more than two years. Sir Thomas Clarke, M.R., contended that trusts must be governed strictly by uses, and as there was no escheat in equity of a use, there could be none of a trust. This principle had been undermined a century before by Nottingham and his contemporaries, giving the husband of a *cestui que trust* curtesy, his judgment creditor a lien, and making equitable interests assets, etc.[1]

Lord Mansfield took a very different line of argument. He refused to accept the analogy of the use, pointing out that "its positive authority does not bind where reason is defective"; but he favoured an escheat in equity on the ground that equity follows the law. He considered that trusts were to follow the law so completely and entirely, that whatever would be the rule of law, if it were a legal estate, should be applied in equity to a trust estate. Indeed, he went so far as to say:

The forum, where it is adjudged, is the only difference between trusts and the legal estates. Trusts here are considered as between the *cestuy que trust* and trustee (and all claiming by, through, or under them, or in consequence of their estates,) as the ownership and as legal estates, except when it can be pleaded in bar of the exercise of this right of jurisdiction.[2]

He cited the case of dower as the sole exception, which proves the rule. He repeated his conviction on the soundness of the principles he had adopted:

Twenty years ago I imbibed this principle, that the trust is the estate at law in this court, and governed by the same rules in general, as all real property is, by imitation. Everything I have heard, read or thought of it since, has confirmed that principle in my mind.[3]

Lord Chancellor Northington, whose intermediate opinions seem most in accordance with sound reason and principle, thought that trusts were to be administered on the footing of uses, but not to the exclusion of the improvements subsequently

---

[1] *Ante*, p. 47.   [2] 1 W. Bl. 160.
[3] *Ibid.* 161.

74   HARDWICKE: THE EQUITY OF

introduced. He emphasized the limitation of the analogy of law, the doctrine of the ownership of the *cestui que trust* in equity being as between privies to the trust only, and not between strangers. The lord by escheat was not privy to the trust, and therefore could neither benefit by, nor be burdened with it, and hence it would not escheat to him. His arguments are summed up thus:

> It is true this court has considered trusts as between the trustee, *cestuy que trust* and those claiming under them, as imitating the possession, but...it would be a dangerous conclusion to say, therefore, this court has considered the creation and instrument of trust as a mere nullity; and the estate in all respects the same as if it still continued in the seisin of the creator of the trust, or the person entitled.... Where there is a trust, it should be considered in this court as the real estate, between the *cestuy que trust* and the trustee, and all claiming by or under them; and the trustee should take no beneficial interest that the *cestuy que trust* can enjoy; but for my part I know of no instance where this court has ever permitted the creation of a trust to affect the right of a third person [i.e. a stranger to the trust].[1]

The actual decision in *Burgess* v. *Wheate* has never come up for consideration afresh. It has usually been regarded as correct, while Lord Mansfield's opinion has often been treated in argument as erroneous.[2] The limitation of the analogy of the law which Lord Northington laid down in this case, that it does not apply in the case of strangers, seems to have been generally accepted as correct.

Hardwicke's judgment in *Casborne* v. *Scarfe* is also noticeable by reason of his use of the expressions, "equitable estate" and "equitable estate in the land", in speaking of both the equity of redemption and the trust. He supports his position with regard to the equity of redemption by constant reference to the trust, classifying both as "equitable estates". Thus he says, "The question then will be reduced to this, whether there can be a tenancy by the curtesy of an equitable estate of the wife; but that has so often been determined, that I take it to be the settled law of this Court, founded on the maxim that equity follows

---

[1] 1 Eden, 250.
[2] 2 Ves. J. 174; 2 Sim. and St. 502.

REDEMPTION AS AN ESTATE IN LAND 75

the law". He then cites *Williams* v. *Wray*[1] and *Sweetapple* v. *Bindon*,[2] both cases where curtesy was allowed of a trust, and continues:

The principal objections relied upon were two: First, that there was a laches in the husband, for that he might have paid off the mortgage money, or brought his bill to redeem, and thereby have gained the legal estate....The clear answer to this objection is, that it equally holds in the case of a trust estate, or of a sum of money to be laid out in the purchase of lands. If it had been a mere trust estate, the husband might, with more ease, have obtained a decree for a conveyance, than, in the case of a mortgage, for a redemption, and in the case of *Sweetapple* v. *Bindon*, the husband might undoubtedly have brought his bill to have the money laid out in a purchase of land. Secondly...that it has been determined that a wife shall not be endowed of an equity of redemption;... and the rule ought to be equal: this proves abundantly too much; for it has been also determined that a wife shall not be endowed of a mere trust estate, of which it is admitted that the husband shall be tenant by the curtesy.[3]

Hardwicke, then, speaks of an equity of redemption as an equitable estate; and, what is more, speaks of it as an equitable estate "in the land". He also speaks in the same terms of the trust. This is a new conception. Estates were recognized in the trust and the equity of redemption almost from their uprising; but they were estates in the "thing", the equity of redemption or trust, and not in the land itself. The estates in the equity of redemption or trust now became equitable estates in the land, the ownership of the land in equity; and the protection of this ownership, so far as equity could do so, now became one of the chief guiding principles of that Court.

Previous to Hardwicke "the estate" in the land, denoting the legal estate, is usually found opposed to the trust or equity of redemption of that "estate". The ideas, "trust of the estate" and "equity of redemption of the estate", were very common in the days of Nottingham and his successors,[4] and are sometimes used by Hardwicke in spite of his conception of an equitable estate.[5] Likewise, a few years later, Lord

---

[1] 2 Vern. 680.   [2] *Ibid.* 536.   [3] 2 J. and W. 198.
[4] 1 Eq. Ca. Abr. 320; 1 Vern. 33, 191; Freem. 115, n.; 1 P. Wms. 278; etc.
[5] As to the equity of redemption see 1 Atk. 487; 2 Atk. 428, 494.

76   HARDWICKE: THE EQUITY OF

Mansfield says: "The trust is the estate", meaning that the trust was much the same as the legal estate.[1]

The conception of the trust and equity of redemption as estates in the land seems to coincide with the appearance of the term "equitable estate" as used by Hardwicke, or "trust estate" when the trust was the subject of consideration.[2] This new terminology seems to have soon superseded the old so far as the Chancery was concerned; but the Courts of Common Law, refusing to take cognizance of the dealings of equity, continued to speak of "the estate" in the land, and this expression is still found to-day. The term "legal estate" was for a long time used in the Courts of Equity only, and only then when contrasted with a similar "equitable estate". Its meaning was always precisely the legal ownership known to the common law.

It is usually stated, by those few modern lawyers who object to the term "estate" in the strict sense being applied to equitable interests generally, that Hardwicke used the word, not in the technical sense, but in a sense merely synonymous with interest; and when he spoke of an estate in land, he meant merely an interest in that land. They contend that the equity of redemption is still a "thing" out of which estates may be carved, rather than an estate in the land itself. They also point out that there are interests in land such as seignories, profits à prendre, rights of entry and rentcharges, which were devisable, alienable, descendible, etc., or partially so, but which have never been regarded as estates in land. There is no reason to suppose, as they suggest, that Hardwicke's chief reason for declaring the equity of redemption an estate in the land itself was its devisability, etc. Certainly he prefaces his judgment by remarking on this fact; but surely it was merely to show that the equity of redemption possessed this feature of an estate.

The expression "equity of redemption of an estate" demonstrates the relation between the equity of redemption and estates at common law at the close of the seventeenth century. At that time the equity of redemption was still regarded as a "thing",

---

[1] *Burgess* v. *Wheate*, (1757–59) 1 Eden, 227.

[2] As to estates tail in the trust see 1 Vern. 13, 41; 2 Vern. 131, 226, 552, 583; Pr. Ch. 228; 1 P. Wms. 90.

REDEMPTION AS AN ESTATE IN LAND 77

the estates carved thereout being estates in the "thing" and not in the land. Hardwicke expressly states that the equity of redemption is an estate in the land, and, even when the context is ignored, it needs a considerable stretch of imagination to construe this to mean a "thing" out of which estates may be carved. The conception that in equity the mortgagor has the same estate as he had before at common law is a very natural extension from the idea conveyed by the phrase, "the equity of redemption of the estate". Hardwicke's use of this latter phrase is easily explained when it is observed how closely the one idea follows the other and how easily the earlier terminology, by a slight alteration in meaning, can be used to fit the new conception of the equity of redemption as an estate in land. One cannot imagine that Hardwicke ever called the holder of such interests in land as an equitable servitude or a rentcharge the owner of the land, or said that such holder had an estate in that land. Likewise he would not have regarded an equitable servitude as giving an equitable seisin. In Hardwicke's day, as to-day, seisin implied the possession, in person or by another on one's behalf, of an estate of freehold, either immediately or in the future. Equitable seisin then meant the possession of an equitable "estate" of freehold, the same estate in equity as the mortgagor had before the mortgage conveyance, but subject now to the mortgagee's chattel interest for the purposes of his security. It is inconceivable that Hardwicke was using three technical expressions, "estate", "seisin" and "ownership", in a most untechnical manner, or that he should go to such lengths to show that an equity of redemption was an interest in land, a matter decided generations before by Hale and Nottingham and never disputed since. No, Hardwicke meant an "estate" in land similar in nature to the "estate" in land at common law, an interest in land limited in point of time, the only difference being that it was an estate in contemplation of equity only.

A few years later Lord Mansfield, referring to *Casborne* v. *Scarfe*, said, "In the eye of this court Lord *Hardwicke* thought the equity of redemption is the fee simple of the land. It will descend, may be granted, devised, etc. This proves it is considered as such an estate, whereof, in the consideration of this

78 HARDWICKE: THE EQUITY OF

court, there may be a seisin; for without such a seisin, a devise could not be good of a trust".[1] This only strengthens the view that Hardwicke was not merely making irresponsible remarks about interests when he spoke of an estate. If he thought of the equity of redemption as a fee simple, the latter being an estate, he must have regarded the equity of redemption as an estate also.

In view of the innumerable examples which may be found, it seems hardly necessary to show that the expression "equitable estate" has been in general use in speaking of the equity of redemption and the trust, and that it is still so used by all, save a few who wish to burden English jurisprudence with an unnecessary technicality by confining the notions involved to legal estates. However, a few quotations in point may be instructive and will serve to illustrate this well-known fact.

In 1796 Arden, M.R., is at pains to show that the equitable estate and the legal estate are quite distinct, but he evidently regarded both as estates in the land. He says:

Where he has the same interest in both, he ceases to have the equitable estate, and has the legal estate.... The equitable estate is a mere creature of this Court, and subsists in idea only as to any legal consequences, that might result from possession of it, but totally distinct from the legal estate. This Court has determined, that such equitable estates are to be held perfectly distinct and separate from the legal estate. They are to be enjoyed in the same condition, entitled to all the same benefits of ownership, disposable, devisable and barable, exactly as if they were estates executed in the party.[2]

Again, in 1809 Sir William Grant says:

The question, whether the right of the tenant in tail of an equitable estate to suffer an equitable recovery can in any case be affected by adverse possession, it is not necessary to determine; [and again] It is now found by the Decree, that Mr and Mrs *Smith* had in them an equitable estate tail at the time the recovery was suffered. The conclusion seems to be, that it was well suffered.[3]

Lord Blackburn, when discussing the doctrine of tacking,

[1] *Burgess* v. *Wheate*, (1757–59) 1 Eden, 225.
[2] *Brydges* v. *Brydges*, 3 Ves. 126; see also *Williams* v. *Owens*, (1795) 2 Ves. J. 595, and *Harmood* v. *Oglander*, 6 Ves. 221, *ante*, p. 71.
[3] *Grenville* v. *Blyth*, 16 Ves. 229.

REDEMPTION AS AN ESTATE IN LAND   79

notes this long usage of the notion of equitable estates. He says:

It would seem that as now for a very long time equitable estates have been treated and dealt with as to all other intents estates, any rules founded on the antiquated law ought to be no longer applicable, and that *cessante ratione cessare debet et lex*; but some rules apparently founded on this antiquated law have been so uniformly and long acted upon that they must be treated as still binding.[1]

There are innumerable other instances of judicial recognition of the term "equitable estate", and an almost uninterrupted usage of the phrase by text-writers. Some of these will appear in subsequent quotations, but those mentioned here will suffice to show the contexts in which it has been freely used with a meaning exactly similar to that of an "estate" in land at law, viz. the enjoyment of land limited in point of time.

Those modern jurists who object to the use of the expression "equitable estate", point out that originally the only "estates" in land were those which existed at common law, long before the trust, or even the use, came into being. It is well for them to point out how at one time there were no equitable estates; but it is ridiculous, in the face of the fact that equitable estates have been spoken of as such with little contradiction for more than two centuries, to try, in a spirit of accommodation to the institutions and habits of a bygone age, to return to a former meaning of the word without any more justification than the fact that such a meaning is historically correct. Even that is not the original meaning, but a meaning which the word had reached at a particular stage of its development. We may re-mark, as Challis does after his attack on the conception of the interest of the termor as an estate in land, "It is too late now", in the face of so much authority, "to dispute it"; unless indeed a better phraseology is to be introduced, or the generally ac-cepted expression is found to be inconvenient or misleading.

The phrase "equitable estate" has unfortunately been used occasionally by both judges and text-writers in a loose sense synonymous with interest. The occasions on which this laxity has been shown are invariably evident from the context; and,

[1] *Jennings v. Jordan*, (1881) 6 A. C. 693, 714.

HARDWICKE: THE EQUITY OF

since this criticism of the term has brought the matter to notice, it is now so infrequent as to be unlikely to cause confusion. The expression "equitable estate" has a generally accepted technical sense analogous to "estate" at law, an interest limited in point of time.

An equitable estate is in general regarded in equity in exactly the same manner as a legal estate is at law. Most of the incidents applicable to the legal estate are applied by analogy to the equitable estate. This is so even in the consideration of a man's status, in the old sense of the term, for it is the *cestui que trust* and not the trustee who is entitled to the Parliamentary franchise.[1]

The various types of equitable estates and their respective differences are almost identical with those of estates at common law. There can be equitable estates for life, in tail, and in fee simple, just as there can be similar legal estates. Above all, the so-called equitable estates conform to the generally accepted technical definition of an estate at law, viz. an interest in land limited in point of time. The equitable life interest, fee tail, and fee simple, are as much limited in point of time as the like legal estates, and have been considered as an interest in land ever since the middle of the seventeenth century.[2] Thus, their classification as estates renders a service by emphasizing the vast similitude of these two great series of interests in land, legal and equitable; and, since those equitable interests generally called estates come within the generally accepted definition of "estate" in the technical sense, a very weighty reason for the exclusion of such equitable interests must be found, before we confine the term to interests of a legal character only. Again, the trust conforms with that idea which the word "estate" brings to the legal mind in the shape of enjoyment, in that the *cestui que trust* has a right in equity to the enjoyment of the rents and profits, and even of possession, subject to the limitations imposed by the terms of the trust. There is no need to refuse to consider trusts as within the accepted definition

---

[1] 7 and 8 Will. III, c. 25, § 7; 2 and 3 Will. IV, c. 45, § 23; 6 and 7 Vict. c. 18, § 74.
[2] *R. v. Holland*, (1648) Styl, 21.

REDEMPTION AS AN ESTATE IN LAND   81

because the right to such enjoyment is equitable and not legal. It is still a right to enjoyment of limited duration.

There are various differences between the ownership of a mere equitable estate, the legal estate being left outstanding, and the ownership of both the legal and the beneficial interest. This is what gives the objector to the term "equitable estate" some colour for his argument. In the same way as there are differences between the ownership of an estate tail and an estate for life at common law, (and there must always be differences between two non-identical subjects classified under one head); yet, because those differences are well known, they do not in the least render dangerous the classification of the two interests both as estates in land; so the well-known differences between so-called equitable and legal estates do not make the phrase "equitable estate" in any way inappropriate or confusing, the more so because these differences are so much emphasized by the prefixes "legal" and "equitable". All that has to be done is to remember that there may be either legal estates or equitable estates and to note the different nature of each. Indeed, the subdivision of estates into legal and equitable is valuable in itself as a further classification of the different forms of estates.

Those who dispute the accuracy of the expression "equitable estate", base their objections to its use, firstly on its inconvenience, a fact which we deny, the reverse being the case; and secondly on its lack of historical foundation, even though it has had the uninterrupted acceptance of the last two centuries. As to the first objection, we deny its existence at all. As to the second, it seems totally inadequate; especially since even the term "estate", as applied to those legal interests to which they wish to confine it, was originally a Latin word with a different meaning altogether; and, even since its appearance as an English word with something of its present meaning, it has undergone further historical change by a process of expansion, and that since the notion of an estate in the use first appeared. Hence we conclude that the question whether such a thing as an equitable estate can truly exist is definitely decided in the affirmative, and we will therefore proceed to examine the interest of the mortgagor in this connection.

82   HARDWICKE: THE EQUITY OF

Most of those who object to the classification of the equity of redemption as an estate in the land object also to the classification of any equitable interest whatever as such an estate. This has now been dealt with. Still, there are others who, while admitting the case of the trust, etc., do not accept that of the equity of redemption. Hence it seems necessary to deal with the latter in particular.

Hardwicke's conception of the equity of redemption as an "estate" in land, as formulated in *Casborne* v. *Scarfe*, has now been a fundamental principle of the Court of Chancery in its dealings with mortgages for wellnigh two centuries, and has held its position as such until disputed by some few modern jurists, in an age when nothing is free from criticism. There are, indeed, one or two *dicta* objecting to the application of the term "estate" to the interest of the mortgagor. Thus in 1821 Sir John Leach, V.C., says, "The equity of redemption is not an estate, but an interest, and may well be conceived as substantially vested in the assignees (in bankruptcy) before a bargain and sale".[1] And again Bacon, V.C., has said of the equity of redemption:

It is said that that is an estate. But it is by a figure of speech only that it can be called an estate. It may be in some instances that a husband may have a title by courtesy, and that gavelkind and borough english may apply to it. All these are necessary consequences of the law which recognises the interest of a mortgagor in his equity of redemption, but they do not alter the nature of the interest or create an estate; and in my opinion it is a mis-application of terms to call an equity of redemption an estate in the proper technical legal sense. That it is a right is beyond all doubt.[2]

This latter is certainly a direct attack, but these *dicta* appear as isolated instances in opposition to the established usage of two centuries. Perhaps one of the strongest cases for the acceptance of this doctrine is that, in spite of its having been a generally accepted conception of the Court of Chancery since the time of Hardwicke, there has been practically no fault found with it until the modern age of criticism. A few examples of favourable *dicta* must now be given.

[1] *Lloyd* v. *Lander*, (1821) 5 Madd. 290.
[2] *Paget* v. *Ede*, (1874) 18 Eq. 125.

REDEMPTION AS AN ESTATE IN LAND   83

In *Shrapnel* v. *Vernon*, 1787, where the question was as to whether the *cestui que trust* was "seised" in fee in possession so as to comply with the excepting section of the Annuity Act,[1] Lord Thurlow declared:

In many Acts of Parliament, an equitable estate is considered the same as if it were a legal estate; the words *seised in* law and equity, in the qualification act show that the word *seised* is applicable to both....I cannot distinguish this from the common case of a mortgage, when the mortgagor continues seised in equity, subject to the charge, and he grants an annuity. The only question is whether the word seisin will extend to being seised of an estate in equity, which, unless I am mistaken in point of law, it will.[2]

Here Lord Thurlow undoubtedly uses the terms "seisin" and "estate" in connection with the equity of redemption, and Lord Ellenborough subsequently held this case sufficient authority for there to be a sufficient "seisin" of an equity of redemption to bring it within the exception to the Act. Lord Eldon remarks that, if the Courts of Law in examining the Statute are authorized to "take notice of equitable interests of one species; why should they not those of another, subject to this qualification; that they must be equitable interests of such a nature as this court regards as substantially equal to the owner-ship in fee or in tail".[3]

In 1816, it was pointed out, "The mortgagee has never any right, in Equity, to the Estate, except as a Fund to pay him his Debt; for every other purpose, the Estate is the Estate of the Mortgagor.... Where the mortgagee is overpaid, he is merely a Trustee holding a legal Estate in the Estate of another".[4]

Sir Thomas Plumer in *Cholmondeley* v. *Clinton*, 1820, a case concerning the period of limitation against the mortgagor's redemption, distinguishes between legal and equitable estates in such a manner as to include an equity of redemption under the latter. He says:

The course of reasoning pursued...appears to me to lead, by in-evitable consequence, to a denial of the analogy, hitherto universally understood to be long and clearly established, between legal and

[1] 17 Geo. III, c. 26, § 8; repealed 53 Geo. III, c. 141.
[2] 2 Bro. C. C. 268.   [3] *Tucker* v. *Thurston*, (1810) 17 Ves. 131.
[4] *Quarrell* v. *Beckford*, (1816) 1 Mad. 278.

6-2

84 HARDWICKE: THE EQUITY OF

equitable estates, and particularly in respect of limitations....If then it is to be clearly established that in all other respects this analogy subsists between legal and equitable estates, and that they are in general governed by one and the same system of law, why should there be an exception made of the Statute of Limitations?[1]

He continues:

Disseisin, strictly speaking, can never take place of a mere equitable estate. The equitable owner has not the entire estate, legal and equitable, but only a limited and partial interest. At law his possession may be said to be precarious and permissive, for law recognises no right to the possession, except that which is vested in the holder of the legal estate. These are the necessary and inseparable incidents to every equitable estate.

Lord Blackburn's observations on the matter of equitable estates when dealing with the doctrine of tacking have already been quoted.[2] Quite recently Kekewich, J., said, in terms approved unanimously by a strong Court of Appeal:

The Court having decided that the mortgagor has that right to redeem, construes it as really an estate in land. It is not a legal estate, but what is termed an equitable estate—as much an interest in land as the real fee simple. It is a fee simple subject to a charge, and is vulgarly styled in legal language the equity of redemption.... The mortgagor has an estate in the land, and he can deal with that estate just as much as if he had never made a mortgage....The next step again is easy and natural: when he conveys away his estate or part of his estate in the land he necessarily gives to each of the persons in whose favour he grants an estate the right to do that which he himself can do, that is, to redeem the mortgage.[3]

Not only has the equity of redemption been accepted by the bench as an equitable estate in the land and as affording an equitable seisin within the statutory conception of the word, but it has been expressly brought within the definition of the word "estate" by several important statutes. In at least three[4] different statutes there is a clause of the following type, "Estate shall extend to an Estate in Equity as well as at law, and an Equity of Redemption". Here the equity of redemption is

---

[1] 2 J. and W. 145 *et seq.*
[2] *Jennings* v. *Jordan*, 6 A.C. 698; *ante,* p. 79.
[3] *Tarn* v. *Turner*, (1888) 39 Ch.D. 459.
[4] 11 and 12 Vict. 48, § 1; 12 and 13 Vict. 77, § 54; 21 and 22 Vict. 72, § 1.

REDEMPTION AS AN ESTATE IN LAND 85

expressly included in the definition of the word "estate". It might be possible to argue that, inasmuch as the equity of redemption was mentioned in particular, it was not considered by the framers of the statute to be a true equitable estate; but is it not much more likely that it was included as an example of an equitable estate? We know how frequently particular terms follow the general in legal documents and statutes for the purposes of example. It may also have been inserted in order to quiet any possible doubt that might conceivably be raised as to whether the general term "estate" included the equity of redemption. One point is certain, the clause seems to presume that there is such a thing as an equitable estate. Turning to text-writers, Coventry, a century ago, described the equity of redemption as "an estate in the land, possessed by the mortgagor in virtue of his ancient and original right without any change of ownership".[1] Likewise Challis,[2] Story,[3] Leake,[4] and Wilshere,[5] all speak of the equity of redemption as an estate in land.

The equity of redemption, then, has been generally treated as an estate in the land in equity over a very long period. The words of Arden, M.R., give us the key to the true position of the mortgagor. "A Court of Equity says he still remains possessed of the estate in equity."[6] Before the mortgage was made he had both the legal estate in the land, be it in fee, for life, or for years, and the beneficial interest or equitable estate as well. By the mortgage deed he then conveyed whatever legal estate he intends to the mortgagee, and then had nothing left him at law after the day fixed for payment was passed, save possibly a reversion if he did not mortgage the whole of his estate. In equity the conveyance was but as a security, and the equitable estate did not pass to the creditor, but a charge only, a chattel interest, which implies certain remedies, such as foreclosure, sale, etc., for the realization of the security. The mortgagor still had left to him the like estate in equity as he had before at law, of the same value in point of time as the legal estate with which he had parted, an estate in fee, for life, or for years, as

[1] Powell, *Mortgages*, 5th ed., p. 342 n.   [2] *Real Property*, p. 45 n.
[3] *Equity Jurisprudence*, par. 1023.   [4] *Property in Land*, p. 203.
[5] *Principles of Equity*, p. 172.
[6] *Harmood* v. *Oglander*, (1800) 6 Ves. 221.

86 HARDWICKE: THE EQUITY OF

the case may be. Various other estates, all limited in duration, analogous to common law estates and all other equitable estates, may be created out of this estate of the mortgagor. This latter is the most elementary feature of an estate; but nevertheless by far the most important. Indeed, in one of the most valuable of recent commentaries, an "estate" is defined as "The fee simple of land and any of the various interests into which it may be divided, whether for life, or for a term of years, or otherwise".[1]

Does this interest of the mortgagor, the equity of redemption, which we would classify as an equitable estate in land, satisfy all the requisites contained in the popular and technical conceptions of that phrase? We have seen that the equity of redemption is an interest in land limited in point of time in exactly the same manner as the legal estate. It also complies with the popular notion of an estate in land, involving some form of proprietary right in the land limited in duration; for in equity the ownership of the land remains in the mortgagor. Certainly the mortgagee is at law entitled to the rents and profits; but if this right is exercised, on redemption by the debtor the mortgagee will be called upon to account for those profits even more strictly than a trustee. This is the main difference between the mortgagor and the holder of an executory interest at law conditional on the payment of a sum of money to the particular tenant. The latter has never been considered as having an estate, but merely the possibility of an estate. On payment of the money the particular tenant is not accountable for the rents and profits received by him prior to payment. Until payment the rents and profits are his own. On the other hand, a mortgagee is called strictly to account, and, until he has foreclosed, the rents and profits strictly speaking belong to the mortgagor, for, should the mortgagee receive them, they are considered a payment by the mortgagor on account of the debt.

The mortgagor has a right in equity to the rents and profits, etc., subject to the chattel interest he has given to the mortgagee as security. He has a right to have back the possession and enjoyment of the land, and also all rent and profits that have been or might have been obtained, on payment of principal,

[1] Halsbury's *Laws of England* (ed. 1911), XXIV, 162.

REDEMPTION AS AN ESTATE IN LAND   87

interest, and costs, a right to the enjoyment of the land subject to a limitation imposed upon that right by the mortgagor himself. Moreover that right of enjoyment is such that it is technically in the power of the owner to make it a present one by the mere payment of a sum of money, and is so strong that it is the custom for the mortgagee almost invariably to allow the debtor to remain in possession unless the security is in danger. This incidentally gives him an "estate" *qua* possession at common law as well as his original estate which remains to him in equity.

The equity of redemption has been generally included within the term "estate" by judges and text-writers for two centuries. It has likewise been frequently spoken of as an "estate", whereof there might be an equitable seisin; and what has seisin implied ever since the equity of redemption came into existence but the possession of an estate of freehold? This equity of redemption is also frequently found in the statute book expressly included in the definition of the terms "equitable estate" or "estate".

What then is the reason for refusing to include the equity of redemption under the term "estate"? True, it is not exactly the same as a legal estate, but neither is the trust estate; nor was the estate in the use. The legal estate in fee simple is not the same as the legal estate for years, nor is the equity of redemption of an estate in fee simple the same thing as an equity of redemption of an estate for years. Likewise the equity of redemption differs in some respects from the trust. In every classification each class has its own special features. Thus each common law estate has its own peculiarities, which are well known and hence do not cause confusion when all are classified together. The differences between both the equity of redemption and the trust on the one hand, and the legal estate on the other, are of the same character, due to their equitable nature; and the sub-classification into equitable estates emphasizes these differences. Obviously the equity of redemption is an estate in the land.

CHAPTER V

THE NATURE OF THE MORTGAGOR'S POSSESSION

IT is a well-known fact that it is the general rule to leave the mortgagor in possession of the premises mortgaged, and that the mortgagee does not eject him, save in extreme circumstances when his security is endangered. This is so in spite of the fact that, if he be allowed to remain in possession, he may take the rents and profits for his own use without liability to account for them to the mortgagee. Since the Restoration the severity with which the mortgagee, when in possession, has been made to account, has prevented him from taking such possession save as a last resort; but the custom of leaving the mortgaged property in the hands of the debtor is of a still earlier date.

The earliest gages of land in English law certainly transferred the possession to the creditor. In the Glanvillian gage he took the rents and profits in reduction of the debt, or else in lieu of interest. In Bracton's day the usual form of mortgage was the conveyance of a term of years to the creditor, who then took possession and farmed the land in lieu of interest, with a further clause that in default of payment the land was to belong to him in fee. The first forms of landed security where possession was left to the debtor were probably judgments and recognizances, followed by statutes merchant and staple; which, being but security for money, only conferred a chattel real on the creditor and left the freehold in the debtor.

It is uncertain exactly at what period the custom arose of leaving the debtor who had made a feoffment upon condition in possession. The bills found in the Calendars of Proceedings in Chancery praying relief concerning mortgages seem to be chiefly bills craving reconveyance, the mortgage being satisfied out of the rents and profits; the mortgagor having filed a bill asking "to have his lands back again". Hence in the fifteenth century it seems to have been customary for possession to be

NATURE OF THE MORTGAGOR'S POSSESSION 89

given to the feoffee on a feoffment by way of mortgage, a possession which became ownership upon default.

By the end of the sixteenth century, the practice of leaving the mortgagor in possession seems to have begun; for in 1615 we have the following report, "If a man do mortgage his land, and yet still continues his possession, no disseisin is wrought by this, and so was *Winnington's case*", (about 1598).[1] There follows a discussion as to whether such possession is fraudulent under Stat. Eliz. c. 5, and the conclusion is, "when the conveyance is conditional, continuance in possession after this shall not, in the judgment of the law, be said to be fraudulent".[2]

About the same time we meet with a proviso that the mortgagee should allow the mortgagor to remain in possession. From the language of the Court in construing the same, covenants of a similar nature seem to have been fairly common at that time, for three different forms of possession are mentioned, according to the nature and existence of the covenant.[3] Early in the reign of Charles I we find a case where the mortgagor claimed to have been in possession, "ever since the making", which latter was in 1616,[4] which shows that the custom seemed well known at the time. We find a further case in the same reign where a mortgage made in 1577 was set up, and the mortgagor and those taking under him claimed to have "enjoyed the Premises for 60 years last past".[5] This latter case is not conclusive evidence of past possession, as the plea may not have been upheld, and it is not clear whether the mortgagor disputed the mortgage or was pleading length of possession as a bar to the action of the mortgagee.

Littleton never mentions any possession by the mortgagor, neither does Coke in his commentary on Littleton. Indeed, the former speaks of him as having a right of entry on fulfilment of the condition, and seems to assume possession by the mortgagee throughout the discussion of the mortgage condition. Since Coke does not notice this leaving of the mortgagor in possession, it may be that the custom did not become general

---

[1] 40 and 41 Eliz.   [2] *Stone* v. *Grubham*, (1615) 2 Bulst. 225.
[3] *Powsely* v. *Blackman*, (1620) Cro. Jac. 659.
[4] *Sibson* v. *Fletcher*, (1632) 1 Ch. R. 59.
[5] *Hales* v. *Hales*, (1636) 1 Ch. R. 105.

THE NATURE OF THE

till the beginning of the seventeenth century, or possibly even later, about the time when the right to a general relief in equity was first established. However, in view of the cases previously quoted, it seems more probable that the growth of this custom of allowing the borrower to hold the land till default, and perhaps in some cases a short while after, may have assisted the Chancellor in treating the mortgage as merely a security for money, and so granting relief in general to all comers; rather than that the custom of leaving the mortgagor in possession followed the extension of relief generally. In spite of the silence of Littleton and Coke, the custom may have been steadily growing all through the reigns of the later Tudors. A creditor entitled to possession could not be expected to leave that possession in the hands of the debtor save in times of tranquillity, and hence the custom was probably the result of the increasing prosperity and quietude of the realm under the guidance of these wise and powerful monarchs. It is interesting to note that in most of the reported cases concerning lands in mortgage during the Civil War, the mortgagee seems to have been in possession.

The prevalence of the custom of leaving the mortgagor in possession is also a matter of speculation. It appears to have been general shortly after the Restoration. We still find a large number of cases where the mortgagee had taken possession, but this is hardly evidence to support a contention that the custom was by no means universal at that time; because the mortgagee would naturally take possession of the land in event of default in payment of interest, or whenever there was any trouble between him and the mortgagor, and would only go to the risk of attempting to obtain a decree for foreclosure from the Chancellor in extreme circumstances. It would always have been these cases of trouble which appeared before the court, and it may naturally be supposed that in these the mortgagee had exercised his legal right to take possession. Hence the prevalence of cases in the early reports where the mortgagee was in possession.

In the Welsh mortgage, where no time for payment was limited, and the mortgagee was to satisfy himself out of the rents, the

MORTGAGOR'S POSSESSION

lender obviously took possession; but the use of this type of mortgage declined during the early part of the seventeenth century and soon afterwards fell into disuse.

Now when this custom of possession by the borrower became general, the courts of common law were faced with a problem. Here was the legal ownership in one person, the mortgagee, and another in occupation of the land. What was the position of this occupier? We have seen that he was not to be held a disseisor. He was not a bailiff; for his possession was for his own benefit. He received the rents and profits for himself and not on behalf of the mortgagee. The only other kind of possession known to the common law was a tenancy of some sort. The common law, then, felt that he must be a tenant of some sort to the mortgagee. Of what estate was he tenant? Obviously not a freehold for he had conveyed his estate to the mortgagee. There remained tenancies for a term of years, at will, or at sufferance. He must be one of these.

At common law the *cestui que trust* in ordinary occupation of the premises seems to have been regarded from very early days as tenant at will to the trustees; because, where the purposes of the trust so allowed, the trustees' consent to occupation by the beneficiary was a matter of course.[1] The possession of the *cestui que use* was similarly regarded before the Statute of Uses.[2] This applied only where the *cestui que trust* or *use* was the actual occupant. Where he was merely allowed to receive the rents, or otherwise to deal with the estate in the hands of the occupying tenants, he stood in the position merely of an agent or bailiff of the trustees, who chose to allow him to act for them in the management of the estate. A practical result was that, if in the second case he allowed a stranger to enter, the stranger was in adverse possession as against the trustee.[3] The suggestion was therefore readily conveyed that, on the analogy of the trust estate, the mortgagor in actual occupation of the land might be regarded as a tenant at will.

---

[1] *Freeman* v. *Barnes*, (1660) Vent. 80, 1 Siderf. 349, 458; *Garrard* v. *Tuck* (1849) 8 C.B. 231, 250.
[2] Y.B. 5 Hen. V, 3, 6.
[3] *Melling* v. *Leak*, (1855) 16 C.B. 652, 669.

92　　THE NATURE OF THE

In 1620 we meet with a case of a mortgage with a proviso that the mortgagee, his heirs and assigns, "shall not intermeddle with the actual possession of the premises or the perception of the rents" until default in a re-payment by instalments. The Court held, "It is not a covenant or agreement with the bargainee, that he should enjoy it during those years, for then it would have amounted to a lease for years"; but it was agreed to leave him in possession, which did not amount to such a lease.[1] This settled that, even where there was a covenant that the mortgagee would not take possession, the mortgagor was not in the position of a lessee. The report of the case is headed, "Proviso not to intermeddle,...the mortgagor is a tenant at sufferance to the mortgagee and not a tenant at will, as he would have been on a covenant that he should take the profits till default". This, as it was written by one of the judges before whom the case was tried, should be a fairly authoritative statement of the effect of the case; though the actual report does not refer to this distinction between a tenancy at sufferance and a tenancy at will, and, according to modern ideas, the mortgagor in this case would seem to be a tenant at will, rather than a tenant by sufferance. It would seemingly not allow the mortgagor's possession to be even a tenancy at will.

It was also said in this case that, if a mortgagor who continues in possession by the consent of the mortgagee make a lease for years, and the lessee enter claiming nothing but his lease, on payment and acceptance of his rent he is a tenant at will, and not a disseisor; and if the mortgagor enter after the expiration of the lease, he shall be a tenant at will again to the mortgagee. The case also greatly strengthens the proposition that the custom of leaving the borrower in possession was well established at this time.

In 1695 a question arose, whether, on the mortgagee assigning his interest, the mortgagor's possession under such a clause did not become a disseisin, turning the assignee's estate into a mere right of entry; for if it did, the assignee could not assign again

[1] *Powsely* v. *Blackman*, Cro. Jac. 659; see also *Evans* v. *Thomas*, (1608) Cro. Jac. 172; Shep. Touch. II, 272.

MORTGAGOR'S POSSESSION

without entry unless the mortgagor joined in the assignment. Holt, C.J., held as follows:

The mortgagor, by the covenant to enjoy, till default of payment, is tenant at will, and the assignments of the mortgagees make him but tenant at sufferance; but his continuing in possession could never make a disseisin, nor devesting of the term: it would be otherwise if the mortgagor had died, and his heir entered, for the heir is not tenant at will (Co. Litt. 56, 7), but his first entry was tortious; or if the mortgagee had entered upon the mortgagor, and he had re-entered, because the mortgagee's entry would have been a determination of the will, and the re-entry of the mortgagor had been merely a tortious entry.[1]

It was also said by Eyres, C.J., in the same year, and so ruled upon evidence, "that when the mortgagee for himself, his executors, administrators and assigns covenants with the mortgagor, that he shall enjoy and take the profits until default of payment, the covenant being for his assigns, this would rule the whole case, and he shall be presumed tenant at will to all the assigns, as well as to the first mortgagee".[2] This disposes of the error suggested by the heading of the report just quoted.

The total effect then seems to be; first, that a covenant by the mortgagee that a mortgagor shall enjoy for a certain definite period makes the latter a lessee for that period; secondly, a covenant that the mortgagor shall enjoy until default, or any consent of the mortgagee to the mortgagor remaining in possession gives the latter a tenancy at will; and that otherwise the mortgagor is a tenant at sufferance.

The construction of this covenant to enjoy until default was undoubtedly connected with the fact that a covenant to allow another to enter one's land, not amounting to a legal easement, was only enforceable at law as a licence to enter, revocable at the will of the grantor, even though the covenant were for a fixed term.[3] The only remedy for the licensee was by action in damages for breach of contract; but in some cases equity would give an injunction restraining the grantor from breach of the covenant. Thus the covenant to allow entry for a fixed

---

[1] *Smartle* v. *Williams*, Holt 478.
[2] Andrew Newport's Case, Skin. 423; Holt 478.
[3] See for instance *Fentiman* v. *Smith*, (1803) 4 East 107, 109.

THE NATURE OF THE

term being but a licence revocable at will, the same notion would apply in the case of a covenant to enjoy until default, which would therefore convey a tenancy at will only, revocable at any time it so pleased the mortgagee.

The general rules relating to the mortgagor's possession seem to have been established before the end of the seventeenth century; but the whole matter was by no means yet settled. The question as to whether, in the absence of the consent of the mortgagee, the borrower's possession was a tenancy at will or at sufferance became a matter of considerable controversy.

For some reason the matter does not seem to have been seriously disputed until brought into prominence in the days of Lord Mansfield, who, having practised almost exclusively at the Chancery bar until he was raised to the Common Law Bench, was always particularly interested in cases closely allied to some equitable ground of jurisdiction. Indeed, it is often stated that, had Mansfield been allowed to have his way, many equitable doctrines would have been incorporated in the common law. Whether the discussion was originated by some careless judicial *dicta* in cases where the mortgagee had consented to the mortgagor's possession, thus constituting a tenancy at will, or whether the question was from its first appearance always one of controversy, does not seem clear. Hardwicke, in *Casborne* v. *Scarfe*, refers to the mortgagor as tenant at will at law, without mentioning any covenant or consent on the part of the mortgagee.[1] Perhaps some careless remarks of Mansfield in *Keech d. Warne* v. *Hall* may have been responsible for much of the trouble.

In that case the action was for the ejectment of a lessee of the mortgagor who had no notice of the existence of the mortgage, but the mortgagee had given him no notice to quit; so that, though the lease was void as against the mortgagee on his bringing an action for ejectment, yet, if the lessee could be regarded as tenant from year to year to the mortgagee, the action must fail for want of such notice. Lord Mansfield, in delivering his judgment, said:

The question is whether, by the agreement understood between

[1] 1 Atk. 606.

MORTGAGOR'S POSSESSION

mortgagors and mortgagees, which is, that the latter shall receive interest, and the former keep possession, the mortgagee has given an implied authority to the mortgagor to let from year to year, at rack rent;...When the mortgagor is left in possession, the true inference to be drawn, is an agreement that he shall possess the premises at will in the strictest sense, and therefore no notice is ever given him to quit, and he is not even entitled to reap the crop,...because all is liable to the debt; on payment of which, the mortgagee's title ceases. The mortgagor has no power, express or implied, to let leases, not subject to every circumstance of the mortgage....The tenant stands exactly in the situation of the mortgagor....Whoever wants to be secure, when he takes a lease, should enquire after and examine the title deeds.[1]

In *Moss* v. *Gallimore*, decided the next year, Mansfield had to explain his words in *Keech* v. *Hall*. In the case then before him he held that a mortgagee, after giving notice of the mortgage, may distrain from the tenant of an underlease made prior to the mortgage for rent in arrear at the time of such notice; and pointed out that, in calling the mortgagor in possession a tenant at will, he was but making a comparison; and that, where he spoke of "a tenant at will in the strictest sense", he meant that the possession of the mortgagor conferred on him at law even fewer advantages than those which belonged to a tenant at will. He says:

A mortgagor, is not properly tenant at will to the mortgagee, for he is not to pay him rent. He is only so quodam modo. Nothing is more apt to confound than a simile. When the court, or counsel, call the mortgagor a tenant at will, it is barely a comparison. He is like a tenant at will. The mortgagor receives the rent by a tacit agreement with the mortgagee, but the mortgagee may put an end to this agreement when he pleases.

Ashhurst, J., in the same case, seems to have been willing to accept the conception of the mortgagor in possession as tenant at will at law, and to apply it in practice, (he is by no means the last one to fall into this error), but he drew a distinction where there was an undertenant, as in the case before him. He says:

Where the mortgagor is himself the occupier of the estate, he may be considered as tenant at will; but he cannot be so considered, if there is an undertenant; for there can be no such thing as an under-

[1] 1 Doug. 21.

96 THE NATURE OF THE

tenant to a tenant at will. The demise itself would amount to a determination of the will....The mortgagor is, therefore, only a receiver of the rent for the mortgagee, who may, at any time, countermand the implied authority, by giving notice.[1]

In *Birch* v. *Wright*, Buller, J., re-stated the two cases last considered and announced that Lord Mansfield desired him to say he stood by his decision in *Keech* v. *Hall*. He then says:

Supposing [the parties] are to be considered as mortgagor and mortgagee....It would be said that there is an implied agreement...that the mortgagor shall hold as tenant at will to the mortgagee....That a mortgagor has often been called a tenant at will to the mortgagee in Courts of Law and Equity is undoubtedly true, but I think inaccurately so; and the expression has been used when it was not very material to ascertain what his powers or interests were, or to settle with any great precision in what respects he did, or in what respects he did not, resemble a tenant at will....

Whenever it is necessary to decide a similar question between the mortgagor and mortgagee it seems to me that it will be quite sufficient to call them so....If a likeness must be found, I think, as it was put by Ashhurst, J. in *Moss* v. *Gallimore*, a mortgagor is as much, if not more, like a receiver than a tenant at will. In truth he is not either. He is not a tenant at will, because he is not entitled to the growing crops after the will is determined. He is not considered as tenant at will in...ejectments brought for the recovery of the mortgaged lands. If he were tenant at will, the demise could not be laid on a day antecedent to the determination of the will. But it is in every day's practice. He is not a receiver; for, if he were, he would be obliged to pay all rents and profits to the mortgagee.

He continues:

A mortgagor and mortgagee are characters as well known, and their rights, powers and interests as well settled, as any in the law. The possession of the mortgagor is the possession of the mortgagee; and as to the inheritance, they have but one title between them. The mortgagor has no power of making leases to bind the mortgagee. He cannot against the will of the mortgagee do any act to disseise him.[2] And the reason is, because the mortgagee, so long as he receives his interest, is virtually and in the eye of the law in possession. The mortgagee has a right to the actual possession whenever he pleases; he may bring his action for ejectment at any moment that he will.[3]

[1] 1 Doug. 282.
[2] Citing Cro. Jac. 660; Cro. Car. 304; 3 Lev. 388; Skin. 424.
[3] 1 T. R. 378.

MORTGAGOR'S POSSESSION

It might be thought that this scathing indictment of the analogy of the tenancy at will would have made the legal profession cautious in making any further attempt to sway the Court by arguments based upon it. Frequent endeavours have since been made to get the Court to apply this analogy to the decision of concrete cases, or to turn the analogy into an identity; and further careless *dicta* still gave ground for these attempts. It has been only after a long series of judicial disapproval, showing the weaknesses of the comparison and denouncing it as totally unsatisfactory, that the effort to establish some definite practical connection between the common law conception of the possession of the mortgagor and that of the tenant at will was finally abandoned.

In *Leman* v. *Newnham*, 1747, Sir J. Fortescue, M.R., says: "The Defendant insists, that there being no principal or interest paid or demanded for 20 years, the presumption of law, if nothing else, is that they are satisfied; and in common cases it is so, but not so in mortgages, because the mortgagee shall be supposed continuing in possession, and the mortgagor's possession shall be his, being tenant at will to him".[1] In 1789, Eyre, C.B., says: "I cannot think that the party would be prevented from shewing the truth of the case in a Court of Equity against such a presumption". And hence he held the mortgage was not satisfied.[2]

Two years later, Thurlow, L.C., in *Trash* v. *White*, took the opposite view, saying that, if there was no payment of interest and no demand, the presumption in equity was "as strong as that at law."[3] In *Christophers* v. *Sparke*, 1820, Sir Thomas Plumer, M.R., mentions both these cases, and then says:

The principle on which the opinions expressed in those cases rests is, that though the mortgagor may continue in possession, he is tenant at will to the mortgagee; there is therefor no adverse possession, and the mortgagee may, at any distance of time, assert his title....I would not have it understood that I intend to decide this point, but I cannot accede that no length of time will operate against a mortgagee....The argument from there being a tenancy at will, arises from a mere fiction; for there is no actual tenancy, no demise,

[1] I Ves. Sen. 51.   [2] *Toplis* v. *Baker*, 2 Cox, 122.
[3] 3 Bro. C.C. 291.

98 THE NATURE OF THE

either express or implied. The mortgagor has not even the rights of a tenant at will; he may be turned out of possession without notice, and is not entitled to emblements. It is only *quodam modo* a tenancy at will, as Lord Mansfield says in *Moss* v. *Gallimore*. We cannot push it to that extent, reasoning on the supposed relation of landlord and tenant, which is not founded on fact.

The relation of mortgagor and mortgagee is peculiar; in a court of equity the former is considered as the owner; and that is the nature of the contract between them; the tacit agreement is, that he is to be the owner if he pays.... If the fiction of the tenant at will is an answer to the objection after 20 years, why will it not be an answer after any other time?...His equity is shut out by the mortgagee being in possession for 20 years without acknowledgment; then why should not this be reciprocal?[1]

In passing, we may note the application of the doctrine that the conscience of equity demands that remedies shall be mutual. This is met with repeatedly all through the development of the law of mortgages, and is constantly applied to solve new cases as they arise, even at the present day.

In *Cholmondeley* v. *Clinton*, 1820, Sir T. Plumer makes further objections:

The mortgagor, who is stated to be tenant at will, when in possession pays no rent, nor is liable to any account of his rents to the mortgagee. The mortgagee,...if he takes possession, is a bailiff without salary, bound to account for all the rents and profits. The tenant at will, therefore, in possession, neither pays, nor accounts for, any rent to his supposed landlord; but the landlord, in the same predicament, becomes an accountable bailiff to his own tenant at will. The possession of the mortgagor, or the person claiming that character, is not adverse to the mortgagee.... The mortgagee is, therefore, not barred by any length of that possession; but the possession of the mortgagor is adverse to every other claimant of the equity of redemption.[2]

Comparing this with his remarks in *Christophers* v. *Sparke*, it seems that Plumer considered that the true ground of any equitable bar to the mortgagee's right to possession was not adverse possession, though he rejected the "fiction" of the tenancy at will; but was a presumption of the satisfaction of the mortgage debt after twenty years' possession of the mortgagor

[1] 2 J. and W. 234.   [2] 2 J. and W. 179.

MORTGAGOR'S POSSESSION

99

without any acknowledgment of the debt, on the principle that equity follows the law.

In the same case Sir T. Plumer shows that this question as to the nature of the possession of the mortgagor at law has no connection with his position in equity, and no effect on the equitable conception of the mortgagor as still owner of the land. He asks, "Is he there", that is in equity, "for any purpose ever considered as a tenant at will?...Is any point better established than that a mortgagor,...after condition forfeited, is still considered to remain the absolute owner of the estate?"[1]

Two years later came the case of *Partridge* v. *Bere*.[2] The action was for diverting a watercourse. The plaintiff averred that the premises by reason of which he brought the action were in the occupation of another as his tenant, he being the reversioner. The defendant objected that the plaintiff was a mortgagee, that the mortgagor was in possession, and that the relation of landlord and tenant did not subsist between a mortgagor and mortgagee. This was not accepted by the Court, and on appeal the decision of the Court was confirmed.

The ground of this decision is explained very clearly by Chief Justice Best in *Doe d. Fisher* v. *Giles*, 1829,[3] where he remarks that in that case "the Court thought that a mortgagee might describe himself as a reversioner, the mortgagor being in possession of the estate, and said that he was a tenant within the strictest definition....But this was not a case between a mortgagee and the mortgagor. The defendant in this case was a wrongdoer". Again in *Hitchman* v. *Walton*, 1838,[4] Baron Parke, referring to the same case, says: "That case establishes that he" (the mortgagee) "may treat his mortgagor, as against a stranger, as his tenant at will: he is not bound to do so, and therefore it is that he may bring ejectment against him as a trespasser, without a previous demand of possession". In this latter case Abinger, C.B., following *Partridge* v. *Bere*, states that the mortgagee could bring ejectment against his mortgagor as reversioner, and need not set out all the special circumstances of the case. He says: "In order to constitute a reversion there must be a portion

[1] 2 J. and W. 178.
[2] 5 B. and Ald. 604.
[3] 5 Bing. 421.
[4] 4 M. and W. 409.

of the estate carved out, on which the reversion shall be incident"; the portion carved out is the "time during which the mortgagor is allowed to remain in possession". These cases establish that, with regard to a stranger, the mortgagee may treat the mortgagor in possession without any covenant to enjoy until default as a tenant at will, he being the reversioner; and again, may bring ejectment against his mortgagor in possession as one holding over against himself as reversioner.

As we have seen, a tenant at sufferance may be ejected by the reversioner in the same way as a disseisor. Powell, in his treatise on mortgages, written at the beginning of the nineteenth century, suggests that a mortgagor in possession without an agreement to that effect is a disseisor. He says that the possession of the lessee of the mortgagor "will make him a wrongdoer as to the mortgagee, his lessor being, as to the mortgagee, a disseisor, and consequently incapable of conveying a good title as against the mortgagee".[1]

Coventry, in his notes to Powell, objects to this fallacy, and at the same time discusses the analogy of the tenant at will. He argues that the mortgagor's possession makes no disseisin, probably because of the tacit agreement, which was formerly understood to exist between the mortgagor and the mortgagee, that the mortgagor should hold as tenant to the mortgagee, paying the interest from time to time, and the principal when demanded.

He then says:

The mortgagor being in the nature of a tenant at will, has no power to create an estate for years, consequently his lessee will, in taking possession of the premises, enter under a wrongful or tortious title, and the mortgagee who has the legal estate of freehold may correctly consider *him*, but not the mortgagor, a wrongdoer and disseisor at election,...The reason why a mortgagor is called a tenant at will to the mortgagee is, because his tenure is of that precarious and permissive nature, that whenever the mortgagee pleases, he may assume the possession, and equity will not interfere to prevent him; and the only point of similitude discoverable between a mortgagor and disseisor may perhaps be, that the mortgagee may assume this possession peremptorily by ejectment, without giving the mortgagor any notice to quit; and it may be said, that because an ejectment

[1] P. 212. See also p. 208 (ed. 5).

MORTGAGOR'S POSSESSION

101

proceeds on an ouster or dispossession, it pre-supposes a disseisin by the mortgagor. This, however, is in fact a mere formality, adopted for the sake of avoiding the circuitous proceedings on a real action, and is the admission of an act which never took place.[1] Hence, therefore, it does appear to be the more correct expression to say that a mortgagee is entitled to his action of ejectment as one of the powers belonging to him in the character of mortgagee.[2]

Again he suggests that the reason why the mortgagor will not be entitled to emblements " Is not because he is a disseisor, but because the crop, as well as the land, is a security for the debt".[3] There seems to be a strong presumption, which is not easily rebutted, that the possession of the mortgagor is not of a wrongful character. The mortgagor, by retention of possession, never becomes a disseisor save under the Limitation Acts, where he is uninterrupted for twelve years without acknowledgment of the debt. Exactly what amounts to an actual disseisin is uncertain, but, until the period prescribed by the Acts has run, there must at least be some act totally incompatible with his position as mortgagor, and not a mere retention of possession.[4]

In the passage just quoted, Coventry speaks of the mortgagor as a tenant at will, but he only says he is of such a nature, and remarks that he was called so because of the precarious nature of his tenancy. He points out in another note, "It is an inaccurate expression, and it was used when it was not material to settle what his powers or interests were "; and it is "Altogether unnecessary to hunt through a vocabulary of technical terms, to affix on the mortgagor a more appropriate name than the one he at present bears, being in itself well understood."[5]

The mortgagor in possession, then, cannot be regarded as having a tenancy or estate at will save under a particular covenant or agreement, express or implied. His possession is, however, frequently spoken of as a tenancy at sufferance, since it is said it must be a common law tenancy of some kind, or else as being in a category peculiar to itself and not a common law tenancy at all. Some observations as to his tenancy being *sui generis* have already been quoted, but many *dicta* can be cited in support of both.

---

[1] See also Abinger, C.B., in *Hitchman* v. *Walton, supra*; and Salk 24 6.
[2] Powell, p. 208 n. B.   [3] *Ibid.* 212 n.
[4] *Hall* v. *Doe d. Surtees*, (1822) 5 B. and Ald. 687.   [5] Powell, p. 208 n. A

THE NATURE OF THE

In 1803 Lord Ellenborough said, "A mortgagor is no more than a tenant at sufferance, not entitled to notice to quit; and one tenant at sufferance cannot make another".[1] In 1828, Tenterden, C.J., remarked, "The mortgagor is not in the situation of tenant at all, or at all events, he is not more than tenant at sufferance; but in a peculiar character, and liable to be treated as tenant or as trespasser at the option of the mortgagee".[2] Ten years later Abinger, C.B., stated that the mortgagor must be a tenant of some kind. He says, "In what character does he stay but that of a tenant, since it is clear he is neither a trespasser nor a servant"?[3] Parke, B., says, "A mortgagor is not in all respects a mere bailiff; he is much like a bailiff; he is not a mere tenant at will; in fact, he can be described merely by saying he is a mortgagor".[4] In 1851 counsel states that the mortgagor is tenant at sufferance to the mortgagee, but Patteson, J., replies, "I can never agree to that. I know there are loose expressions in the books as to his being tenant at will, or tenant at sufferance; but he is not, in truth, a tenant at all".[5] Watson, B., in 1859 says, "Many loose expressions are to be found in the books as to the position of a mortgagor. Sometimes he is said to be the agent of the mortgagee; sometimes to be tenant to him". He says the true ground is, "that the mortgagor is not a tenant at all; he has no interest".[6] It seems that an attornment clause creates a tenancy at will.[7] Vaughan-Williams, J., after dealing with this, points out that, "a mortgagor in possession is not necessarily more than a tenant on sufferance, and occupation and payment of interest necessarily connected with the mortgage is not necessarily referable to a tenancy other than a tenancy on sufferance".[8]

There does not seem to be any actual decision in which a mortgagor, having made an absolute conveyance of his estate by way of mortgage and remaining in possession without any consent of the mortgagee, has been considered in any light

---

[1] *Thunder* v. *Belcher*, 3 East 449.
[2] *Doe d. Roby* v. *Maisey*, 8 B. and C. 767.
[3] *Hitchman* v. *Walton*, 4 M. and W. 409.
[4] *Litchfield* v. *Ready*, (1850) 20 L.J. (N.S.), Ex. 51.
[5] *Wilton* v. *Dunn*, (1851) 17 Q.B. 299.
[6] *Hickman* v. *Machin*, (1859) 4 H. and N. 722.
[7] *Turner* v. *Barnes*, (1862) 2 B. and S. 435.
[8] *Scobie* v. *Collins*, (1895) 1 Q.B. 377.

MORTGAGOR'S POSSESSION 103

contrary to the conception of him as tenant at sufferance, whatever *obiter dicta* may have been expressed to the contrary. He seems to answer strictly to the usual definition of a tenant at sufferance, being one who comes in by right and holds over without right. The mortgagor cannot maintain an action of ejectment; but neither can a tenant at sufferance, because, like the mortgagor, in the eye of the law he has no estate at all apart from possession, and if he loses that he loses all. Again, the mortgagor who retains possession seems to be in the same position as regards the mortgagee as the lessee is against his lessor when holding over after the termination of his lease. Coke[1] and Hale[2] both stated that if a tenant for years surrenders, and still continues possession, he is tenant at sufferance or disseisor at election. This is exactly the position of the mortgagor.

Though the mortgagor's possession seems to fit in with that of a tenant by sufferance, we see that a large number of very able judges consider it better described as peculiar in itself. The incidents of such possession are well worked out and the implications raised by the phrase "possession as mortgagor" as well defined as a tenancy by sufferance. It is of much greater frequency. In addition to the rights ordinarily incident to a tenancy by sufferance, the mortgagor's possession confers on him some further common law rights and a number of very important Statutory powers and remedies, the latter due to the endeavour of the Legislature to complete the work begun by Equity of making the mortgagor more nearly owner of the land.

Thus, while in possession he may hold the manor courts,[3] he is entitled to the parliamentary franchise provided the clear yearly value to him is still sufficient, he is within the Statute of Sewers,[4] and he may be fined for the non-repair of sea banks.[5] He may receive the rents and profits for his own use, and may, since 1875, bring an action in respect of the mortgaged property save against his mortgagee. He may commit waste provided he does not thereby make the security insufficient, and he may have an express power to make leases, subject to certain restrictions.

---

[1] Co. Litt. 57.
[2] Hale MSS.
[3] 1 Scriven, 73 n. (ed. 5).
[4] 23 Hen. VIII, c. 5, § 3.
[5] *R.* v. *Baker*, L.R., 2 Q.B. 621.

THE NATURE OF THE

Yet the mortgagee may treat him as a trespasser, in one character to be sued for injuring the reversion, in the other to be ejected without notice or claim to rents in arrear or to emblements.

The chief difference between the two ideas seems to be that one school contends that this possession must raise some sort of tenancy recognized by the common law, or be a disseisin; for the mortgagor is not a mere bailiff, and since he seems to correspond to a tenant at sufferance, that is what he must be. The other school regards the attempt to fit the mortgagor's possession into the old scheme of common law tenancies and estates as fixing it with a fictitious label, which, though it may appear to suit for all practical purposes, yet is unnecessary, and may eventually prove an inequitable bond.[1] They point out that it is really much safer to call him mortgagor and to leave it at that, thus giving the judges of the future a free hand, than to run the risk of forcing upon the Court any rules which may relate either at the present time or at any future date to the common law tenancy by sufferance, and which do not necessarily, or ought not equitably, to apply to mortgages. They are apt to remark upon the position of the parties in equity, and to notice how the common law rules are effected to some extent by this equitable position, which they point out is the real position; and hence they regard the application of the system of common law tenancies, a system established long before the question of the nature of the mortgagor's possession had ever arisen, as attempting to impose an obsolete feudal classification on an interest which originally grew up by tacit agreement without any regard to the law of tenure, and which, in these days of so stereotyped a legal system where the Court's discretion must be jealously guarded, is making for an unnecessary fixation of the law.

The theory of each school seems reasonable. The question as to which shall prevail really rests with the judges and jurists of the future in their determination, when it becomes necessary, whether the analogy of the tenancy at sufferance is to be pursued to its furthermost limits. The negative view seems the more

---

[1] See Holmes, C.J., in *Guy* v. *Donald*, (1906) 27 Supp. C.R. 63, 64; 203 U.S. 406, and *Hyde* v. *U.S.* (1911) 225 U.S. 347, 391.

MORTGAGOR'S POSSESSION

favourable, in that it avoids an unnecessary technicality and gives a wider scope for discretion. The evolution of the possessory estate of the mortgagor may well outstrip that of the tenancy at sufferance if it be not checked by the analogy between them, especially in view of the modern statute law strengthening the mortgagor's possession in a manner hardly compatible with a tenancy by sufferance.

The Law of Property Act 1925 does not appear to alter the nature of the mortgagor's possession. Under the Act he has the legal freehold as well as possession; but there is an intervening term of years belonging at law to the mortgagee, the mortgagor being still a tenant to him, at will, by sufferance, or *sui generis*, as the case may be. His remedies as freeholder and those which he has *qua possession* or which have been annexed to his possessory estate by statute are still quite distinct. His possessory estate does not merge in his freehold because of the intermediate term of the mortgagee.

The mortgagee, when the debt is completely satisfied, becomes a constructive trustee for the mortgagor.[1] The relation of mortgagor and mortgagee ceases, and that of trustee and *cestui que trust* begins. Fry, J., recently expressed this view of the situation, adding, that under such circumstances the mortgagor becomes in reality a tenant at will, being no longer mortgagor, but *cestui que trust*. He says:

It appears to me that upon that payment being made the mortgagee clearly became a trustee for the mortgagor, and the mortgagor became tenant at will to the mortgagee.... The exact relation between mortgagor in possession and mortgagee, whilst the relation of mortgagor and mortgagee is subsisting...has sometimes been described as the relation of tenant at will; sometimes it is said to be purely anomalous and *sui generis*. It appears to me that after payment was made, and the true relation of mortgagor and mortgagee had come to an end, the mortgagor was tenant at will to the mortgagee who had the legal estate.[2]

The *cestui que trust* has an estate at will because the consent of the trustees to his occupation under an ordinary trust cannot

---

[1] See Chap. VIII, B, *infra*.
[2] *Sands to Thompson*, (1883) 22 Ch. D. 614.

106 THE NATURE OF THE

generally be withheld. Thus far the courts of law seem to take notice of the equitable relationship of trustee and *cestui que trust*.[1] If, however, the *cestui que trust* while in possession grant a lease to a stranger, inconsistent with the terms of the trust, the latter becomes a tenant at sufferance or a disseisor at the pleasure of the trustees; while if the beneficiary grant such a lease while in receipt of the rents and profits merely, and not in occupation, the lessee seems to be in as an adverse possessor, the *cestui que trust* in receipt of rents being considered a bailiff only and not a tenant to the trustees.

It is interesting to note that, although the *cestui que trust* was from the earliest times regarded as a tenant at will to his trustees, little use seems to have been made of this fact in the arguments of counsel attempting to bring forward the identity of the mortgagor's possession and a tenancy at will. Apparently the difference between the *cestui que trust* and the mortgagor in possession at law was always realized, namely, that whereas the trustee has no power to eject his *cestui que trust* as a disseisee without notice to quit, the mortgagee may do so at pleasure. The analogy between the trust and the mortgage continues to hold in the case of a lease by the mortgagor in possession without the consent of the mortgagee. Such a lease is *prima facie* contrary to the terms of the mortgage in that it tends to prevent the mortgagee realizing his security, and the lessee becomes a tenant at sufferance or a disseisor at the pleasure of the mortgagee, just as he would in the case of a lease by a benificiary in possession contrary to the terms of the trust.

The discrepancies to be noted in the *dicta* from the bench concerning this conception of the mortgagor as tenant at will were often more apparent than real. This was due to the fact that if there could be found any agreement, either expressed or implied by such circumstances as payment of rent, that the mortgagor was to retain possession of the premises, that possession would be construed as a tenancy at will. The courts were ever ready to find such an agreement and to affix such a character to the mortgagor's possession. Coventry speaks of "the tacit agreement, which was formerly understood to exist

---

[1] *Freeman* v. *Banes*, (1660); *ante*, p. 91.

MORTGAGOR'S POSSESSION 107

between" mortgagor and mortgagee;[1] and this remark suggests that in his time this leaning was less noticeable than formerly. Again, where there was such a tenancy at will, if mortgagor or mortgagee assigned without the consent of the other, or the mortgagor died and his heir or devisee entered, the tenancy was determined, and the new possessor, not being a party to the agreement, was a mere tenant at sufferance, and might be treated as a disseisor. Thus, a dictum which appears in a general form, stating that the mortgagor is a tenant at will, can often be explained by reference to the case in hand, where such an implied agreement is often found to exist.

We have seen that the actual occupation and possession of the land is hardly ever taken over by the mortgagee until his security seems to be in danger or the mortgagor is in arrear with the payment of his interest; and also, that it was common to find a clause inserted in the mortgage deed, that until the day fixed for the payment of the mortgage money, or default in payment of the interest, or in the performance of the covenants, the mortgagor shall retain possession and receive the rents. Similar covenants seem to have become very common by the end of the eighteenth century. Coventry observes this, referring to, "the mere possessory tenancy, which is generally conferred on him by the last clause in the mortgage deed, or by the tacit understanding of the parties".[2] A clause of this nature can hardly now be spoken of as general, though it is by no means obsolete.

A covenant for the mortgagor to enjoy the rents and profits for a definite period of fixed duration, as is stated in *Powsely* v. *Blackman*,[3] operates as a redemise for a term. Bovill, C.J., says of this: "If there be an express agreement in the mortgage deed that the mortgagor shall remain in possession for a certain time, he has an interest in the nature of a term of years during such time; but, upon expiration of such period, if there be default in payment of the money, the mortgagor becomes a tenant at sufferance".[4]

---

[1] Powell, *Mortgages* (5th ed.), p. 208 n. B.　　[2] *Ibid.* p. 378 n.
[3] (1620) Cro. Jac. 659; *ante*, p. 92.
[4] *Gibbs* v. *Cruikshank*, (1873) L.R., 8 C.P. 461.

108 THE NATURE OF THE

The line of distinction taken with reference to these various covenants seems to be that, in order to create a term of years in favour of the mortgagor, there must be a covenant that he is to hold for a definite period. In the words of Denman, C.J.: "Though the words imply some right of possession in the mortgagor they will not amount to a redemise unless some certain time be fixed during which the mortgagee is to hold".[1] A covenant merely restricting the right of the mortgagee to immediate possession implies merely a tenancy at will or quasi at will, as in *Powsely* v. *Blackman*.[2] With regard to mortgages of chattels personal, covenants of this nature appear to have a different effect; for instance, a proviso that the mortgagor shall hold till default in payment has been held to amount to only a licence to consume.[3]

The position of the mortgagor in possession at law may be summed up as follows:

By a covenant in the mortgage deed that the mortgagor shall continue in possession till a day certain, he has an estate for the intervening term. At the determination of that term he becomes a tenant at sufferance.

Where the mortgagee has expressly or impliedly consented to his possession, the mortgagor has a tenancy at will.

Where there is no such consent he is a tenant at sufferance; or it is preferable to call his interest simply possession as mortgagor, which latter seems to conform to all the rules of a tenancy at sufferance, so far as is yet known.

In either of the last two cases, if some other person takes possession under the mortgagor, he is a tenant at sufferance to the mortgagee, though he may become a tenant at will by an express or implied agreement as before; but receipt of interest by the mortgagee, or mere notice from him to the new possessor to pay the rents to him and not to the mortgagor, is not evidence of such new agreement.[4]

The mortgagor in possession, then, has two distinct estates or interests. He still has the same estate in equity as he had

---

[1] *Doe d. Parsley* v. *Day*, 2 Q.B. 147; see Bac. Abr. Leases K.
[2] *Roylance* v. *Lightfoot*, (1841) 8 M. and W. 559.
[3] *Gale* v. *Burnell*, 7 Q.B. 150. See also *Doe d. Parsley* v. *Day, supra*.
[4] *Evans* v. *Elliot*, 9 Ad. and E. 342.

MORTGAGOR'S POSSESSION

before the mortgage relationship began, and he has also an estate or interest *qua possession* at common law, for years, at will, by sufferance or as mortgagor, according to the circumstances of the possession. The classification of tenancies at will or by sufferance as "estates" is sometimes the subject of objection, on the ground that the term "estate", which was originally applied at common law to freehold interests only and which has been but gradually extended to include leasehold and equitable interests, should not be applied to interests of so precarious a nature as tenancies at will and by sufferance. There is certainly some practical sense in this contention, and it is supported by a few dicta, one or two of which have special reference to the possession of the mortgagor. Thus Parke, B., says, "The possession of a mortgagor is at law, no estate at all", whereupon Platt, B., continues, "That must be so, for the mortgagee may bring ejectment, and lay the demise on a former day. If the mortgagor had any estate, however precarious, the demise should be laid after it was determined".[1] These *dicta* can usually be explained with reference to the context, which in the above case was the question whether the mortgagor's possession was such an estate as would support a rent charge. This tenancies by sufferance or at will cannot do.

On the other hand, Blackstone speaks of an "estate at sufferance", and the phrase has been used with frequency from his time to the present day;[2] though some judges and text-writers seem to avoid the expression, using the phrases "tenancy at will", etc., instead. A tenancy at sufferance is certainly an interest in land limited in point of time, and confers enjoyment of the land itself. So far as an "estate" can be defined, it seems difficult to exclude such a tenancy from a definition without special explanation. By excluding these tenancies from the theory of estates, a certain form of very limited enjoyment of the land is excluded from the general definition, and its exclusion then has to be explained by placing an unnatural limit on the meaning of the word, enjoyment. It is really a protest made because "estate" still conveys to the mind some vague sugges-

---

[1] *Freeman* v. *Edwards*, (1848) 17 L.J. (Ex.) 258.
[2] See, for instance, Powell, *Mortgages*, p. 208 n. (5th ed.).

110 NATURE OF THE MORTGAGOR'S POSSESSION

tion of limited ownership. A tenancy at will obviously does not confer a real ownership of the land, even of a limited character. Ownership at will is no ownership, though it may be said that a tenancy for a definite period does confer ownership for the period, be it but a week. Thus ownership might be connected with the theory of estates. Certainly at one time tenancies at will and by sufferance were not considered "estates"; but it seems unnecessary to alter established usage and place a limitation upon the generally accepted test of an estate with reference to duration, a limitation requiring an explanation, merely to serve a purpose which seems totally inadequate.

The possession of the mortgagor, whether a tenancy by sufferance, or *sui generis*, would seem, in relation to estates, to stand in the same position as such a tenancy, by reason of the closeness of the analogy between them. It is, then, an estate by sufferance or *sui generis*. True, it was in itself formerly of little value; but with all the statutory powers and remedies which have been annexed to it during the last century, it has in practice assumed a character much stronger than that of an ordinary tenant by sufferance, and, as has been said, may well outstrip the latter altogether. It is an estate *sui generis*, the possessory estate of the mortgagor.

CHAPTER VI

THE INFLUENCE OF ROMAN LAW AND THE MOVEMENT TOWARDS *HYPOTHECA*

THE Greek and Roman conceptions of pledge of land are sometimes said to have been derived from the Jews, who, in the earliest period, exercised a species of pledge, as far as their laws would allow, by mortgaging their lands until the ensuing jubilee. The old Roman mortgage was transfer of ownership with possession, with an understanding, *fiducia*, for its reconveyance, something similar in effect to the original English common law mortgage.

By the time of Justinian the conveyance with *fiducia* had fallen out of use, having been displaced by the superior simplicity and convenience of the *hypotheca*. In the *hypotheca*, the ownership did not pass, nor did the possession; but in the *pignus*, or pledge of moveables, the possession was transferred to the creditor. The general effect of both *pignus* and *hypotheca* was the same.[1] The word *pignus* was often used loosely to describe both species of security;[2] but in the exact sense it was properly applied to moveables, and *hypotheca* to immoveables,[3] just as the corresponding term "pledge" is sometimes used in a general sense to include mortgages of land. The property pledged was considered merely as a security; and when the debt was discharged, the *pignus* or *hypotheca* was extinguished. There was no need for a reconveyance, the transaction being of a similar nature to what in English law is called a "charge". An attempt seems to have been made to make the property subject to forfeiture or foreclosure on non-payment at a day named, but Constantine, on the grounds of public policy, declared all such stipulations void as being oppressive.[4]

The proper remedy of the creditor was seizure and sale, reimbursing himself his debt, interest, and expenses. The residue of the proceeds of the sale then belonged to the debtor, to whom the creditor was personally liable,[5] and to whom he

---

[1] Dig. 20. 1. 5. 1; 13. 7. 9. 2. [2] Dig. 13. 13. 1.
[3] Dig. 50. 16. 238. 2. [4] Cod. 8. 33. 8. 35. 3.
[5] Dig. 13. 7. 42.

112 INFLUENCE OF ROMAN LAW AND

had to pay interest if he made use of it or refused to pay it on demand.[1] In the exercise of the Roman power of sale, the debtor was in a rather better position than he is in our law. He had to be given notice of the sale, and in some extraordinary cases, or where no notice could be served, a decretal order of the *Praeses* seems to have been necessary.[2] An agreement between the parties prohibiting sale was so far invalid that a decretal order for sale could even in this case be obtained upon application of the creditor;[3] and where a sale could not be effected, a decree, in the nature of a foreclosure, could sometimes be obtained, vesting the property absolutely in the creditor.[4] As the ownership was in the debtor, the buyer was not absolutely secure. If his title proved defective, the rule was laid down by Ulpin that, apart from fraud or knowledge of the defect, the creditor selling under his powers is safeguarded;[5] but if the sale were in excess of his powers, as where the money was not yet due, it was simply void; and if the buyer were party to a fraud or unfairness, damages could be obtained from him when the creditor's estate was insufficient.[6] The Conveyancing Act, 1881, is a distinct advance on this position.

Besides this remedy of selling the pledge the creditor had also the remedy of suing the debtor personally for the debt, just as he has in English law. Again, the rules relating to subsequent incumbrances were much the same. Any one incumbrancer, subject to certain statutory regulations, might sell his interest and destroy the rights of all subsequent ones, except as to any surplus in the price.[7] This could only be prevented by redeeming the one about to sell.[8] Conversely, a subsequent incumbrancer could not sell the thing absolutely, so long as there were prior incumbrancers unredeemed.[9] He who was prior in time had precedence in payment. There was no legal estate to complicate the relations of the parties, hence there was no tacking; but a right similar to consolidation seems to have existed between mortgagee and mortgagor.[10]

[1] Dig. 13. 7. 6. 1. 7.
[2] Cod. 8. 34. 3. 1–3.
[3] Cod. 8. 28. 14; Dig. 13. 7. 4.
[4] Cod. 8. 34. 3. 1–3.
[5] Dig. 19. 1. 11. 16.
[6] Cod. 8. 29.
[7] Cod. 8. 18. 1. 3; Dig. 20. 4. 12. 7.
[8] Cod. 8. 19. 3.
[9] Dig. 20. 5. 1. 3.
[10] Cod. 8. 27. 1; Dig. 20. 4. 20.

THE MOVEMENT TOWARDS *HYPOTHECA* 113

The mortgagee in possession was in at least as difficult a position in Roman law. He could not draw any benefit from the property unless there was an agreement that he might take the proceeds in lieu of interest. This suggests that the *vivum vadium*, where there was a similar agreement, and hence probably the *mortuum vadium*, or ordinary mortgage, also, were conceptions borrowed directly from the civil law. The creditor in possession was liable if the property were stolen from him, perhaps even without fault of his own,[1] and he was liable to account for fruits which he might have received had he been careful, as well as those which he had actually received.[2] Other points appear in the development of both legal systems. The same test of the mortgage appears, with the same difficulty in determining whether the transaction is intended as a security or as a sale with special conditions.[3] In the former case collateral terms were allowed which would tend to destroy or hamper the right to redeem. A stipulation to raise the rate of interest if not punctually paid was valid as to interest accruing after default in payment of the principal, but void as to that which accrued before default,[4] but the evasion which appears in English law does not seem to have occurred to the lawyers of Rome.

The various forms of land gage prior to Littleton do not show any fundamental resemblance to the Roman mortgage, although particular incidents of the various early forms all show the application of divers civil-law principles in the course of their development. Littleton expressly puts the mortgage as an estate upon condition, a basis far removed from the civil law. Exactly how this came about is uncertain. It is sometimes suggested that Littleton was himself responsible for the change and that he held a view different from that of his predecessors; but it is difficult to understand why this should be so. It seems much more likely that his theories represent the ideas of his time and of the ages which immediately preceded him, than that he was personally responsible for establishing an entirely new conception of English landed security.

Whether the mortgage developed in England as a common-

---

[1] Dig. 13. 7. 13. 1, 14.   [2] Cod. 4. 24. 3; 8. 24. 2.
[3] Dig. 18. 1. 18.   [4] Dig. 22. 1. 12.

INFLUENCE OF ROMAN LAW AND

law condition or not, it had then reached a stage very similar to the Roman *Mancipatio cum fiducia*, described by Gaius, before the *hypotheca* took the place of the *fiducia* and became the mode of landed security at Rome. Then in both legal systems a change took place, the final result of which was in general the same, but the steps by which that result was attained were very different. In the *hypotheca* the ownership was not transferred, and often not even possession, though the right to the latter was given to the creditor. In English law the Court of Chancery effected much the same result so far as it could do so. The legal ownership was still transferred; but the creditor did not take possession until his security was in jeopardy, owing to the onerous terms placed upon him if he did.

The equity of redemption was not a direct borrowing from Rome, though its later development was much influenced by the knowledge of the civil law still prevalent among the legal fraternity. It appeared as an extension of relief given to bond debtors and mortgagors who had incurred forfeiture owing to hard circumstances; and there is no reason to suppose that the Chancellor, in extending his jurisdiction by an almost imperceptible increase in the types of cases in which he would grant relief, followed by a final decision to grant relief in almost all cases, bothered to go to Roman law for a precedent in so doing; and, even if he did go there, the idea that he found what he was seeking in the Roman *hypotheca* seems fantastic. The *hypotheca* and the common-law mortgage were very different types of security, and it is a bold statement to make without authority that the Chancellor was influenced by the *hypotheca* in his decision to relieve forfeitures of bonds and mortgages generally, and a still bolder statement that he was intentionally turning the common-law mortgage from the *fiducia* stage of development to that of the *hypotheca*.

In the first place the early relief afforded to mortgagors does not in any way give us the impression of a change in the direction of *hypotheca*. There is no mention in the reports of these early cases of any analogy from Rome. The granting of the relief to forfeited mortgages was almost certainly an accident so far as the movement towards *hypotheca* was concerned. Thus

THE MOVEMENT TOWARDS *HYPOTHECA* 115

the chief remedy of the creditor under the civil law was seizure and sale, whereas in the English system the appearance of sale as the most effective remedy is of comparatively recent date and shows no sign of derivation from the civil code. The foreclosure may have been strengthened by the authority of the elder system, but in its early stages it was not regarded as a decretal order vesting the ownership in the creditor. It was the closure of the chance or right of the debtor to obtain relief in equity on the desire of the Chancellor to see justice done. The movement towards *hypotheca* appeared later in the development of the new interest so formed on lines which drew in towards the Roman analogy. It was not until a century later, under Hardwicke, that the stage of *hypotheca* can be said to have been reached in the principles of English equity. Again, the movement which began more than a century before and was pronounced by Hardwicke in terms parallel to the Roman idea of *hypotheca*, was pronounced with no mention of any comparison between Roman and English law. Indeed, the comparison does not seem to have occurred to Hardwicke at all. A change which was so gradual as to take more than a century to be definitely pronounced in parallel terms, and even then with no direct mention of the parallel, a change which commenced in such a very tentative and in a manner so widely divergent from the final result, cannot be called a direct result of the Roman example.

Although we cannot accept the suggestion that the equity of redemption was based upon the Roman *fiducia* or *hypotheca* without some definite authority to show that the Chancellor, in his gradual establishment of a right to obtain relief in equity from mortgage conditions, was influenced by Roman law, it seems quite certain that, once the equity of redemption had been established, some rules which were then applied to it, and which were of a similar nature to those found in the Roman precedent, were directly borrowed from Rome. There are no means of telling exactly how far the English Courts borrowed directly from the civil law in the development of this branch of our land law, and as to how far the general similarity between the two systems is the result of accidental development on parallel lines. The great respect for the authority of Roman law

116   INFLUENCE OF ROMAN LAW AND

probably assisted a close comparative development; for, when a principle similar to the Roman counterpart was once laid down, whether the initial conception was borrowed from Rome or not, subsequent lawyers soon noticed the Roman parallel, which at once gave the rule an authority difficult to overcome.

By the time the Chancellors began relieving mortgages, they had long ceased to be ecclesiastics brought up in the atmosphere of the civil law. Indeed, the great Lord Ellesmere pleads his ignorance of Roman principles.[1] Yet the majority of lawyers were still well versed in Roman law, and that system must have exercised a general influence from time to time. The Chancellor, even if not learned in civil law himself, often called in judges and masters to his assistance, many of whom had a first-class knowledge of the civil code, and these must often have gone to Rome for parallels when meeting a difficult situation. Probably this borrowing from Rome did not take place until the equity of redemption had been recognized as "A title inherent in the land" after the Restoration, and the Chancellors were endeavouring, with the assistance of the judges, to settle the incidents of the relationship between the mortgagor and the mortgagee; the power of redemption having become merely one of the incidents of that relationship, surrounded by numerous others invented to preserve it intact.

The influence of Roman on English law was on the whole general rather than particular. The atmosphere of men learned in the civil law was all around the Courts, especially the Court of Chancery; and, since theories of the Roman law were so well known, there is no doubt that in some cases they were applied unconsciously to difficult problems. The unconscious application of the ancient *hypotheca* was probably responsible for some of the similarity in the two species of landed security; but much also must have been due to a chance development on similar lines. In the development of legal systems, lawyers unconsciously evolve similar ideas. It has been found to be so in law, in science, in religion and in art. When they have read and studied that other system and have thus had the precedent set before them, how much more is that precedent

[1] *Calvin's Case*, (1609) 2 S.T. 673.

THE MOVEMENT TOWARDS *HYPOTHECA* 117

likely to have at least an unconscious effect in the working out of a new problem? To give a modern example of development on parallel lines without deliberate intention: the Property Acts of 1925 go a long way to further the change from *fiducia* to *hypotheca*; but it can hardly be said that they were copied from the Roman law, nor that the legislature was actively influenced by Roman precedent. It is chance development in similar channels, aided perhaps by the fact that the pilots of the second system have the knowledge that another system has gone the same way before them, and hence are aware that there is a passage in the direction.

In the Roman system we have the theory that the pledge was but a security for money; we also find it, previous to its appearance in Chancery, in the common law. Doubtless the Chancellor knew of this Roman conception of the pledge, as did also the common-lawyer. Yet it is more than probable that when they evolved the theory for their present purpose, they did not consciously adopt the Roman precedent, but rather applied what they thought was an English principle, perhaps unconsciously derived from the Roman system. The foreclosure, in its early stages considered as barring a right to relief, does not seem to find much of a parallel in the Roman decretal order of like nature; but, when after the Restoration it came to be regarded as the extinguishing of the interest of the mortgagor, then probably the Roman parallel was used as an authority for this species of remedy, thereby ensuring its permanence. For a time, the fact that the foreclosure was merely permission to the mortgagee to exercise his legal rights was almost lost to sight. The chief remedy of the creditor under the civil law, a right of seizure and sale, does not appear in the English mortgage as established by Littleton until a comparatively recent date, and only during the last century has it superseded the foreclosure. The one great difference between the English and Roman systems, that the mortgagor does not have the legal estate, whereas in the Roman *hypotheca* there was no *dominium* in the creditor at all, has prevented, and, so long as it exists, must prevent the English mortgage from becoming a true parallel of the Roman *hypotheca*.

118   INFLUENCE OF ROMAN LAW AND

The best type of security is that which combines the most efficient protection of the creditor, the least interference with the rights of the debtor, and the security of third parties against fraud. What can be done by mortgage in securing a debt, can be done equally well by way of charge or lien, and this avoids all the disturbance of legal ownership which is essentially involved in the mortgage. It is often stated that a registered charge, conferring merely a group of powers to secure the money lent, such as to sell, to take possession, etc., is the ideal form of landed security, giving the creditor such rights and powers as are necessary for the safety of his security, which rights lapse *ipso facto* on the payment of the debt, and meanwhile leaving the owner what he is meant to be, owner subject to his fulfilling his obligations. This is practically the Roman *hypotheca* with the addition of registration.

The English mortgage, before 1926, was by no means such an ideal type of landed security. It is sometimes considered unfortunate that the equity of redemption was ever brought into existence. Lord Bramwell speaks of its disadvantages thus:

Whether it would not have been better to have held people to their bargains, and taught them by experience not to make unwise ones, rather than relieve them when they had done so, may be doubtful. We should have been spared the double condition of things, legal rights and equitable rights, and a system of documents which do not mean what they say. But the piety or love of fees of those who administered equity has thought otherwise. And probably to undo this would be more costly and troublesome than to continue it.[1]

This is all very true. The result has been to complicate the English law of landed security to a great extent. Many like criticisms are to be found of the establishment of such strict and extensive rules concerning clogging the equity of redemption, another fetter upon the free contract of the parties; but the objections were to the extent of the rules and not to their existence.[2] It is impossible to say what the result would have been, had the Chancellor not interfered when he did. Perhaps some sort of relief of forfeited conditions would have been given

---

[1] *Salt* v. *Marquess of Northampton*, (1892) A.C. 1, 19.
[2] *Samuel* v. *Jarrah Timber Co.* (1904) A.C. 323, etc., *post*, p. 180.

THE MOVEMENT TOWARDS *HYPOTHECA* 119

later at common law, which would have led to much the same result as that at which the combination of the two systems of law and equity has eventually arrived, but without the complication of the dual conception of the nature of the transaction and the corresponding incongruities in the position and relationship of the parties. We have seen that the relief given to mortgagors by the Court of Chancery was at first not at all popular, and was threatened with what was tantamount to extinction by the legislature during the Commonwealth. Hence it is unlikely that any change in that direction would have been attempted by the common law, if at all, until sometime after the Restoration; but it is unreasonable to suppose that, if the Chancellor had not stepped in and granted relief, the mortgage would be in much the same state to-day as the common law conditional feoffment of the sixteenth century. Nor would the law be any the better if it were. It is probable that a forfeiture on non-payment at the day would have been found extremely unsuitable for modern commercial conditions, and would have long ago fallen into disuse, or have changed with the times almost beyond recognition. What form out of all the possible forms the English pledge of land would have taken seems mere idleness to attempt to conjecture.

Whatever might have happened, had not the Chancellor commenced relieving unfortunate mortgagors, the creation of the equity of redemption has eventually brought about an advance in the English conception of the land gage very similar in effect to the change in Roman law from the *fiducia* to the *hypotheca*. This has been the conception of the mortgage transaction in equity for nearly two centuries; but, as the ownership was still transferred to the creditor at law, and all the ensuing consequences could not be obviated by equity with its mere jurisdiction *in personam* and principles of conscience, the debtor's ownership was of a very superficial character.

The movement of the pledge of land in English equity from the mortgage, with its transfer of ownership, and sometimes possession also, to the charge, securing the money lent, but involving no change of ownership, seems to have come about rather by an unconscious application of principles, similar in

120   INFLUENCE OF ROMAN LAW AND

nature to those applied in the civil law, than by any direct effort to turn the mortgage into a charge. We can follow these unconscious movements towards *hypotheca* from the beginning of the seventeenth century. About this time, or before, the custom of the creditor taking possession as well as ownership was largely discarded, and has since become a mere last resort when he cannot successfully realize his security otherwise. Soon after this the debtor was given a right to redeem the property in equity; and this in a century ripened into a theory that the debtor was the owner so far as equity could make him so. From the time of Hardwicke to the first decade of the nineteenth century, when the rules of equity became stereotyped, the Court of Chancery was occupied with doing all its limited jurisdiction would allow it to do to overcome the effects of the transfer of ownership at law, and to enforce its conception of the mortgage transaction as a mere charge for the purpose of security.

When equity ceased to have a reforming influence on the law of mortgage, the Legislature began to make attempts to remedy the defect which still existed by reason of the mortgagor's lack of legal *dominium*. The general policy adopted, however, was not to alter in any way the theoretical basis of the mortgagor's position, but to give to the mortgagor in possession a number of common-law remedies for the protection of the property and certain powers of management. This gave the mortgagor something more in the nature of a *dominium* so far as practice was concerned, but did nothing to simplify the theory of the English pledge of land by removing the complication of the dual system of law which is a historical anomaly in our law of mortgages. The result, as in the majority of our legal and constitutional reforms, was to patch and strengthen the existing structure, rather than to pull down and build afresh.

The inconvenience of the dual system of law and equity was recognized as early as 1734. The Statute 7 Geo. II, c. 20, gave the common-law Courts a limited jurisdiction to order a reconveyance where the right of redemption was not disputed and,

Any Action shall be brought on any Bond for Payment of the Money secured by such Mortgage, or Performance of the Covenants therein

THE MOVEMENT TOWARDS *HYPOTHECA* 121

contained, or where any Action or Ejectment shall be brought...by any Mortgagee...[or those claiming under him], and no Suit shall be then depending [in any Court of Equity] touching the foreclosing or redeeming of such mortgaged Lands, [if the mortgagor pay principal interest and costs].

A wider enactment might have robbed the Court of Chancery of its exclusive jurisdiction over mortgages just as it had previously lost its jurisdiction over common money bonds,[1] but the act was too limited in scope, and little use was made of it. Lord Mansfield is sometimes credited with an intention to do away with the dual system on the authority of such expressions as, "the trust is the estate" and "the forum where it is adjudged is the only difference between trusts and legal estates";[2] but this seems doubtful when his judgments are studied as a whole, and, since he was previously at the Chancery bar, it is unlikely that he was consciously attempting such a change.

Perhaps one of the most important steps in the movement towards *hypotheca* has been the gradual increase in the popularity and effectiveness of the mortgagee's remedy of sale, until it is now the dominating factor in the choice of a mortgage security. At one time there was some discussion as to whether an express power of sale by the mortgagee in the mortgage deed would not be regarded as a clog on the equity of redemption.[3] Subsequently these express powers of sale became so frequent that one of the provisions to simplify conveyancing passed under Lord Cranworth's Act, 1860, was that a power of sale should be incident to every mortgage made by deed, unless a contrary intention was expressed. The usual conservatism of the legal profession still continued the custom of inserting an express power of sale in mortgage deeds, until this provision was repealed and re-enacted on a larger scale in the Conveyancing Act, 1881, such power being still liable to extension, variation, or even exclusion, by the express terms of the mortgage deed. For more than half a century the chief remedy relied on by the mortgagee for the realization of his security has been a power

---

[1] (1704) 6 Mod. 11, 61, 101; 4 and 5 Anne, c. 16; 8 and 9 Will. III, c. 11, § 8; 1 Wils. 157; 1 T.R. 629; Str. 1271; 3 T.R. 657; 4 T.R. 10.
[2] *Burgess* v. *Wheate*, (1757–59) 1 Ed. 224; see also *Eaton* v. *Jacques*, (1780) 2 Doug. 455.   [3] See Chap. VIII, C, *infra*.

122   INFLUENCE OF ROMAN LAW AND

of sale, statutory or otherwise. It is a cheap and speedy remedy which has paved the way for the time when it is felt that, provided the mortgagee is given sufficient remedies of a speedy and efficient character, there is no need for the transfer of ownership at all.

We have a striking example of the working of the charge, with sale as the most important remedy, in the Roman *hypotheca*. The efficiency of the English remedy of sale has been greatly increased by the Conveyancing Act, 1881, which enacted that the title of a purchaser from a mortgagee selling in the professed exercise of his power of sale is not impeachable on the ground that no case for sale has arisen, and the purchaser is not concerned to enquire whether such a case had actually arisen. This enactment exceeds the advantages of the Roman counterpart. It enables the mortgagee selling under a power of sale to confer a title readily accepted, and hence enables him the more easily to realize his security.

In spite of the perfection of the mortgagor's position in equity, the common law, save in the interpretation of some few statutes, would in general take no notice of the equity of redemption. In the reign of Elizabeth the Court of Common Pleas held that, "Forbearance of a suit in Equity, is a good consideration at law to maintain an *assumpsit*";[1] and in 1703, "all the Court held, that without a doubt a release of an equity of redemption is a very good consideration, and the common law will take notice, that the mortgagor has an equity to be relieved in Chancery".[2] In 1759, however, the whole Court held, "a release of an equity of redemption was nothing at all in the eye of the law", and was therefore accord without satisfaction.[3] In this case counsel argued from Littleton's statement that the land "is taken from him for ever, and so is dead to him upon condition",[4] as showing that an equity of redemption was of no value at law.

In 1790, where a lessee of the mortgagor and mortgagee entered into certain covenants with the mortgagor, it was held

---

[1] *Dowdenay* v. *Oland*, (41 Eliz.) 1 Cro. 768.
[2] *Thorpe* v. *Thorpe*, 1 Ld Raymond, 664.
[3] *Preston* v. *Christmas*, 2 Wils. 86.   [4] Co. Litt. § 332.

THE MOVEMENT TOWARDS *HYPOTHECA* 123

without hearing any argument that the covenants, "not being made with the person who had the legal estate, did not run with the land", and hence were *in gros*.[1] The decision was affirmed by Lord Loughborough.[2] In 1794 Lord Loughborough stated, "a court of law has nothing to do with the disposition of the equity of redemption; for it takes no notice of such an interest".[3]

Again in 1804, where there was a covenant by the purchaser in a conveyance by the mortgagee containing a clause of confirmation by the mortgagor that the mortgagor and his heirs might enter to dig for coal, etc., Lord Ellenborough, stopping the counsel for defence, held that a reservation to a person having an equity of redemption only is not possible in law, saying, "This case appears to me to involve no point of difficulty. In contemplation of the law the mortgagor was a perfect stranger, as to any legal estate, and therefore could neither *grant* the *legal* estate, nor consequently *reserve* to himself anything out of it".[4] Lastly in 1851 Lord Campbell, C.J., remarks, "There is great difficulty in our noticing, at law, the nature of the equitable interest of the mortgagor". This seems to be the correct view, save where Statute has given the common law jurisdiction over mortgages, or the common-law courts, in giving effect to the obvious meaning of Statutes, have been forced to take notice of equitable interests; namely, that the mortgagor has no estate or interest whatever at law apart from possession.

Before the legislature intervened, the mortgagor's equitable ownership was protected in the Court of Equity only, and then only upon the antecedent condition of redemption. The common law gave the mortgagor only those remedies available for the protection of his tenancy, which, if he were a tenant at sufferance, were almost non-existent. Hence the mortgagor, if he wished to sue a trespasser who threatened to become a disseisor, must first have persuaded the mortgagee to join in the action with him, or if the latter would not join, redeem the property by payment of principal, interest and costs, so as to

---

[1] *Stokes* v. *Russell*, (1790) 3 T.R. 678.   [2] 1 H.Bl. 562.
[3] *Brydges* v. *Chandos*, (1794) 2 Ves. J. 428.
[4] *Cheetham* v. *Williamson*, 1 Smith, 278.

124   INFLUENCE OF ROMAN LAW AND

have a right to sue in his own name. The mortgagor then, viewing the resultant effect of his position at law and in equity, whether as against the mortgagee, or as against strangers, could only be considered the owner in any sense of that term, subject to redemption.

The Legislature has attempted to rectify this defect by strengthening the position of the mortgagor in possession in giving to him the right to use in his own name various common-law remedies for the protection of his interest without the consent of the mortgagee, thus greatly strengthening his claims to ownership as against strangers. Even as against the mortgagee, his "ownership" has been reinforced by the powers of leasing and management granted to a mortgagor in possession under provisions first extended by the Conveyancing Act, 1881, and now codified by the Law of Property Act, 1925.

The first of these changes which must be noticed was a matter of administration. The procedure of the Courts concerning mortgages was greatly simplified in 1875 by the establishment of one single High Court of Justice administering both law and equity together; but the principles of the two systems underwent no change as a direct consequence, save that both systems of law were now applied in one single Court.[1]

At common law the equity of redemption was held to be no such reversion as would entitle the owner to sue for an injury to the mortgaged property.[2] Nor would the mortgagor's possession entitle him to maintain trespass, for in general he was at most but a tenant at sufferance. Where there was an agreement making him tenant at will or for years, it was otherwise. Again, although the mortgagor was allowed to distrain for rent due under a tenancy commencing before the date of the mortgage, as long as he was permitted by the mortgagee to receive such rent, for such permission was held to authorize him, *presumptione juris*, to distrain for it;[3] any action to recover that rent must be brought in the name of the mortgagee, to whom it belonged in the eye of the common law.[4]

---

[1] Judicature Act, 1873, 36 and 37 Vict. c. 66.
[2] *Mamford* v. *Oxford W. and W. Ry. Co.* (1856) 1 H. and N. 34.
[3] *Trent* v. *Hunt*, (1853) 9 Ex. 22.
[4] *Doe d. Marriott* v. *Edwards*, (1834) 5 B. and Ad. 1065; *Trent* v. *Hunt, supra*

THE MOVEMENT TOWARDS *HYPOTHECA* 125

By § 25 (5) of the Judicature Act, 1873, where the mortgagee has not given notice of his intention of taking possession, the mortgagor may sue for the possession of the land, or for the recovery of the rents and profits, or to prevent or recover damages in respect of any trespass or other wrong relative thereto, in his own name only, unless the cause of action arises upon a lease or other contract made by him jointly with any other person. Under this clause he may sue in his own name for an injunction to restrain a tenant, whose tenancy commenced before the mortgage, from breaking a covenant in his lease, provided such breach would seriously affect the mortgaged premises;[1] and under § 10 of the Conveyancing Act, 1881, he can sue and enforce the covenants under such Lease.[2]

Cotton, L.J., sums up the result of these enactments as follows:

If the mortgagee does not assert his right to possession, and the mortgagor is left to manage the property, he has a right to insist, without reference to the mortgagee, on the observance of any obligations, the non-observance of which would injuriously affect the premises...unless there is a probability that the relief for which the mortgagor sues will injuriously affect the interest of his mortgagee.[3]

Even so, the possessory remedies of both mortgagor and *cestui que trust* are deprived of some of their value by the fact that, in an action brought by an equitable owner, the legal owner must be made a party to the action in order to be bound.[4] It may be added, he must also be found and served. Indeed, if the equitable owner is claiming possession it may be that the legal owner must be brought before the Court for proceedings to be maintained.[5] § 25 of the Judicature Act seems to be limited in a curious manner. It does not seem to include the assignee of the mortgagor, nor any incumbrancer of the equity of redemption.[6] Save for the statutory power of the second mortgagee to appoint a receiver, and the regulations relating to registered charges, statute law seems in general to have con-

---

[1] *Fairclough* v. *Marshall*, (1878) 4 Ex. D. 37.
[2] *Turner* v. *Walsh*, (1909) 2 K.B. 484.
[3] *Fairclough* v. *Marshall*, 4 Ex. D. 37, 47.
[4] *Bowden's Synd. Ltd.* v. *Smith*, (1904) 2 Ch. 86, 91.
[5] *Allen* v. *Woods*, (1893) 68 L.T. 143.
[6] *Mathews* v. *Usher*, (1900) 2 Q.B. 539.

126   INFLUENCE OF ROMAN LAW AND

templated only one effective mortgage of the same land. Under the Property Acts of 1925, however, sub-mortgages, second and subsequent mortgages have all received consideration.

Again, as the mortgagor's equity of redemption was an estate in the contemplation of equity only, it did not enable him to create any legal estate or interest in the mortgaged land; and in general a lease granted by him for any term, however short, might be avoided by his mortgagee. In some cases, however, there was inserted in the mortgaged deed, by agreement between the parties, a power for the mortgagor to grant leases, which operated under the Statute of Uses in the same manner as a power of leasing given to a tenant for life by a settlement. It may seem curious that equity, having recognized the mortgagor as the owner of the land, did not allow him some power of making suitable leases at a rack rent in his capacity as owner; but equity has interfered very little with the common-law rules as to the creation of terms of years, for these rules did not suffer from technicalities as to form. Also we may presume that a lease by the mortgagor would have been regarded as depriving the mortgagee in some measure of his remedies for the realization of his security, as it would have prevented him from taking over the possession and management of the estate.

Further, the mortgagee in possession was not allowed by the Court of Chancery to grant leases against the mortgagor's redeeming in the absence of express agreement to that effect, because such a lease would prevent the mortgagee from returning the land to the mortgagor in the same form as he had pledged it. Thus it was not safe to accept a lease from either mortgagor or mortgagee without the consent of the other. However, under the Conveyancing Act, 1881, § 18,[1] various powers of leasing, to be exercisable by the mortgagor, while in possession or until the appointment of a receiver, or otherwise by the mortgagee, are to be implied in the mortgage deed; but these with the various other powers of management granted to the mortgagor in possession or the mortgagee by that Act, are subject to exclusion of variation by the express contract of the parties in writing. On a mortgagor's exercising this statutory

[1] Extended by Law of Property Act, 1925, §§ 99, 100.

THE MOVEMENT TOWARDS *HYPOTHECA* 127

power of leasing, his lessee obtains a legal term in the land valid at law in the same manner as the lessee of an equitable tenant for life on the exercise of the power of leasing given him by the Settled Land Act, 1882.[1]

A beginning in the attempt to popularize the charge was made under the Land Transfer Acts, 1875 and 1897,[2] which created a registered charge of land in those counties which adopted the system of land registration as indicated by those Acts. The chargee was given all the remedies of the legal mortgagee, and the incidents of this charge were in practice the same as in the mortgage, save that, in general, priority of registration gave priority of interest. The property remained in the debtor until the creditor exercised his power of foreclosure or sale, in which case the lands were registered in the names of the mortgagee or purchaser respectively; the need for reconveyance, one of the worst disadvantages of the mortgage, being thus removed altogether.

A further experiment was made under the Yorkshire and Middlesex Registry Acts, 1884 and 1891,[3] whereby registration of title in these counties became compulsory, giving priority to mortgagees according to the date of registration, and in the latter county giving priority of registration precedence even over a subsequent mortgagee who has the legal estate.

The substitution of a registered charge for the ancient mortgage was also effected in the case of ships by Merchant Shipping Act, 1894,[4] and a mortgage of personal chattels in effect gives no more than a charge under the Bills of Sale Acts, 1878 and 1882, save that the property in the goods has to be redelivered to the debtor after the debt is paid, in order to give him a good legal title to them.

The usual practice on a mortgage of copyholds also foreshadows the charge. The mortgagor surrenders to the use of the mortgagee upon condition, and when that condition is forfeited at law, he retains a mere equity of redemption. The mortgagee, however, seldom requires an admittance from the

---

[1] 45 and 46 Vict. c. 38, § 20; now 15 Geo. V, c. 18.
[2] 38 and 39 Vict. c. 87; 60 and 61 Vict. c. 65.
[3] 47 and 48 Vict. c. 26; 54 and 55 Vict. c. 64.
[4] 57 and 58 Vict. c. 60.

128   INFLUENCE OF ROMAN LAW AND

lord unless he wishes to enforce his security, contenting himself
with the right to admittance conferred upon him by the surrender. The fines payable to the lord of the manor on every
admittance are therefore avoided, and, when the debt is repaid,
all that is then necessary is to procure the steward to insert on
the Court Roll a memorandum of acknowledgment by the mortgagee of satisfaction of the principal money and interest secured
by the surrender.[1] If the mortgagee should have been admitted
tenant, on repayment he must, of course, surrender again to
the use of the mortgagor, who will then be readmitted.

The movement towards *hypotheca* which the Courts of Equity
had carried out as far as they were able, and which was continued in part by recent experimental legislation, has now been
accelerated by the new Property Acts of 1925. These acts
make a fundamental change in the theoretical position of the
mortgagor, but do not thereby alter the practical effect so
much as might at first sight be supposed. Whereas previously
the Legislature, save in its experimental dealing with a very
limited field of subject-matter, had, as it were, accepted the
theoretical position of the English mortgage, but had tried to
remedy its weakness by giving the mortgagor and mortgagee
a number of special powers of management and remedies; the
new acts for the first time since the days of Nottingham and
Hardwicke have somewhat altered the fundamental basis of the
mortgage relationship.

Without any regard for the intention of the parties, they
convert all existing and future mortgages of freeholds into long
terms of years, (in case of mortgages purporting to convey the
fee simple, a term of 3000 years), and all mortgages of leaseholds
into subdemises, (in the case of mortgages purporting to be by
way of assignment, for a derivative term less the last ten days).
Thus, if the estate mortgaged be freehold, the freehold reversion
will remain in the mortgagor. He will still retain the seisin,
and a leasehold, or chattel interest, will be all that is conveyed
to the mortgagee. Likewise, if the original estate be leasehold,
the mortgagor will retain the head term. A submortgage will be

[1] 1 Scriv. Cop. 242; 1 Watk. 117, 118; *Hopkinson* v. *Chamberlain*, (1908)
1 Ch. 853, 855.

THE MOVEMENT TOWARDS *HYPOTHECA* 129

made by means of a subdemise of a term slightly shorter than that of the original mortgage. The result is to make the mortgagor who has conveyed the legal estate a reversioner at law, with all the legal remedies of a reversioner for the protection of his interest, in addition to those which equity or statute had previously conferred upon him.

The ordinary incidents of the relation of mortgagor and mortgagee remain in general unaltered. There will still be a technical forfeiture of the leasehold term on failure to perform the condition, and hence there will still be an equity of redemption, an equitable estate for a term of years, subject to the debt. The mortgagor will still be viewed as owner in equity subject to the debt, even of the leasehold interest conveyed to the mortgagee, but he will retain a reversion at law as well. The effect of the theoretical change made by the new Acts is merely to alter the position as regards third parties, in that the mortgagor will have a legal reversion in the land as well as his equity of redemption, and can use all the common-law remedies for the protection of that reversion without the consent of the mortgagee. The result is somewhat similar to that produced by the form of mortgage at one time in use in the days when seisin meant much more than it does now, and it was customary to grant mortgages in the form of long terms of years, thus securing to the mortgagee his right to possession, and the mortgagor his seisin and the remedies therefor. Such mortgages are only common to-day when trustees mortgage a long term of years to raise portions for younger children.

It appears that the new Acts not only made the mortgagor a reversioner immediately on the conveyance of the leasehold term to the mortgagee, but also intended to make a legal reversion an inseparable incident of the equity of redemption of a legal mortgage. It is laid down that legal mortgage shall only "be capable of being effected" in this manner; but from the tenor of subsequent passages it would seem intended to apply for as long as the mortgage relationship lasts. There would seem no reason, however, why the mortgagor should not deal with his legal reversion in the same manner as with any other legal estate, by granting further estates subject to the mortgage

TER

9

130   INFLUENCE OF ROMAN LAW AND

term; nor is there any express prohibition against his granting to another the whole reversion while retaining to himself the equity of redemption of the mortgage term. Any person interested in the reversion has a right to redeem the mortgage, subject to any prior right. Hence, even if what appears to have been the intention of the legislature does not seem to have been properly carried out, the time may come when this rule will be inverted into the theory that the equity of redemption of a legal estate must be appurtenant to some larger legal estate in the same parcel of land.[1]

The retention of a legal reversion by the mortgagor as a necessary incident of the mortgage transaction is undoubtedly a great advance in the direction of *hypotheca*. Perhaps the greatest practical step in that direction is the abolition of the necessity for a reconveyance of the property on the satisfaction of the debt. On payment of the debt, the mortgage term becomes satisfied and is merged in the freehold without reconveyance. All that is now necessary for conveyancing purposes is a receipt for payment by the mortgagor of the amount due endorsed on the mortgage deed and signed by the mortgagee. This has long been the case with equitable mortgages, from which the idea was originally borrowed, and has already been made sufficient by Statute in the case of legal mortgages by certain Building and Friendly Societies.[2]

Again, dealings with the mortgage property are facilitated by allowing the mortgagee to effect a conveyance of the mortgage term by means of a deed purporting to transfer the mortgage, such deed implying, unless a contrary intention appear, a legal conveyance of the term and an assignment of the mortgage debt and all securities for the same. Likewise on sale or foreclosure by the mortgagee, or the extinguishment of the equity of redemption in any other manner, the order of foreclosure will vest the fee simple in the mortgagee, or the latter may on sale convey the fee simple to a purchaser, thus extinguishing the reversion and operating as an enlargement of the mortgage term.

An equitable mortgage can still be created by a deposit of

[1] Law of Property Act 1925, §§ 85, 86.
[2] See, e.g., *Crosbie-Hill* v. *Sayer*, (1908) 1 Ch. 866.

THE MOVEMENT TOWARDS *HYPOTHECA* 131

title deeds, but the Acts bring into use second and subsequent mortgages of a legal character. It will henceforth be possible to make a legal second mortgage by a demise for a slightly longer term than is comprised in the first mortgage. This alters the rules as to tacking. The first mortgagee is allowed to tack further advances as before; but, where the mortgage takes effect by way of a legal term of years, the third mortgagee has now no right to tack by reason of his acquisition of the first legal mortgage, for the second mortgagee has a legal estate.[1] Hence a second mortgage is a somewhat safer investment, as there is less danger of tacking and also the advantage of a registered legal estate. Consolidation is in no way affected.

A further attempt has been made to popularize the charge at the expense of the mortgage by the creation of a "charge by the way of legal mortgage", which is to have the same effect as that of a mortgage by grant of a legal term of 3000 years, or, in the case of leaseholds, as if a subdemise had been made by way of mortgage. The owner of such a charge has all the rights and remedies available to a legal mortgagee, the only difference between his position and that of the latter is that technically he has no estate, legal or equitable, vested in him until he chooses to realize his security.

It seems unfortunate, from the jurisprudential point of view, that it was found necessary to emphasize the fact that the owner of a legal charge under the new Acts is in exactly the same position as a legal mortgagee. It was obviously the easiest way to specify the remedies available to a chargee, without making an unnecessary complication by giving the creditor different remedies according to his taking the legal estate or a legal charge; and further, in the face of the well-known conservatism of the general practitioner and the desire of the creditor to obtain the safest security possible, even though the additional security be one of shadow rather than of substance, the fact that there is no practical difference between the legal charge and the mortgage will help to satisfy these conservative tendencies. A charge which operates as if it were a mortgage does away with the transfer of ownership and simplifies the form of the necessary

[1] Sched. II, 8, §§ 2 and 3.

132 INFLUENCE OF ROMAN LAW AND

documents; but it still retains the complicated dual system of law applicable to mortgages, and, since under the new Acts there is no need for a reconveyance, the practical effect of this new charge is merely the substitution of the word "charge" for that of "mortgage". The emphasis which is placed on the fact that the chargee has all the remedies of a mortgagee is rather stating that the ownership is left in the hands of the debtor, but that the charge takes effect as if it did not.

The new Acts are certainly a very big step towards *hypotheca*. They give the mortgagor some sort of ownership both in law and equity, and at the same time abolish all necessity for reconveyance. Yet the change is only partial. A leasehold ownership at law is still conveyed to the creditor. Under the new Acts further covenants and powers are implied in the mortgage deed unless contrary intention is expressed; but there is still left a suggestion that the English mortgage document does not mean what it says, and the relations of the parties are still subject to two diverse systems of law. Englishmen, and English lawyers too, have a great dislike for sweeping changes in their institutions, and are therefore much more ready to reclothe an old system than to abolish it, and build afresh. This is what they seem to have done with the mortgage in the new Acts. Few of the incidents attached to the mortgage have been touched. The old model has been put into a new dress, and it remains to be seen exactly what the result will be. How the change of vesture, a change to a newer fashion, will stand the wear and tear of the needs of commerce and the exigences of the courts cannot be foreseen.

We cannot say that of recent years the effect of an Act of Parliament has always been that which was intended. Every great Statute of the past relating to property has had far-reaching effects, legal and economic, many of them unforeseen at the time the Statute itself was passed, and most of these Acts have at least been partially evaded by cunning conveyancing or judicial legislation, so that the result achieved was far different from that which was intended by the framers of the Statute. We cannot say that this will not be the case when the vast change brought about by the Acts in matters other than

THE MOVEMENT TOWARDS *HYPOTHECA* 133

mortgages come to be judicially construed in connection with them, and attempts are made to violate its spirit and alter its tenor by documents drawn by skilful lawyers intent on evading the objects of the Legislature, nor can we state with certainty the form of landed security which will eventually become popular under the new state of affairs; but everything points to continued progress towards the establishment of the charge, registered as under the Land Transfer Acts, 1875 and 1897, or unregistered, as the type of the English land gage of the future.

Registration, a movement towards bureaucracy which obtained no footing in Rome, was brought into existence in an experimental form by nineteenth-century legislation, the necessity and effect of registration being changed to and fro by each succeeding Act without any apparent consecutive design. These innovations met with little support, probably because of the general aversion both of legal practitioners and the public at large to dealings with a government bureau in any shape or form. At various times during this period it was necessary for complete security to register judgments, writs of *elegit*, debts due from the Crown, *lites pendentes*, annuities, deeds of arrangement and other charges affecting land with results differing in each case. Also registration of title was made compulsory in Middlesex, Yorkshire and London, but the voluntary registration of title, either by the individual, or by the county as a whole, for which provision was made under the Land Transfer Acts 1875 and 1897, met with no response at all.

Under the new Acts the various provisions as to registration have been collected and codified, and registration has been made necessary for many other interests in land, including equitable easements, contracts for the sale of land, and all charges or mortgages not secured by deposit with the chargee of the documents of title to the legal estate. Further, there is provision for the compulsory extension of the area of registration of title without resolution on the part of the County Council concerned, any time after ten years from the coming into operation of the Acts. There is no doubt that in the minds of some of our legislators this is but an intermediate step to general registration of title throughout the country. It remains

134 INFLUENCE OF ROMAN LAW AND

to be seen whether the Legislature will overcome the popular and professional aversion to registration.

It is said that registration of title will simplify and cheapen conveyancing. This has not been found to be the case where such registration exists. The solicitor is still a necessary safeguard and must be so. If all the complicated rights in land that exist are all to be registered, the register will tax the present methods of indexing to the fullest and threaten to increase the universal outcry against the dilatoriness of officials. A solicitor will still be necessary to examine the register and explain the meaning of what is there found. If, as at present, in order to escape these difficulties, many of these rights are not registrable, a solicitor will be necessary to see whether they exist. In either case, judging by the present system, the labour of solicitors at a distance from the registries is increased, while their fees diminish, in order to provide for the Registry fees paid to feed the army of civil servants who will run this colossal government bureau.

Under the 1925 Acts, unless a mortgage or charge on land where the chargee or mortgagee does not take possession of the documents of title to the legal estate is registered, it is void as against a purchaser of the land, whether he has notice of the charge or not, and registration of a charge gives notice thereof to all persons subsequently dealing with the land. This is a great safeguard to a purchaser, and also to a second mortgagee without the deeds, in that it eliminates most of the trouble which may arise by reason of constructive notice. A second mortgage becomes a much safer investment.

The present method of registration and search is not satisfactory, notwithstanding the amendments contained in the Act of 1926. In order to be safeguarded, the legal profession, especially the country branch, must incur much unnecessary expense in telegraphic searches, which expense naturally falls on the public, or render themselves responsible for departures from the strict rule of searching within two days of the date of completion against every person who is able to deal with the title. If the strict rule were observed by the profession, the completion of a number of interrelated transactions would be

THE MOVEMENT TOWARDS *HYPOTHECA* 135

a work of art. The hitches and postponements of completions are only too well known. The necessity of multiple searches by mortgagee and purchaser within two days of completion creates an almost impossible burden. An alteration of the completion day means a fresh series of searches, if the client is to be truly safeguarded. This difficulty is increased because a prompt official search is in no way assured unless a special telephone fee and cost of telephone is paid. A country solicitor cannot rely on the result of a search by post arriving on the correct day unless the application is made more than a week before, especially during the quarter-day period. Even the lesser telegram fee does not mean search will be made on receipt of application.

The period of two days' grace should be lengthened or the work of the Registry expedited, and some method should be found of making search against the last purchaser sufficient or registration should be made with reference to an official plan so as to avoid multiple searches. Unless something is done, the question will arise whether the additional protection of purchasers and second mortgagees in the very few cases where trouble ensued for them under the old law is worth the creation of a host of Registry officials, more fees, a check on speedy transfer of property, and an increase of work and responsibility for the solicitor. (Recent changes may lessen these evils.)

It is interesting to speculate what the effect of the substitution of the charge, registered or unregistered, for the mortgage with its transfer of ownership will be on the usage and meaning of the terms "charge" and "mortgage". The word "charge" seems to have two meanings; first, a pledge of property which in general binds that property into whosesoever hands it may come as well as the person of the debtor with repayment of the debt; and secondly, a meaning opposed to mortgage in that the property is not conveyed to the creditor. In the first sense the word "charge" includes the mortgage, in the second it is opposed to it and is used in the sense of *hypotheca*. In this chapter it has been used with the second meaning only. The new Acts establish a new species of charge, a "charge by way of legal mortgage", operating as if it were a mortgage;

136   INFLUENCE OF ROMAN LAW AND

but the time may be approaching when the word "charge" will itself imply both to the legal and non-legal mind the various remedies attached, without having recourse to the intermediate, explanatory word, "mortgage". This would undoubtedly be a further step forward in the direction of *hypotheca*.

At present the new Acts create the difficulty of the existence of two different species of charge, the charge by way of legal mortgage under the Acts, and also those various charges on land which are to be carefully differentiated from equitable mortgages, charges which do not allow of the remedy of foreclosure, many of which have to be registered under the Acts. The word "mortgage" is at present infinitely more widely known as implying landed security than the word "charge", as witness the expression, "charge by way of legal mortgage", and it may well be that on the abolition of the mortgage proper, the expression will be extended to include what is technically an *hypotheca*.

It seems certain that the present state of things is only a transition stage and that, when at length the charge has become the general mode of pledging land, the mortgage with its transfer of ownership and its dual system of law and equity will finally disappear. With the fall of the conditional conveyance in the face of the simple and more convenient form of landed security, the charge, it seems the equity of redemption, which only came into existence by reason of the legal forfeiture involved on failure to perform the condition, must also become obsolete and cease to exist; but as long as a transfer of ownership is the usual form of land gage, or the charge of land is said to operate as if there had been a mortgage by conditional conveyance, even though a legal reversion is left in the mortgagor, so long will there be an equity of redemption, an equitable estate in the hands of the debtor who has lost his leasehold interest at law. When this legal conveyance and forfeiture and the corresponding equity of redemption are abolished or fall into disuse, the English law of landed security will be very similar to that of the Roman *hypotheca*, with a few added advantages as a result of 2000 years' legal experience, and some small variations to meet the special needs of the times.

There is something satisfactory in the fact that in the evolu-

THE MOVEMENT TOWARDS *HYPOTHECA* 137

tion of the pledge of land our courts have at length arrived at a position approaching that of the Roman law. This satisfaction is not lessened by the fact that though the law of Rome had some indirect effect on the corresponding English conceptions of the pledge, the evolution of the two systems, especially since the Chancellor assumed jurisdiction over the mortgage, has moved in widely divergent lines, but is now approaching the same conclusion. There is a feeling that as in two of the greatest legal systems of the world, where the lawyers of the second system were not deliberately trying to bring about a change corresponding to that which took place in the first, the end achieved is to a large extent the same, the conceptions upon which the rules in application are based are sound in character and little short of the ideal.

Our system of land gage is not yet as fully developed as that of the Roman law, in that we still have the unnecessary complication of dual ownership; yet at the same time it cannot be said that the creation of the equity of redemption, the cause of the dual ownership, was a mistake; for we have no idea what the result would have been had such an equitable power to redeem never existed. All that can be done is to point out the heavy complications which have resulted from the basing of our law of landed security, be it charge or mortgage, upon the sixteenth-century condition and the seventeenth-century equity of redemption; and to hope that the time may come when this theoretical position of the mortgagor, caused by a transfer of the legal ownership followed by forfeiture, will completely disappear.

CHAPTER VII

THE EQUITY OF REDEMPTION AND RIGHTS *IN REM* AND *IN PERSONAM*

DURING the first half of the last century, a large number of distinguished analytical jurists, whose leader was Austin, and who controlled legal thought almost completely from the early years of the last century down to a few decades ago, brought into prominence a classification of so-called "rights" into those *in rem* and those *in personam*, the terms being taken from the Roman classification of actions. This classification has assumed a place of some juridical importance, and much learned discussion has been spent in placing under these two headings the various so-called rights, and in particular equitable rights, recognized by the English law.

The whole matter is complicated at the outset by a divergence and vagueness of definition and user of the terms involved. For instance, the various senses in which the word "right" has been used has caused much confusion of thought. Technically a right is one of the means of supporting an interest. When used in this sense, as Professor Gray remarks, "The right is not the interest itself, it is the means whereby the interest is secured". In the strictest sense, the *cestui que trust*, the mortgagor, and the owners of any valuable interest whatever, have not one right connected with that interest, but many; and a large number of powers, liberties, and privileges, and even duties, etc., as well. However, the word "right" is often used indiscriminately to describe such powers, privileges, etc., which are distinguished from a right in the strict academical sense of the term by other writers. This seems to have been done in all cases where the classification *in rem* and *in personam* has been under discussion, and hence in this work this strictest differentiation of rights from liberties, etc., will be abandoned.

There are two conceptions of a right which figure with reference to this classification. The first is obtained by assembling

RIGHTS *IN REM* AND *IN PERSONAM* 139

together all the rights, liberties, powers, etc., appertaining to a given interest, viewing the total effect, and then calling the resultant sum so obtained one single right. This makes "right" and "interest" almost convertible terms, the difference being perhaps that the term "interest" emphasizes the idea of ownership of a species of property, corporeal or incorporeal, whereas a right emphasizes that of the various remedies protecting that interest.

In the second case it is laid down that no one has a right until the interest supported is threatened with violation, whereupon the right arises against the particular person or persons who are about to violate that interest; for law must be regarded, not as a scheme of abstract ideas, but of concrete relations between men, and until men come into such a position that a legal relation is established the law has nothing whatever to do with them. Thus it is one's interest to enjoy an estate in land, or to walk along the highway, but no one has a right to do so until someone else proposes to interfere. In other words, right is here synonymous with remedy. It is a means of protecting an interest when that interest is assailed.

The distinction between a right as a means of supporting an interest, and a right as the interest itself may be further illustrated as follows. When *A* and *B* contract together that *A* shall have the right to some service to be done by *B* in return for a sum of money, *A* has by reason of the contract a valuable interest, the extent of which is the services to be performed by *B*, an interest, or in the latter sense a right, which in most cases he can assign to another during his lifetime, and which will, unless the services concern his person, pass to his personal representatives on his decease. That interest, or right, is quite distinct from his right against *B* arising out of the contract, to make the latter perform those services, from his subsidiary right that *B* shall pay him damages if he does not do so, or from his further right that no one else shall induce *B* not to perform them. These last three rights are the means of supporting *A*'s interest, that is, remedies.

As its Latin phraseology suggests, the classification *in rem* and *in personam* was borrowed from the Roman law; but in

140 EQUITY OF REDEMPTION AND

Roman law the terms were confined to actions, and had nothing whatever to do with the right or interest supported by the actions at all. The Romans broadly classified their law of things into obligations, which were enforced by means of an *actio in personam*; and property, which was upheld by an *actio in rem*. An *actio in personam* supported a relation between two persons only, both of whom were named parties to the action; whereas in an *actio in rem* the plaintiff claimed a particular thing as his own, and he had to be prepared to vindicate his claim against all the world; there was no other party to the action. There does not appear to have been any suggestion in Roman law of the application of the terms to the interest supported by the remedy, but only to the action, or remedy itself.

The Austinian School, as the followers of Austin may for convenience be called, have taken over the Roman classification of actions, which had a strict technical meaning in Roman law, but in this technical meaning was valueless in English law, since in the latter all actions, both at common law and in equity, were essentially *in personam* in this sense; for in English law there are no actions truly against a thing, but merely actions between individuals concerning their relationship *inter se*. They then argue as to whether the *cestui que trust* or the mortgagor, etc., has a "right *in rem*" or a "right *in personam*". What can they mean? Obviously they have defined all the terms afresh and have adopted an arbitrary classification which is by no means identical with, but merely analogous to that of Rome. The Romans had no idea that a right, in the sense of interest, could be *in rem* or *in personam*, and, according to their conception, all remedies in English law are *in personam*.

The so-called Austinian School accepted Austin's definition of rights *in rem* as rights available against the world at large, which they interpreted as rights available against all classes of legal persons, save perhaps a definite number of individuals who were exempt by grant or otherwise; and rights *in personam* as rights available against particular individuals, which they interpreted as rights available against certain definite types of legal personages only. They then stated that a right *in rem*, as defined by Austin, was the only true proprietary right.

RIGHTS *IN REM* AND *IN PERSONAM*   141

This classification they applied to rights in the sense of remedies. They noted that the trust was originally a matter of agreement, and that the right of the *cestui que trust* rested merely upon the obligation of the trustee, that, as Coke said, the *cestui que trust* had neither *jus in re*, nor *jus ad rem*; but merely a *jus in personam*. They held that the right of the *cestui que trust* (and we may presume the rights of the mortgagor also, for their arguments cover equitable interests generally, often expressly so, though they usually adopted as their guide the most prominent of all equitable interests, that of the *cestui que trust*), although appearing like ownership, was not a true proprietary right, but a right *in personam*. They showed that gradually this right came to look like a right of a proprietary nature by reason of the increase in the number of classes of persons against whom it could be enforced, as the *cestui que trust* was enabled to recover the thing, first in the hands of the heir of the trustee, then in the hands of his personal representative, his doweress, his creditors, volunteers taking under him, and lastly, in the hands of a purchaser for value from him, provided the latter had notice, actual or constructive of the trust. They pointed to this gradual increase in the number of persons against which the right of the beneficiary would prevail, but observed that it would not prevail against that of a purchaser of the legal estate for value without notice, nor perhaps, until the Legislature intervened, that of a lord by escheat, nor against a disseisor. Hence they came to the conclusion that, though his position was like ownership, yet he really had only a right *in personam*, available against particular classes of persons only, and no true proprietary right; for the right *in rem*, the right available against all the world, was to them the only true proprietary right.

Let us for a moment examine exactly the position to which their reasoning has led them. They state that, from a jurisprudential point of view, the right of the *cestui que trust* is *in personam*, and therefore, though it has all the appearance of conveying ownership, that is not the case. If we leave jurisprudence, as they have learnt it, alone, and turn to the practical position of the *cestui que trust*, we find him to all intents and purposes the owner, for the trustee cannot exercise any of his

142 EQUITY OF REDEMPTION AND

powers, etc., save for the benefit of the beneficiary. Further, we find the beneficiary continually spoken of by judges and text-writers as the real owner of the land. Again, according to the Austinian School the trustee seems to have a right, or rights, *in rem*, available against everyone except the *cestui que trust*. He then has ownership; but it is a poor type of ownership. It is an ownership which gives no benefit whatsoever, for the trustee is not allowed to take any advantage of his position. Yet, accepting their conceptions of ownership and of the meaning of the term, *in rem*, it does not seem possible that they could have come to a more satisfactory conclusion; and if we are going to accept their hypotheses, we cannot but concur in the result.

If this classification of rights in the form laid down by the Austinian School be accepted, the result then is as follows. The trustee has a right *in rem*, in general a true proprietary right according to their hypothesis. Yet we are taught almost as soon as we open a book on the English law of property that the trustee cannot legally take any benefit by reason of his ownership. Again, the *cestui que trust*, continually spoken of by learned judges and text-writers as the real owner, is denied ownership in jurisprudence, for he has only a right *in personam*, which is not a true proprietary right. Practitioners tell us that the trustee with the legal estate, though apparently the owner, yet is not really so, for in equity he holds merely for the benefit of another; but then we are told that the trustee has the true proprietary right, a right *in rem*, whereas the *cestui que trust*, although his rights are generally regarded as equivalent to ownership, yet is really not an owner at all. Obviously the result attained is unsatisfactory; and, although any criticism of the Austinian School, by reason of their contradiction of the practical position of so-called equitable owners, would probably be met with the answer that theirs is the true technical position, and that the economic standpoint cannot be allowed to cloud a legal system of thought; yet the upholders of any juris-prudential theory which produces such an unhappy result as this can scarcely expect their thesis to be accepted without a general endeavour to find a flaw in their hypotheses.

RIGHTS *IN REM* AND *IN PERSONAM*   143

Prior to 1926, apart from possession the mortgagor and *cestui que trust* both have an equitable estate protected by one single remedy, available against the mortgagee or trustee and a certain number of legal personages taking under or through them, a remedy *in personam*. The *cestui que trust* has no remedy against a stranger, until he has obtained possession of the property from his trustee and the relationship of trustee and *cestui que trust* is at an end, and he can obtain a conveyance or possession only from the trustee, a volunteer under the trustee, or persons with notice of the trust, etc. The mortgagor cannot by reason of his equitable estate bring action against a stranger until he has redeemed the mortgage. Hence he can only protect his equitable interest by means of an action for redemption, available against the mortgagee and certain classes of persons only, a right *in personam*. Even when the mortgagor has redeemed, as regards strangers he is merely in the position of a purchaser, the mortgagor being trustee of the legal estate for him until conveyance. The relation of mortgagor and mortgagee has ended and the relation of the trustee and *cestui que trust* arises until the conveyance is executed. After conveyance, the newly acquired title of the mortgagor does not entitle him to bring an action of trespass by relation, but only for such trespass as has occurred since he acquired the legal estate.

The mortgagor or *cestui que trust* in possession has another "estate" or interest also by reason of that possession. This is a legal estate or interest; in the case of the *cestui que trust*, a tenancy at will, protected by trespass, nuisance, etc., rights *in rem*. Formally the possession of the mortgagor, in general only a *quasi* tenancy by sufferance, would not support an action for ejectment, nor even trespass, without the aid of the mortgagee, and hence protecting remedies were practically non-existent; but it has been greatly strengthened by the statute law of the last century, which enables the mortgagor by reason of his possession to bring both an action for trespass and for ejectment, both remedies *in rem*. It may be said that the mortgagor did not acquire a right *in rem*, *qua* possession, until it was given him by Statute, unless the consent of the mortgagee had turned his possession into a tenancy at will.

144   EQUITY OF REDEMPTION AND

We have seen that the Austinian position with regard to equitable estates brings about results contrary to the practice of ordinary phraseology in denying to the holders of those estates a true ownership of the land. This is largely owing to their use of the hypothesis that a right *in rem*, as defined by them, is the only true proprietary right. They sometimes admit that some rights *in rem* are less than ownership, but they state that ownership involves the protection of at least one right *in rem*.

First of all they have somewhat confused the issue by occasionally referring to the interest supported by the remedy as a right, and speaking of this interest as being *in rem* or *in personam*, when they are really referring to some remedy protecting that interest. This they have naturally done more frequently in discussing equitable interests, since in that case there was only one protecting remedy, and hence it was very easy to falter between the two different conceptions of right.

Again, they are unfortunate in having to deal with a term used with such varied degrees of meaning as ownership. Obviously, if they make the terms ownership and rights *in rem* convertible, they are not using that term in the sense of the right to exclusive enjoyment and disposition of a concrete thing, land or goods. Carried to its logical conclusion, their hypothesis would make a tenant at will the owner by reason of his flimsy estate which his landlord may put to an end at his pleasure, since a tenancy at will is protected by a right *in rem*. Likewise under this hypothesis he who has an easement would then have a proprietary right, ownership, and he who has a mere possession of goods would then be considered the owner of them.

The meaning of ownership which the Austinian School have adopted would seem to be the enjoyment of any valuable interest whatever, a right of way, a cheque, an estate by sufferance, a patent, or an action for breach of contract. Yet, in order to make their arbitrary classification serve some useful purpose, they have to limit this definition of ownership to the enjoyment of those interests protected by a right *in rem*. This is very unsatisfactory in practice. Some refuse the term owner to the mere possessor of goods, and likewise to a tenant at will, by

RIGHTS *IN REM* AND *IN PERSONAM*   145

abandoning the theory that all rights *in rem* imply ownership; while all would deny ownership to the trustee and mortgagor, who have interests in the land of much greater importance than even a tenant for life, because the trust and the equity of redemption are not protected by a right *in rem*. They have pronounced this connection between rights *in rem*, as defined by them, and ownership without really examining the logical conclusion to be drawn from such a hypothesis; and, when a thorough examination is made, the connection will not stand. The distinction thus established between ownership and non-ownership is quite absurd. The only way in which the Austinian School can hold its ground at all is by abandoning the connection altogether; for jurisprudence becomes mere idle reasoning when a result attained by the introduction of a number of exceptions does not even then fit in with the true practical position.

In order to probe further into this classification, let us examine the history of the terms, "right *in rem*" and "right *in personam*" in English law. The terms, *in rem* and *in personam* found their way into English law before the days of Coke, for we find that great lawyer stating, "An Use is a Trust or Confidence reposed in some other, which is not issuing out of the Land, but as a Thing collateral annexed in Privity to the Estate of the Land, and to the Person touching the Land;...Cestuy que trust had neither Jus in re, nor Jus ad rem, but only a Confidence and Trust".[1]

A *jus in re* was a medieval term synonymous with *jus in rem*, and a *jus ad rem* was a legal right to obtain possession and enjoyment against all others, perhaps for a specific purpose only. The Latin word *jus*, as used in Roman law, conveyed an idea something between right and law in English, with varied shades of meaning, sometimes very like the English ideas of right, and sometimes like those of law.

Since the expressions *in rem* and *in personam* were imported from the civil law, we must expect a lawyer such as Coke, at a time when the law of Rome was still greatly studied and highly esteemed, to use them with the Roman meaning. Certainly many such phrases borrowed from the Roman law have become

[1] Co. Litt. § 464 n.

TER

146 EQUITY OF REDEMPTION AND

distorted after passing into the English system; and, in view of the perverted conception adopted by the Austinian School, it might be argued that the perversion had already taken place at the time of Coke. This, however, does not appear probable. His words quoted above fit the Roman conception better than the Austinian. The terms *in rem* and *in personam* were not of frequent occurrence in the Reports, nor were they used save with a vague meaning much the same as in the civil law. It is more probable that Coke's *jus in re* contained more of the Roman conception of an *actio in rem* than that, at a time when lawyers were dealing with relations between persons concerning physical objects and were not much given to jurisprudential speculation, juristic thought had developed to such an extent as to conceive of a right *in rem* in such an abstract form as that put forward by Austin.

During the formative period of English equity, nobody seems to have paid much attention to the question as to whether a trust estate or an equity of redemption was a right *in rem* or a right *in personam*, much less a right *in rem* as adopted either in theory or in effect by the Austinian School. The one maxim which appears to have arisen out of the Roman classification is "Equity acts *in personam*", in other words, the Court of Chancery acts by means of remedies, all of which are, according to the Roman conception, *in personam*. The maxim was used to show that the Court did not issue a decree against the property itself, but only against the defendant personally. The form of the Chancellor's decree was an order that the defendant shall do or forbear to do something, whereas the decree of the Court of Common Law was often an order to the executive to see that a definite thing, such as putting the plaintiff in possession, was done.

Save for this one exception the expressions *in rem* and *in personam* do not appear to have been used at all frequently; and even when they were used it was with an undefined meaning somewhat after the style of Coke, a meaning which was not considered very material until the Analytical School of Austin brought it into prominence. Hence it seems that the adherents of that School largely made the classification for themselves,

RIGHTS *IN REM* AND *IN PERSONAM*

giving the terms a new meaning for the purpose of classifying a different subject-matter. In particular, they commenced their examination of equitable interests, such as the equity of redemption, hampered by the fact that these interests had been built up by the Court of Chancery with little or no regard for classification under which, if possible, they were now to be placed. In 1900 Holmes, C.J., speaking of the term *in rem* says: "No phrase has been more misused".[1]

Not only were the Analytical School historically inaccurate in their definition of the terms *in rem* and *in personam*, but they were also unfortunate in their choice of the word "right" with which to denote the subject-matter they intended to classify. The meanings of the word, both legal and popular, are legion, and in almost all cases indefinable. They are so interwoven that the word is rarely used in sustained legal argument without appearing in several different forms, tending to confusion of thought or to a false appearance of clever reasoning. Almost every jurist and every individual lawyer has his own different conception of its meaning. Each has a vague idea as to the true meaning; but each would fix its limits in a different place.

As to the meaning of the word when used in conjunction with the phrase *in rem*, even the School which have coined the combination and have thrust it upon the world of jurisprudence are hopelessly disagreed. Many of them shun a definition altogether. The bolder ones make an attempt and hope for the best. All the efforts which have been made to form a satisfactory definition have something in common and something upon which they disagree.

Professor Roscoe Pound ruthlessly attacks this hopelessly indefinite phraseology, where he says:

The attempt at exact definition of legal rights broke down because the idea was not a simple one, as was supposed, but involved a number of distinct things, and also because the compromises and adjustments which were called for could not be derived from the simple idea of freedom....."Right" had come to mean too much. All the

---

[1] *Tyler* v. *Court of Registration*, 175 Mass. 71, 76; see also Franklin, J., in *Hook* v. *Hoffman*, (1915) 16 Ariz. 540, 554.

148 EQUITY OF REDEMPTION AND

juristic writing of the last century is obscured by the ambiguity of that overworked word. We called the *de facto* claim or interest, an idealization of the *de facto* claim, as we thought it ought to be asserted and ought to be recognized, the legally recognized and legally delimited claim after the law on a balance of claims or interests had come to some practical adjustment, and a bundle of legal institutions by which that recognized and delimited claim is made effective, all by the name of right.[1]

English law was not worked out from the idea of the adjustment of conflicting rights, in spite of the attempt of the Analytical School to make it fit such a conception. In its early stages it was entirely concerned with the availability of remedies, and doubtless, had the phrases *in rem* and *in personam* been imported from the Roman law at that date, it would have been easy with the aid of a small amount of judicial legislation to have made the various remedies fit in with the Roman classification of actions. But when in the nineteenth century a parallel classification is attempted, not of actions, but of the indeterminate and abstract idea of "rights", the jurisprudence of the Austinian School is found trying to put the square peg into the round hole.

The true basis of English law is the conception of a relationship between the parties. Thus Professor Pound writes:

The common lawyer sees almost all problems,—all those, indeed, in which he has not been led to adopt the Romanist's point of view in the last century—in terms of a relation and of the incidents in the way of reciprocal rights and duties involved in or required to give effect to that relation. Magna Carta, the foundation of our public law, is not an expression of the idea of individual freedom but a formulation of the rights and duties incident to the relation of the king and his tenants in chief....On every side we think not of transactions but of relations. We say law of landlord and tenant, not of the contract of letting. We say master and servant, not *locatio operarum*....We think of the claims and duties involved in a fiduciary relation and of the legal incidents that give effect to trusteeship or executorship as a relation of good faith, not of the implications of the declaration of will involved in accepting or declaring a trust or qualifying as executor....We do not think of giving effect to the will of the parties to a contract of hypothecation.

[1] *Interpretations of Legal History*, 159.

RIGHTS *IN REM* AND *IN PERSONAM* 149

We consider what incidents are involved in the relation of mortgagor and mortgagee and the reciprocal claims and duties that give effect thereto.

We must remember that the analogy which was ever before the lawyers and judges of the formative period of our law, the typical social and legal institution of the time, was the relation of lord and man, still represented in our law by the relationship of landlord and tenant. Continual resort to this analogy, consciously or subconsciously, has made the idea of relation the central idea in our traditional mode of juristic thought.[1]

As an instance, this conception of the relation of the parties to one another and the incidents involved therein has enabled the Courts of Chancery to state that the equity of redemption is a reasonable and proper incident in the relation of mortgagor and mortgagee, and later, that this incident must at all costs be maintained unimpaired. The lawyers of the seventeenth century did not consider the question as to whether the mortgagor had a right to have the property back unimpaired, but as to whether, in equity and conscience, the relationship of the parties was not such that the mortgagor ought to be protected from the sharp practices of the mortgagee. In the Chancery Reports of the seventeenth and early eighteenth centuries we do not often find such phrases as "right of redemption". Nor is the word "right" found with any frequency in the common-law reports. The central idea in both is relations, not rights. The true standard of English law was the working out of these various relationships, not the weighing of abstract rights.

The classification of the Austinian School, then, does not seem to rest upon any true historical basis, but is rather an attempt to explain seventeenth and eighteenth-century legal phenomena in the terms of nineteenth-century doctrine. The School's jurisprudential juggling with an arbitrary classification of its own making has not produced anything which might be considered creative or explanatory. When the right *in rem* as defined by Austinians is connected with ownership, they are in open opposition to all practical ideas of ownership; while, as soon as their claim to connect ownership and rights *in rem* is destroyed, although it can no longer be said that their position

[1] *Interpretations of Legal History,* 57.

150 EQUITY OF REDEMPTION AND

offends against general legal experience, the small practical value of the result and the fictionary basis of their whole argument open it to the criticism that the whole matter is a piece of juristic skittles of little or no importance. All the Austinian School have achieved is an arbitrary classification of remedies which does not explain anything, but tends to confuse both itself and other matters by reason of an increase in the already numerous definitions of the phraseology involved, and which has led to inaccuracies in itself by reason of the same difficulty of the ambiguity of most of its terms.

There is a variation of the Austinian conception of "rights *in rem*" and "rights *in personam*" which must yet be considered. Sometimes a right *in rem* is defined as a right availing against all the world, which is explained as an interest which each person in the world, taken singly, save possibly a few particular individuals exempted by grant or otherwise, may at some time or other be in a position to violate; and a right *in personam* as an interest which only a certain definite number of persons can be in a position to violate. This is a classification of interests, not of remedies; and right in this case is used in the sense synonymous with interest.

Here the interest of the mortgagor is a right *in rem*, even when viewed as an equitable estate only, apart from possession; for anyone in the world may violate the mortgagor's right to redeem, either by sitting on the land and obtaining a squatter's title, or by taking under the trustee and refusing to submit to redemption. Again, the mortgagor in possession has a legal interest *in rem qua* possession, for anyone save his mortgagee may violate that right to possession.

In any system of law where new interests of various kinds have been allowed to develop gradually by virtue of judicial interpretation resulting in a policy of trial and error, there must be a tendency for interests to commence as interests *in personam* in this sense, for these interests become more and more important, and then for other remedies to spring up protecting the original interest, thereby turning that interest into an interest *in rem*. This seems to be true both of the equity of redemption and the trust. The latter originally rested upon a mere moral

RIGHTS *IN REM* AND *IN PERSONAM*   151

obligation, which later was enforced against the trustee of the Court of Chancery. Both were at first a mere remedy against mortgagee or trustee personally and could be violated by them alone; but in a short time the equity of redemption was recognized by Lord Hale as an "equitable right inherent in the land, and binds all persons in the post or otherwise",[1] and a little later Nottingham spoke in similar terms of a trust.

This classification cannot be considered much more satisfactory than that more usually adopted by the Austinian School. It is usually stated by those who put forward this variation that in this case interests arising out of contract and tort are the only interests *in personam*. Accepting their statement for a moment, may we not question as to whether the discussion of a classification which merely distinguishes interests arising out of contract and tort from all others is really worthy of much consideration? Further, it is also questionable whether the interests arising from obligations are truly interests *in personam* in this sense.

A contract certainly gives a remedy for performance, or damages in event of failure of performance, available against the other party or parties to the contract only, a right *in personam* in the usual Austinian sense of that term. This primary right can only be violated by a definite number of persons. In many contracts anyone may become an assignee and so be in a position to violate that contract. It is necessary to explain that there can only be a definite number of assignees at one and the same time. There has developed, however, a secondary remedy protecting the interest of the contracting party, an action against anyone who induces a breach of that contract, on the authority of *Bowen* v. *Hall*[2] and *Lumley* v. *Gye*,[3] a remedy which all the world taken singly may bring into operation; and hence the interest in the benefit of a contract is truly an interest *in rem*.

In the same way at first sight no one can interfere with a right of action save possibly the King in Parliament. Hence it is sometimes stated that a right *in rem* or right *in personam* is an interest violable, etc., "if violable at all", thus excluding a right of action. Again, there is a secondary remedy protecting

---

[1] *A.-G.* v. *Pawlett*, (1667) Hard. 469, *ante*, p. 51.
[2] 6 Q.B.D. 333.   [3] 2 El. and Bl. 216.

152 EQUITY OF REDEMPTION AND

a right of action. This is the action of Maintenance and Champerty, available against anyone who interferes with that interest by assisting the other parties to the action, a remedy *in rem* in the usual sense of the term. All the world may be in a position to render assistance of the prohibited character to the parties, and hence the interest in an action is also truly *in rem*. Occasionally the difficulty created by these secondary remedies is countered by the fiction that these latter protect a different interest, that the obligor has one interest against the obligee which is *in personam*, and another interest against the world which is *in rem*. This is at its best a fiction, and can hardly be said to meet the case satisfactorily. It is tending to separate the interest in a thing into a number of interests equal to the number of remedies protecting that interest, a confusion of right as synonymous with interest and right as synonymous with remedy.

The classification in its varied form, then, tends to become one in which all the subject-matter is in one class, and really ceases to be a classification at all unless the subject-matter is divided into two classes by the use of subsidiary fictions. The results attained are of too doubtful a value to be worth the manufacturing of an arbitrary classification of no historical significance, involving a series of new definitions of terms already possessed of a large variety of vague meanings and subsidiary fictions which still further complicate the definition of the terms involved. It is a moot question whether the whole discussion raised by these arbitrary classifications borrowed from Roman law and distorted to fit in with new facts is not a mere academical tourney with no real bearing upon the practice of the law, and, being faulty in hypothesis and unsatisfactory in result, would be better abandoned altogether.

The question whether the interest of the mortgagor in particular can be said to confer on him the "ownership" of the land is sometimes a matter of discussion. The *cestui que trust* has a right to enjoy and alienate the land subject to the terms of the trust, he has likewise a similar right to a conveyance of the legal estate; his trustee has no beneficial interest whatever, nor has anyone else save by his special grant or favour. It is

RIGHTS *IN REM* AND *IN PERSONAM*   153

ridiculous to deny him ownership just because he has no remedy against a few rare classes of persons such as a purchaser of the legal estate for value without notice. It is just as absurd as to suggest that the holder of an estate in fee simple has not ownership because he has no remedy against a person whom he has allowed to squat on the land for twelve years. The ideas of property and ownership cannot be so strictly limited without making them useless technical ciphers which must eventually fall before popular usage in a wider sense.

We have seen that, on the Austinian basis, the mortgagor and the *cestui que trust* were both denied true ownership. The question as to whether a mortgagor can be regarded as a true owner of the land, taking a broad view enclosing the respective effect of the legal and equitable conceptions of the matter, depends somewhat on the scope of the term ownership. It has a variety of meanings. A technical definition often adopted, especially in connection with land or goods, is "the right to the enjoyment and disposition of the thing owned and the benefits accruing therefrom, subject to such rights of a limited nature as the owner may have granted to others, and subject also to limitations imposed by law".

Taking this definition of ownership, the mortgagor obviously has a right to enjoy and alienate the land subject to the rights he has himself conferred on the mortgagee to hold the land for the purposes of security. The question really is whether these rights of the mortgagee prevent the mortgagor's being regarded as owner of the land. It is clear that, where a fee simple owner gives another possession of the land for a short term of years, he is still generally regarded as owner. Is the mortgagor who mortgages a fee simple to his creditor likewise owner of the land?

His position is somewhat similar to that of B where land is limited to A in fee simple, but if B pay A a debt he owes him of £5000, then to B in fee simple. He has a right to the enjoyment of the land on payment of the debt. There is, however, this important difference, that the mortgagee has to account very strictly for any rents and profits he has received before payment of the debt, and the mortgagor can take into consideration

EQUITY OF REDEMPTION AND

such receipts in the computation of his debt. These rents and profits belong to the mortgagor, though the mortgagee has a right to receive them for the purposes of security. There are other minor differences. Thus, such executory interests confer a present right of action to restrain equitable waste, which is not so in the case of a mortgage; while, on the other hand, the particular tenant is not liable to account on payment of the debt, nor liable for careless management as is a mortgagee. The particular tenant cannot in general be prevented from selling the property under the Settled Land Acts save by performance of the condition of defeasance; whereas sale by a mortgagee will be improper and he will be liable to account therefor unless due cause for sale has arisen.

We have seen that an executory interest such as described above is not an estate in the land, but a mere possibility of an estate.[1] The "ownership" of the land is really divided between the particular tenant and the holder of the executory interest, the ultimate issue depending solely upon the payment of the money. Till then the particular tenant is entitled to the rents and profits for his own purposes without liability to account. In the case of a mortgage, however, the mortgagor is really the owner of the rents and profits. The mortgagor is, then, owner of the land.

The true position, then, is more similar to an executory interest where land is given to A in fee simple liable to cease on B doing a certain act (sale or foreclosure) which A can prevent on payment of a sum of money, and then to B in fee simple; but if the money is paid before B does that act, then to A absolutely. There are, of course, differences in the incidents of such a relation from that of a mortgage, such as the mortgagee's right to take possession; but this is a dangerous remedy only used as a last resort, and in general effect the position is very similar in both cases. An executory interest such as B's would appear to convey some fragmentary ownership of the land concurrent with that of the particular tenant, the final determination as to who has absolute ownership depending on circumstances. This is exactly the position in the case of a

[1] See p. 5.

RIGHTS *IN REM* AND *IN PERSONAM*   155

mortgage. The mortgagee has some shadowy form of ownership which is treated as far as possible as a *jus in re aliena* for the purposes of security, but which is nevertheless very real.

The truth is that the mortgagor and mortgagee are in practice concurrent owners, the issue depending on the subsequent action of the mortgagor, for he can prevent the mortgagee proceeding to sale or foreclosure by payment of the money. We have seen that the *cestui que trust* is both judicially and generally spoken of as the owner of the land, and that it does not seem reasonable to deny him that ownership, because he has no remedy against a purchaser of the outstanding legal estate for value without notice. The mortgagor has been generally regarded as owner of the land from the time of Hardwicke to the present day. His interest possesses all the necessary characteristics of ownership. The fact that he has no remedy against a purchaser of the legal estate without notice can make no more difference in his case than in that of the *cestui que trust*. The mortgagor is owner of the land subject to the payment of his debt.

In popular parlance, the possession of the land without rack rent or receipt of rents is often made the test of ownership. As regards mortgages this is more practical than appears at first sight; for the mortgagee rarely takes possession save as a last resort, and such possession is therefore usually followed by sale, foreclosure, or the acquisition of a squatter's title. Likewise possession confers upon the party the parliamentary franchise and many extensive powers of management, statutory and otherwise. Yet the possession of the mortgagor is at the will of the mortgagee and that of the mortgagee is fettered with liability to account and hence cannot be regarded as the decisive factor.

Under the Law of Property Act, 1925, the mortgagor cannot part with the whole of his estate at law by way of mortgage, but retains the freehold or head term subject to a long term of years or a derivative term conveyed to the creditor as security, a term of which in equity the mortgagor is still considered the owner subject to the debt. A question at once arises whether a long term of years confers ownership of the land. Historically it did not, but it would seem that now any long term capable of immediate enlargement into a fee simple does confer owner-

156 EQUITY OF REDEMPTION

ship of the land. In the case of a mortgage under the Act the position *inter se* between the parties remains substantially the same. On sale or foreclosure the mortgagor loses both his legal and equitable estate. The mortgagee is still entitled to possession, but is still called as strictly to account. The mortgagor is still owner of the land subject to the debt. He may extinguish the rights of the mortgagee by payment thereof. If anything, his ownership is increased somewhat by reason of the freehold or head term he now has at law and the abolition of the necessity of reconveyance.

CHAPTER VIII

A. INCIDENTS OF ANALOGY WITH THE TRUST

A FEW comparisons of the growth of specified rules relating to the equity of redemption and the trust are worthy of study in order to show the extent to which the growth of the one followed the growth of the other, and the points at which the analogy could no longer be continued, owing to a fundamental difference in the nature of the two interests.

In 1681, shortly after the mortgagee's interest had been finally determined to be personalty,[1] Nottingham continued his work on the same lines and held that a devise by the mortgagee of all his lands would not pass those held by him on mortgage; for his interest in them was but a chattel interest in equity for the purposes of his security.[2] Later this was held to be so even though the mortgages were afterwards foreclosed,[3] and Hardwicke quoted this decision with approval in *Casborne* v. *Scarfe*, saying, "By a devise of all lands tenements and hereditaments a mortgage in fee shall not pass".[4]

In 1730 the question of the intention of the testator was brought into consideration, and it was held by a strong Court that lands held on mortgage would not pass on such a devise, unless he had no other lands wherewith to satisfy it, or unless it could be inferred from particular circumstances that the mortgaged lands were intended to pass.[5] Until the end of the century not even the legal estate passed by such a devise except where an intention could be inferred. The trust estate, however, was regarded in a different light. In *Marlow* v. *Smith*, 1723, Sir Joseph Jekyll, M.R., held that, in a trust estate, "The legal estate being in the devisor in the eye of the law, it is *his* estate and *his* property, and therefore passes by the devise of his estate; and if he had devised *all the land which he had been seized of*, these lands would certainly have passed".[6]

---

[1] *Thornbrough* v. *Baker*, (1676) 1 Ch. Ca. 284.
[2] *Littleton's Case*, 1 Vern. 4, 2 Vent. 351.
[3] *Strode* v. *Russell*, (1708) 2 Vern. 621.   [4] (1738) 2 J. and W. 195.
[5] *Chester* v. *Chester*, (1730) 3 P.W. 62.   [6] 2 P. W. 198.

158 INCIDENTS OF ANALOGY WITH THE TRUST

For almost a century the fact seems to have been overlooked that, just as the trustee, so had the mortgagee the legal estate, which should pass as realty by a general devise. In the exercise of their jurisdiction over administration of estates the Chancellors appear to have considered the position in equity only, and to have forgotten that at law the mortgagee had the estate in the land. It is possible that the reference in the cases cited is to the beneficial interest of the mortgagor, the legal estate passing as a matter of course to the devisee, who then held it upon trust; but surely this would have been mentioned in precise terms in the discussion which arose when the matter came finally to be decided.

Saunders, in his notes to Atkyns, published in 1794, seems the first text-writer to give the matter any serious consideration. He quotes Hardwicke's remark, "By a devise of all lands tenements and hereditaments a mortgage in fee shall not pass",[1] and then says:

This rule as laid down by Lord *Hardwicke*, and by the reports of *Wynn* v. *Littleton*[2] and *Litton* v. *Russell*[3] deserves some consideration.... The question is, Whether we must understand his Lordship's meaning to be, that the general devise of all *lands, tenements, and hereditaments* will neither pass the *legal* nor *beneficial* estate of mortgagees in fee after forfeiture, or whether those words are only incompetent to pass the *beneficial* interest? If the latter, the rule, generally speaking, is certainly right: because the *beneficial* interest, being in fact nothing but the money due on the mortgage, and the lands mortgaged being considered in equity merely as a security for a personal debt, it is very evident that such *personal* or beneficial interest cannot pass by words peculiarly adapted to transfer *real* property; unless in some particular instances, as where the testator has no other lands than those mortgaged to him. (*Clarke* v. *Abbot*.[4])... But I take it, that this is a very obvious distinction between the *legal* estate of a mortgagee in fee after forfeiture, and his *beneficial* interest, as to the operation of a devise. The latter would certainly pass by a esiduary bequest of all his personal estate; yet it is clear, that the ormer would not; which, if not vested in some particular person by the will, would in such case descend to the *heir at law* of the testator as a *trustee* for the devisee of the personal estate. (*A.-G.* v. *Meyrick*[5] and *Wynn* v. *Littleton.*) But as the *mortgagee* is considered as to the

[1] *Casborne* v. *Scarfe*, 1 Atk. 605.   [2] 1 Vern. 3.   [3] 2 Vern. 621.
[4] Barn. C.C. 457, 461.   [5] 2 Ves. 46.

INCIDENTS OF ANALOGY WITH THE TRUST 159

legal estate and inheritance, merely as a trustee,[1] if he should devise *all and every his real estate* to *A*. and his heirs, this would, according to the determination in *Marlow* v. *Smith*, pass the *legal* estate, and if he should likewise bequeath all his *personal* estate to *B*., this would pass the mortgage debt, and *A*. would thereby become a trustee for *B*.

Obviously he is trying to show that the legal estate will pass by such a devise, but in the last paragraph quoted he appears to argue from the identity of the mortgage and the trust instead of from the analogy between them. A few years later the discrepancy in the doctrines applied to the two interests appears to have been realized. The question becomes the subject of litigation; and, after several attempts, the analogy of the trust was applied, though at the same time an attempt was made to bring the trust estate into line with the equity of redemption.

In 1797 Hardwicke's remark in *Casborne* v. *Scarfe*, interpreted in the sense that a general devise did not pass even the legal estate, was regarded as conclusive by the Attorney-General.[2] In the next year both Loughborough and the Master of the Rolls were "inclined to think" that the legal estate in mortgaged premises passed by a general residuary devise.[3] About the same time some expressions used by Loughborough and Eldon created a grave doubt as to the passing of even the legal estate of the trustee by a general devise, unless special evidence of intention could be found in the will. Loughborough, L.C., speaking of a devise by a trustee, said, "I take the rule to be, that general words will not pass trust estates, unless there appears to be an intention, that they shall pass. Perhaps the most convenient rule would be the reverse".[4] However, in 1803, upon consideration of all the cases, Lord Eldon decided that a general devise would pass a trust estate, unless the contrary intention be expressed, explaining that his previous remark only referred to the special circumstances of the particular case then in hand, whereas it was otherwise in the case of "a mere, dry, naked, devise, with no one word denoting an intention, that what undoubtedly the Law would pass, should

---

[1] *Casborne* v. *Scarfe*, 1 Atk, 606; 2 Vern. 401.
[2] *Leeds* v. *Munday*, 3 Ves. 348. [3] *Ex parte Sergison*, 4 Ves. 147.
[4] *A.-G.* v. *Buller*, (1800) 5 Ves. 340; *Ex parte Brettel*, (1801) 6 Ves. 577.

160 INCIDENTS OF ANALOGY WITH THE TRUST

not pass, and to narrow the construction in *Marlow* v. *Smith*".[1]

This judgment of Lord Eldon seems to have settled the matter both as to a devise by the trustee and the mortgagee. As to the latter, there seems no direct decision, but it has been taken for granted ever since by the legal profession that the mortgagee's legal estate would pass by such a general devise. Similarly, the legal estate in the mortgaged premises had always since been considered as passing to the heir;[2] but the heir or the devisee was considered in equity as a mere trustee thereof for the deceased's personal representatives.[3] This inconvenience has now been remedied by the Conveyancing Act, 1881, which enacts that on the death after that year of a sole trustee or mortgagee of any freehold estate of inheritance, his estate, notwithstanding any testamentary disposition, shall devolve like a chattel real upon his personal representatives.[4] The working of the analogy between the two equitable estates is here very evident, and seems to have resulted in a clearer realization of the nature of the mortgagee's legal estate. Coventry, in a note to Powell on Mortgages,[5] shows the strength of the analogy with reference to this question of a general devise by the mortgagee, in that he quotes *Marlow* v. *Smith* and other like cases relating to trusts as having a very important bearing on the subject.

The position of judgment creditors of the mortgagor and *cestui que trust* is also illustrative of this analogy.

We have seen that it was Nottingham who first allowed the judgment creditor, unable to use the ordinary legal process of execution by reason of a trust, to avail himself of an equitable *fieri facias* against the *cestui que trust* of a leasehold estate.[6] The question of such a creditor using an equitable writ of *elegit* does not seem to have come before him; but the matter was taken out of his hands by the Legislature, which made lands and inheritances held upon simple trust liable to the legal writ

---

[1] *Braybroke* v. *Inskip*, 8 Ves. 417.
[2] *Ex parte Morgan*, (1804) 10 Ves. 101.
[3] Note to *Casborne* v. *Scarfe*, 1 Atk. 605 (3rd ed.).
[4] 44 and 45 Vict. c. 41, § 30.   [5] 5th ed., 445 n.
[6] *Pit* v. *Hunt*, (1681) 2 Ch. Ca. 73; Anon. case cited 1 P.W. 445, etc.

INCIDENTS OF ANALOGY WITH THE TRUST 161

of *elegit* under § 10 of the Statute of Frauds, 1677. Nottingham seems to have allowed redemption by judgment creditors in 1673;[1] but Lord Keeper North nine years later showed some hesitancy in the matter.[2] In 1685, however, such a creditor was definitely allowed to redeem a mortgage in fee.[3] This seems to have been generally accepted as applying to a leasehold also, for we soon find it regarded as of course, and a century later it even had to be decided that the equity of redemption of a term of years could not be taken in execution under an ordinary legal writ of *fi. fa.*, but that resort must be made to a Court of Equity.[4]

No one seems to have attempted to use the writ of *elegit* against an equity of redemption of a mortgage in fee under § 10 of the Statute of Frauds.[5] Coventry explains this by stating that § 10 does not extend to any constructive trusts, and if not to these, it would obviously not extend to the equity of redemption.[6] About the same date Sir John Leach, V.C., said:

A Judgement Creditor has at Law, by the Statute of Frauds, execution against the equitable Freehold Estate of the Debtor in the hands of his Trustee, provided the Debtor has the whole beneficial interest; but if he has left, a partial Interest only in his equitable Freehold Estate, the Judgement Creditor has no execution at Law, though he may come into a Court of Equity, and claim there the same Satisfaction out of the equitable Interest as he would have been entitled to at Law, if it were legal.[7]

The crux of this development of the equity of redemption and the trust seems to have been the Statute of Frauds. There was undoubtedly a general desire that creditors should have some form of execution against the owners of equitable interests, a desire which had apparently caused Nottingham to allow a creditor to redeem. Within the next few years after the passing of the Statute, the defect caused by the limited operation of

---

[1] *Mole* v. *Franklin*, (1673) Rep. T. Finch 51.
[2] *Child* v. *Stephens*, 1 Vern. 101.
[3] *Greswold* v. *Marsham*, 2 Ch. Ca. 170; see also *Crisp* v. *Heath*, (1714) 7 Vin. Abr. 52.
[4] *Lyster* v. *Dolland*, (1792) 3 Bro. C.C. 478; 1 Ves. J. 435.
[5] *Plunkett* v. *Penson*, (1742) 2 Atk. 290.
[6] Powell, *Mortgages*, (ed. 5), p. 341 n.
[7] *Forth* v. *D. of Norfolk*, (1820) 4 Mad. 503.

TER

162 INCIDENTS OF ANALOGY WITH THE TRUST

§ 10 was obviated by the provision of an equitable execution for judgment creditors, where a legal execution was not conferred upon them by the Statute, the ground of this extension being the doctrine, "Equity follows the law". Thus the only difference between the trust estate and the equity of redemption in this respect is a statutory one, enabling the creditors of the *cestui que trust* in some cases to obtain execution at law instead of in equity. The trust and the equity of redemption seem to have followed each other in this matter as of course; for it must be remembered that at this time the doctrine of precedent did not exist as we know it to-day, but that there was a doctrine of custom of the court, or as we might say, accumulated precedent, one isolated decision being of little authority.

Notwithstanding an early authority to the contrary, where the point does not seem to have been discussed,[1] the judgment creditor could under the old law extend a moiety only of a trust estate upon an *elegit*, as a moiety of the lands only was liable under the writ.[2] It was otherwise as regards an equity of redemption. Before the end of the seventeenth century it was clear that the creditor, once he had taken out execution, had a lien on the property which entitled him to redeem. So far as he was concerned, it was to redeem a moiety only, since "Equity follows the law"; but, since a mortgagee could not be compelled to part with the smallest portion of his estate until the debt was completely satisfied, the creditor must of necessity redeem the whole.[3] Again, having paid the mortgage debt in full and having taken a transfer of the security, it was only equitable that he should be allowed the full benefit of it, so that he now held the property both for the mortgage money and his judgment. Thus at the suit of a judgment creditor Hardwicke ordered a sale of the whole of lands in mortgage, but gave possession of a moiety only of the lands in trust.[4]

The question as to whether, on the death of the mortgagor, the equity of redemption should be assets for the benefit of

---

[1] *Compton* v. *Compton*, Reg. Lib. A. 1711, fol. 134, cited *Stileman* v. *Ashdown*, (1743) 2 Atk. 477, 608.   [2] *Shirely* v. *Watts*, (1744) 3 Atk. 200.
[3] *Sish* v. *Hopkins*, (1730) Amb. 793; *Stonehewer* v. *Thompson*, (1742) 2 Atk. 440.   [4] *Stileman* v. *Ashdown*, *supra*.

INCIDENTS OF ANALOGY WITH THE TRUST 163

bond creditors has been closely argued from the analogy of the trust. The trust of a chattel was always assets in equity.[1] It was determined, by the advice of the judges in the case of *Bennett* v. *Box*, 1662, that on analogy with the use a trust in fee should not be assets;[2] and this case was followed as to trust estates by Lord Hale[3] and Lord Keeper Bridgeman,[4] though the latter seems to have been uncertain whether he would be bound by the authority of the decision in the case of an equity of redemption.[5]

Section 10 of the Statute of Frauds declared a trust in fee simple to be assets at law by descent; but, in the same limited way as in the case of judgment creditors, it was held to apply to simple trusts only, and not to complicated trusts or equities of redemption;[6] so that the question, as to whether such interests might upon the general principles of equity be treated as assets by analogy of the law, still remained to be settled. Nottingham is reported as declaring that an equity of redemption was not assets at law, and seemingly not in equity either; but the report of the case is a mere note and may be inaccurate.[7] It seems to have been overlooked by all text-writers. However, the year after the passing of the Statute of Frauds, Nottingham declared trust estates to be assets in equity,[8] and, in spite of the subsequent inclination to the contrary by Lord Guildford,[9] the more liberal principles of Nottingham prevailed.

The question as to the equity of redemptions being assets occurred twice in 1686. In *Cole* v. *Warden* it was argued:

The mortgage being but a mortgage for years, the reversion, which attracts the redemption,...was adjudged assets in this court in the case *Davie* v. *Dabinett*,...but it was admitted there was a difference between a mortgage in fee, and a mortgage for years: for in the case of *Bennett* v. *Box*, which was resolved with the advice of Judges, they would not allow, that the equity of redemption of a mortgage in fee should be assets in equity to pay a bond creditor.

[1] *A.-G.* v. *Sands*, (1669) Freem. 131, Hard. 490; *Barthrop* v. *West*, (1672) 2 Ch. R. 62; *D. of Norfolk's Case*, 3 Ch. Ca. 10.
[2] 1 Ch. Ca. 12.   [3] *A.-G.* v. *Sands*, *supra*.
[4] *Prat* v. *Colt*, (1669) 1 Ch. Ca. 127; 2 Freem. 140.
[5] *Trevor* v. *Perryor*, (1669) 1 Ch. Ca. 148.
[6] *Plunkett* v. *Penson*, (1742) 2 Atk. 293; *Solley* v. *Gower*, (1688) 2 Vern. 61.
[7] *Freeman* v. *Taylor*, (1674) 3 Keb. 307.
[8] *Grey* v. *Colvile*, (1678) 2 Ch. Rep. 143.
[9] *Creed* v. *Colville*, (1683) 1 Vern. 172.

164 INCIDENTS OF ANALOGY WITH THE TRUST

The Chancellor directed the Master to certify the matter specially, "His present opinion being...it should be assets to answer bond-debts".[1] No decree can be found. *Bennett v. Box*, a case on trusts, seems to have been quoted as directly in point, or else the judges in *Bennett* v. *Box* examined the analogous case of the mortgage, though we have no report of their so doing.

In the second case, *Plucknett* v. *Kirk*, the Statute of Frauds, making simple trust estates assets in the hands of the heir of the *cestui que trust*, was regarded as a powerful authority for the proposition that the equity of redemption should be likewise assets in equity. As reported, "The point chiefly disputed was, whether the equity of redemption of a mortgage in fee, since the statute of *Frauds* and *Perjuries*, should be assets in equity to satisfy a debt by bond; and the *Lord Chancellor* inclined that it was".[2] It was finally so decreed.[3] So it has always been held since.

These cases seem to have decided the matter so far as the equity of redemption was concerned. In 1734 an attempt was made to argue that the equity of redemption was legal assets on the analogy of the trust, but it was pointed out that at law the heir had nothing, the whole estate being in the mortgagee.[4] Since 1686 it has always been assumed that the same rules applied to complicated trusts and every equitable interest upon the same ground, viz. "Equity follows the law".[5] Here we have an instance of the trust estate in general following a rule laid down for the equity of redemption; and this rule was established, or, at any rate, its foundation was greatly assisted by a statutory enactment applying only to a certain species of trust. The argument in *Creed* v. *Colville*, 1683, a case concerning trusts, is worthy of notice in this connection. After a disparagement of the decision in *Bennett* v. *Box* it was pointed out that "An equity of redemption is every day made

---

[1] 1 Vern. 410. [2] 1 Vern. 411.
[3] R. L. 1686, B, fol. 181, 844.
[4] *Case of Creditors of Sir C. Cox*, (1734) 3 P.W. 341; see also Reg. Lib. 1740, B, fol. 125, 134.
[5] *Anon.* (1690) Freem. 115; *Acton* v. *Pierce*, 2 Vern. 480; *Solly* v. *Gower*, (1688) 2 Vern. 61; *Baden* v. *Earl of Pembroke*, (1688) 2 Vern. 54.

INCIDENTS OF ANALOGY WITH THE TRUST 165

assets in equity ". Lord Guildford did not accept this statement. He said:

> As to an equity of redemption, if a man had a mortgage and a bond; before the mortgage should be redeemed of the heir the bond ought to be satisfied; but he did not know that an equity of redemption should be assets in equity to all creditors....He should much be governed by the precedent of *Bennett* v. *Box*, unless they could shew, that the latter precedents had been otherwise.[1]

This they do not appear to have been able to do;[2] and, as we have seen, the matter was finally decided the other way a few years later.

The question is now of little importance, as by the Administration of Estates Act, 1833, it was enacted that all a person's "estate or interest" (which includes any trust or equity of redemption) in lands, etc., should be assets for the payment of simple contract debts as well as debts by specialty;[3] and by the Administration of Estates Act, 1869, it was provided that simple contract and specialty creditors should be in equal degree, and be paid accordingly out of the assets, whether legal or equitable.[4]

The statutory enactments of the seventeenth century have caused a further divergence between the trust and the equity of redemption in this matter of assets which is well brought out by Lord Hardwicke in *Plunkett* v. *Penson*, where he says:

> I do agree that if a mere trust descends upon an heir at law, that it will be considered as legal, and not as equitable assets; and this is founded upon the third section of the statute [3 and 4 W. and M. c. 14,] which gives a specialty-creditor his remedy at law by an action of debt against the heir of the obligor, but it has not made a mortgage in fee of a trust estate subject to the same thing.
>
> If there was a mortgage in fee for 1000 years, and the reversion in fee left in the mortgagor, it will be legal assets, (*secus* when the mortgagor has himself but a term of years, *Creditors of Sir C. Cox, Hartwell* v. *Chitters*,) because the bond-creditor might have judgment against the heir of the obligor, and a *cesset executio* till the reversion come into possession: but where it is a mortgage of the whole inheritance, I do not see what remedy a bond-creditor can have to make it assets at law; and if the specialty-creditor should

---

[1] 1 Vern. 172. [2] R. L. 1683, A, fol. 166; 1684, A, fol. 210.
[3] 2 and 3 Wm IV, c. 45. [4] 32 and 33 Vict. c. 46.

166 INCIDENTS OF ANALOGY WITH THE TRUST

bring an action against the heir, he may plead *riens per discent*. Therefore if the plaintiff is under a necessity of coming here for relief, this court will act according to its known rule of doing equal justice to all creditors, without any distinction as to priority.[1]

In some cases it has been considered that the fact that the property was equitable at the owner's death sufficed to make it equitable assets,[2] but this is clearly erroneous, the question being, not whether the assets could be recovered at law or in equity, but whether the creditor can obtain payment thereout only from a Court of Equity.[3] In respect of specialties binding the heir, a simple trust was made assets in a court of law in the hands of the heir by the Statute of Frauds, and hence was legal assets in equity,[4] whereas the trust of a term was not. A further remedy was given the creditor by 3 and 4 W. and M. c. 14, but complicated trusts and equities of redemption were not touched by the statute. It seems that, as after these enactments the Court of Equity subjected all trusts to specialty creditors by analogy of the law, observing the analogy throughout, it adopted the legal course of administration; but provided the mortgagor had conveyed his whole interest as security, the equity of redemption was considered as equitable assets only.

B. THE MORTGAGEE AS A TRUSTEE

Hardwicke's pronouncement of the equity of redemption as an "equitable estate" in the land naturally had a powerful effect in strengthening the analogy of the trust. From time to time numerous attempts have been made to fix upon the mortgagee the character of a trustee and so to turn the analogy into an identity. Counsel essayed to do this as early as the year of the Restoration. In a case where "a Mortgagee assigns his Mortgage over for his due Debt. But it was much insisted by the Plaintiff's Counsel, That there was a Breach of Trust; and it was decreed that *Foyle* should account for all the Profits both before

---

[1] *Plunkett* v. *Penson*, (1742) 2 Atk. 293. As to the equity of redemption being equitable assets, see *Solly* v. *Gower*, (1688) 2 Vern. 61; *Cox's Case*, (1734) 3 P. W. 341; *Hartwell* v. *Chitters*, (1756) Amb. 308; *Sharpe* v. *Scarborough*, (1799) 4 Ves. J. 538; *Deg* v. *Deg*, (1727) 2 P. W. 416.

[2] *Cox's Case; Hartwell* v. *Chitters; Clay* v. *Willis*, (1823) 1 B. and C. 372.

[3] *Cook* v. *Gregson*, (1856) 3 Drew. 549.   [4] *King* v. *Ballett*, (1691) 2 Vern. 248.

THE MORTGAGEE AS A TRUSTEE 167

and after the Assignment ". The decree was, however, afterwards discharged on other grounds.[1] A number of careless dicta are to be found calling the mortgagee a trustee or a kind of trustee; and so, despite numerous decisions to the contrary, continual attempts have been made to base decisions and arguments upon that fact. Each attempt has been severely dealt with either by other judges sitting on the case in hand, or by their successors; and we now have a mass of dicta objecting to the use of such a term for the relation between mortgagor and mortgagee.

Nottingham appears to have considered a mortgagee who had been satisfied by payment of principal, interest, and costs to be a trustee for the mortgagor, and based this upon the ground that the mortgage is but a security. He says, "The land was never more than a security; and after payment of the money, the law keeps a trust for the mortgagor". This is as far as the conception of the mortgagee as a trustee can strictly be carried; that, when the money is paid, he is a trustee of the legal estate for the mortgagor, who is then complete owner of the beneficial interest; for in equity he had the legal estate but as security for the debt, and, now that the debt has ceased to exist, the reason for his retention of the legal estate is at an end. This seems to have been Hardwicke's real conception of the mortgagee as trustee. In *Richards* v. *Syms*, 1740,[2] he says, "Where a Mortgage is made of an Estate, that is only considered as a Security for Money due, the Land is the Accident attending upon the other; and when the Debt is discharged, the Interest in the Land follows of Course. In Law the Interest in the Land is thereby defeated, and in Equity a Trust arises for the Benefit of the Mortgagor".

There is one particular instance, that of an advowson, where the mortgagee before redemption has been said to be a trustee for the mortgagor; for, when the church is vacant, instead of his being able to present a person of his own choice, he must present the nominee of the mortgagor, and so appears a trustee. He is so only when the church is vacant. At all other times he can exercise his power of sale for his own benefit. Yet since this matter was decided early in the history of the equity of

---

[1] *Venables* v. *Foyle*, 1 Ch. Ca. 3. [2] Barn. 93.

168   THE MORTGAGEE AS A TRUSTEE

redemption,[1] it gave some colour of authority for statements that the mortgagee was but a trustee. Thus in 1700 it is said, "The mortgagee can make no profit by presenting to the church, nor can account for any value in respect thereof, to sink or lessen his debt, and the mortgagee therefore in that case, until a foreclosure, is but in the nature of a trustee for the mortgagor ".[2]

A few examples of the loose language of some judges are worthy of notice. Both Nottingham and Hardwicke have failed in this respect. Nottingham speaks of the heir of the mortgagor as "in a Nature of a Trustee for the Mortgagee till the Money is paid,"[3] and Hardwicke says in *Casborne* v. *Scarfe*:

It is true that a mortgagee is not barely a trustee; but it is sufficient for this purpose that he is in fact a trustee. He is owner of the charge or incumbrance on the mortgaged premises, and is entitled, in his own right, to hold the same as a pledge for his debt; but as to the inheritance descendible, the real estate in the land, he is a trustee for the mortgagor till the equity of redemption be foreclosed.[4]

Chief Baron Richards says:

In Equity, as in common sense, a mortgagee has the legal estate in the mortgaged premises only as a pledge for securing to him his money...subject to such security, he is a trustee for the owner of the equity of redemption; and although he may devise the legal estate as such pledge, yet it always continues subject to the owner's right of redemption. A mortgagee has not, any more than any other trustee, a right, either substantially or in equity, to apply the legal estate in the mortgaged premises to any purposes of his own.[5]

Again Arden, M.R., calls the mortgagee a trustee, though he was in reality only drawing an analogy between them. He says:

A. seised in fee, devises to *B.* in fee, charged with the payment of debts; then makes a mortgage in fee; then pays that off: and takes back the estate from the mortgagee to him and his heirs. This would fall directly within Lord *Hardwicke's* rule; that taking the legal estate from a trustee is not a revocation.[6]

---

[1] *Jory* v. *Cox*, (1697) Prec. Ch. 71; Reg. 1697, lib. A. 901.
[2] *Amhurst* v. *Dawling*, (1700) 2 Vern. 401; see also *Hobart* v. *Selby*, (1704) Freem. 273.   [3] *Burgh* v. *Francis*, (1673) R. t. Finch, 28.
[4] 2 J. and W. 196. See also Saunders in note to 3rd ed.
[5] *Silvester* v. *Jarman*, (1822) 10 Pri. 84.
[6] *Harmood* v. *Oglander*, (1800) 6 Ves. J. 221.

THE MORTGAGEE AS A TRUSTEE 169

It has been stated time and again by most eminent authorities, both judges and text-writers, that a mortgagee is not a trustee while so much as sixpence remains owing to him. A number of reasons why the mortgagee is not a trustee have been collected and set out with great care in a scathing indictment against such a conception by Sir Thomas Plumer in *Cholmondeley* v. *Clinton*, 1820. He limits the notion to where the mortgage debt is satisfied, and then admits an implied trust only. He says:

It is only in a secondary point of view, and under certain circumstances, and for a particular purpose, that the character of trustee constructively belongs to a mortgagee. No trust is expressed in the contract; it is only raised by implication, in subordination to the main purposes of it, and after that is fully satisfied; its primary character is not fiduciary.... He (mortgagee) acquires a distinct and independent beneficial interest in the estate; he has always a qualified and limited right, and may eventually acquire an absolute and permanent one to take possession, and he is entitled to enforce his right by adverse suit *in invitum* against the mortgagor; all which can never take place between trustee and cestuique trust. They have always an identity and unity of interest, and are never opposed in contest to each other.... The mortgagee, when he takes possession, is not acting as a trustee for the mortgagor, but independently and adversely for his own use and benefit. A trustee is stopped in equity from dispossessing his cestuique trust, because such dispossession would be a breach of trust. A mortgagee cannot be stopped, because in him it is no breach of trust, but in strict conformity to his own contract, which would be directly violated by any impediment thrown in the way of the exercise of this right.

Upon the same principle the mortgagee is not prevented, but assisted in equity, when he has recourse to a proceeding, which is not only to obtain the possession, but an absolute title to the estate, by foreclosure. This presents no resemblance to the character of a trustee, but to a character directly opposite. It is in this opposite character that he accounts for the rents when in possession.... The ground on which a mortgagee is in any case, and for any purpose, considered to have a character resembling that of a trustee, is the partial and limited right, which, in equity, he is allowed to have in the whole estate legal and equitable. He does not at any time possess, like a trustee, a title to the legal estate, distinct and separate from the beneficial and equitable. Whenever he is entitled at all to either, he is fully entitled to both, and to the legal and equitable remedies incident to both; but in equity, his title is confined to a particular

170 THE MORTGAGEE AS A TRUSTEE

purpose. He has no right to either, nor can he make use of any remedy belonging to either, further than and as may be necessary to secure the repayment of the money due to him. When that is paid, his duty is to reconvey the estate to the person entitled to it; it never remains in his hands cloathed with any fiduciary duty. He is never entrusted with the care of it, nor under any obligation to hold it for any one but himself, nor is he allowed to use it for any other purpose. The estate is not committed to his care, nor has he the means of preventing or being acquainted with the changes which the title to the equity of redemption may undergo, either by the act of the mortgagor, without his privity, or by operation of law....

The mortgagee is a mere indifferent stakeholder. The real contest lies between the competitors for the estate, which, in the hands of either, must continue subject to the mortgage till paid off; when paid off, the mortgage title ends, and then, and not before, the implied trust, to surrender the estate to the person entitled to demand it, begins.[1]

The words of Lord Parker when this case came before him in the House of Lords express the matter more concisely. He

[referred to] the vast difference between trusts, some being express, some implied; some relations...in which it could hardly be said that one was trustee and the other cestuique trust, and yet it could not well be denied that for some purposes they were so. Of this kind he took the relation between mortgagor and mortgagee to be. In the case of a strict trustee, it was his duty to take care of the interest of his cestuique trust, and he was not permitted to do any thing adverse to it; a tenant also had a duty to preserve the interests of his landlord, and many acts therefore of a trustee and a tenant, which, if done by a stranger, would be acts of adverse possession, would not be so in them, from its being their duty to abstain from them. But the case of a mortgagee was different, he being at liberty to hold possession; and not becoming strictly a trustee till the money was tendered to him, and having a right, if he continued in possession for 20 years without acknowledging the mortgage, to turn round on the mortgagor and say the estate was his own.[2]

It might well be imagined that such a decisive opinion as was given in this case would have closed the matter entirely. Certainly from this period onwards we rarely find the bench making the same loose statements as before, but advocates have repeatedly submitted the question to the Court in one form or

2 J. and W. 183, 188.   [2] 2 J and W. 190.

THE MORTGAGEE AS A TRUSTEE 171

another, always with the same result, thus adding continually to the mass of opposing authority.

Thus in 1865 Lord Cranworth, when forced to deal with the question, says:

Sir Edward Sugden said that the relation between trustee and cestuique trust, although in one sense existing between mortgagee and mortgagor, has never been so held to exist as that the mortgagee cannot purchase from the mortgagor. That is not disputed.... Being in possession could only make a difference if it created an obligation between the mortgagee and the mortgagor which would not have existed if he had not been in possession.... No duty arises on being in possession, except, to account to the mortgagor in a way onerous to the mortgagee, but there is no duty which would prevent the relation between the mortgagee and mortgagor different from what would have existed if he had not been in possession.[1]

The point was also brought before Vice-Chancellor Wigram, who said:

That a mortgagee is in some sense a trustee for the mortgagor may be admitted; for every person in whom the legal estate is vested, with a beneficial interest for another person, in a sense, is a trustee for that person. In some sense a mortgagee is in a worse position than a trustee, for a trustee in an ordinary case is not liable to a decree for wilful default, unless a special case be proved against him; whereas such a decree is merely of course as against a mortgagee in possession. On the other hand, a trustee can never make a benefit to himself by any dealing with the trust property; but if a second mortgagee should buy in the first mortgage for half the amount, or even obtain an assignment without consideration from the first mortgagee, I have no doubt he would be entitled to charge the mortgagor with the full amount of the first mortgage in addition to his own. And other cases of a like kind might be put.[2]

Again, Lord Herschell says:

It is quite a different proposition and one which I think is wholly untenable to assert that a mortgagee is trustee for the mortgagor. It is admitted that a mortgagee may create such estates as he pleases, he may convey, by way of sub-mortgage, to whom and in as many

[1] *Kirkwood* v. *Thompson*, 2 De G. J. and S. 613.
[2] *Dobson* v. *Land*, (1850) 8 Hare, 216, 220; quoted with approval by Lord Hatherly, *Kirkwood* v. *Thompson*, 2 H. and M. 400, Kay, J., *Banner* v. *Berridge*, (1881) 18 Ch. D. 267, and James, L.J., *Locking* v. *Parker*, (1878) L.R., 8 Ch. 30.

172   THE MORTGAGEE AS A TRUSTEE

parcels as he pleases. This seems to me to show that L's representatives cannot be regarded as holding the legal estate as trustees for the appellants. If the conveyance to the respondent was a breach of trust on the part of L's representatives, as against the appellants, they could I presume have come to a Court of Equity for an injunction to prevent the conveyance being executed. But had they done so, the answer would surely have been, "Come and redeem".[1]

Lewin has laid down in his treatise on trusts that a mortgagee in possession is constructively a trustee of the rents and profits, and cites a number of old cases in support of his contention. In none of these cases is any express mention made of the matter in hand, and they do not seem to be authority for his proposition. All were concerned with accounts of profits against a first or subsequent mortgagee. As has been pointed out by Vice-Chancellor Wigram in the passage just quoted, a mortgagee is in a worse position than a trustee with respect to accounts, and, in the preceding passage quoted, Lord Cranworth denied that possession can make the mortgagee a trustee. The mortgagee in possession is, in general, liable to the same extent as a trustee in the matter of accounts, and sometimes even further. This is doubtless what led Lewin to make such an inaccurate statement. A mortgagee is never a trustee until his debt is satisfied; for until then, besides holding the legal estate, he also has an equitable interest in the property for the purpose of his security, which gives him rights over the property, such as sale and entry, in opposition to his mortgagor. This can never take place in the relationship of trustee and *cestui que trust*. On satisfaction of the debt the equitable interest for the purposes of security vanishes. The mortgagee is no longer mortgagee, but is trustee of the legal estate for the persons entitled to it. As is stated by Lord Herschell, "The first mortgagee, on being paid off, becomes a trustee of the legal estate for any subsequent incumbrancers according to their priorities".[2]

This is not all. It has been held that, "a mortgagee is strictly speaking not a trustee of the power of sale. It is a power given to him for his own benefit, the better to realize his

[1] *Taylor* v. *Russell*, (1892) (H.L.) A. C. 255.
[2] *Ibid.*

THE MORTGAGEE AS A TRUSTEE   173

debt";[1] and again, that the fact of the mortgage being in the form of a trust for sale did not make the mortgagee a trustee. As to this latter, after quoting numerous cases, Kay, J., concludes:

I have, therefore, a series of decisions[2]—there are other cases to the same effect, but none that I am aware of in the least degree contradicting these...shewing that even where the words of the mortgage express a trust in the most clear and emphatic manner, the Court is very loth to hold the mortgagee to be a trustee to all intents and purposes. As I read this last case, where under an express trust of the moneys to be received by the mortgagee, that is not a trust which the mortgagor can enforce at all except as to the surplus. Where a trust is so expressed, he may say the mortgagee is a trustee for me of the surplus....But I take the true result of these decisions to be this, that in this particular case, where there is no trust expressed either in writing or verbally of the proceeds of the sale, no trust can possibly arise until it is shown there is a surplus, and then I should be disposed to hold that there is sufficient fiduciary relation between the mortgagor and the mortgagee to make the mortgagee constructively a trustee of the surplus, in case it is shewn there is a surplus. But that seems to me to be a case not of express trust at all but of constructive trust, that is to say, a trust which only arises on proof of the fact that there was a surplus...the ordinary rule of a Court of Equity would apply, that nobody would be allowed to enter into evidence to raise a case of constructive trust after the statutory period had expired.[3]

In the same case he points out that the deed of conveyance or mortgage may be so worded as to create "an express trust with reference to the sale moneys, exactly in the same way as where a mortgagee sells under the powers of a common mortgage. In that case, when the estate has been sold there is an express trust of the surplus money for the mortgagor".[4]

It seems, then, that on a sale by the mortgagee, he is only a constructive trustee of the surplus, unless an express trust of such surplus has been declared by the deed. This was laid down

---

[1] *Warmer* v. *Jacob*, (1881) 20 Ch. D. 223, per Kay, J.

[2] *Locking* v. *Parker*, (1878) 8 Ch. D. 30; *Kirkwood* v. *Thompson*, (1865) 2 H. and M. 392, 400; *Dobson* v. *Land*, (1850) 8 Hare, 216, 220; *Tanner* v *Heard*, 23 Beav. 555 distinguished.

[3] *Banner* v. *Berridge*, (1881) 18 Ch. D. 269; see also Lord Hatherly in *Kirkwood* v. *Thompson*, 2 H. and M. 392, 402.

[4] James, L.J., in *Locking* v. *Parker*, *supra*, quoted by Kay, J.

174 THE MORTGAGEE AS A TRUSTEE

by Sir Thomas Plumer in *Cholmondeley* v. *Clinton*, and even as early as 1740 by Lord Hardwicke, who says when the debt is discharged, "There arises a Trust by Operation of Law for the Benefit of the Mortgagor, and that Case is within the Exception in the Statute of Frauds".[1]

That this is still correct law may be seen from the case of *Sands to Thompson* in 1883. Section 25 of the Real Property Limitation Act, 1833,[2] contains a proviso that, "No mortgagor or *cestui que trust* shall be deemed to be a tenant at will within the meaning of this clause, to his mortgagee or trustee". In this case[3] Fry, J., held that on satisfaction of the debt the mortgagee had become a trustee for the mortgagor, and the relation of mortgagor and mortgagee was at an end; that it had already been decided that the word "trustee" in the clause only applied to a trustee under an express trust;[4] that therefore, as this was not an express trust, the section applied, and the mortgagor gained a squatter's title thirteen years after the commencement of the new relationship. It should be noticed that the expression "trust" in the Trustee Acts of 1850 and 1893, "does not include the duties incident to an estate conveyed by way of mortgage";[5] but a mortgagee, on being paid off, is no longer holding in the character of mortgagee, but as trustee,[6] and a mortgagee having surplus proceeds of sale has been relieved as a trustee under the Judicial Trustees Act, 1896.

This seems to be the result of the whole matter. When the debt is satisfied the relation of the mortgagor and the mortgagee is at an end, and that of trustee and *cestui que trust* takes its place by the construction of the law. It is quite a different relationship, and each party may be said to be in of a new estate. So long as a single farthing of the debt remains owing, the comparison between the mortgage and the trust is but an analogy.

The Court, to a certain extent, controls in each case the exercise of the legal incidents of the estate or interest, making it subservient to the purposes for which it is assumed it was

---

[1] *Richards* v. *Syms*, Barn. 93. [2] 3 and 4 Will. IV, c. 27.
[3] 22 Ch. D. 614.
[4] *Doe* v. *Rock*, Carr and M. 549; *Drummond* v. *Sant*, L.R., 6 Q.B. 763.
[5] 56 and 57 Vict. c. 53, § 50; 13 and 14 Vict. c. 60.
[6] See *Re Osborn's Mortgage*, (1871) 12 Eq. 392.

THE MORTGAGEE AS A TRUSTEE 175

created; but there is this material difference, that in the case of the equity of redemption the holder of the legal estate is not completely at the command of the Court, for the mortgagee does not acquire it in the character of a trustee, or merely for the purposes of the mortgagor, or that it may continue to be subservient to the equitable title, but for the purposes for which equity assumes it was created, namely, that of security. So long as the mortgagee suffers the equitable interest to exist, which, unlike a trustee, he may at his pleasure bring to an end, the relations of the two parties, both of whom have interests in equity, the one to redeem, the other for his security, are moulded and directed by the Court of Chancery according to rules and doctrines of its own, though often adapted from those applied to the trust.

C. THE THEORY OF CLOGGING THE EQUITY OF REDEMPTION

We have seen that as soon as the mortgagor's power of redemption became an established right, the Chancellor allowed the mortgagee to apply to him for an order for foreclosure. The relief given by the Chancellor, as soon as it became general, was in reality a direct interference with the express agreement of the parties, and mortgagees at once set to work to find some means for its evasion. As the mortgagee was generally in a position to dictate terms, the obvious method was by an express agreement in the mortgage deed prohibiting or curtailing redemption. This the Court of Chancery refused to allow, and a principle was soon established that any agreement or stipulation forming part of the mortgage bargain which attempted to restrict or hamper this power of redemption in equity in any way was void in so far as it had such limiting effect. This general principle of the Court has since been crystallized into three doctrines, usually represented by three catch phrases; viz. "Once a mortgage, always a mortgage", "There shall be no clog or fetter upon the equity of redemption", and, "The mortgagor shall be given back exactly what he has parted with".

It cannot be definitely ascertained whether these rules were established solely as a protection to the borrower, who in both

176 THE THEORY OF CLOGGING

English and Roman equity was always regarded with tenderness and guarded against all possible forms of oppression; or how far they were established as a protection of the newly won jurisdiction of the Court of Chancery over mortgages, preventing the use of clauses evading redemption in equity, in order that the common-law principle of forfeiture should not take its course. Considering the completeness with which all such clauses were declared void, it is quite possible that this latter consideration may have influenced the Court to some extent in its dealing with the matter.

The Court appears to have objected to attempts to clog the right of redemption almost as soon as the right was established,[1] and it seems probable that a like course was pursued in such isolated cases which may have come before the Court prior to the Chancellorship of Nottingham, who quickly enunciated this general objection as a definite principle of the Court and with his customary breadth and decision. In *Newcomb* v. *Bonham* he is reported as saying, the deeds "Being but a security, the same could not be extinguished by any covenant or agreement at the time of making the mortgage",[2] and again he said, "It was a general rule, *once a mortgage, and always a mortgage*; and in regard the estate was expressly redeemable in the mortgagor's lifetime, it must continue so afterwards".[3] Two years later, in the argument for the plaintiff in *Howard* v. *Harris* the same principles are cited as customs of the Court. Thus it was argued:

First, that restrictions of redemption in mortgages have been always discountenanced in this court...; that there was no more in this case against a redemption, than there was in every mortgage. It is true, here is an express covenant, that none but H. or the heirs male of his body, should redeem: and in every mortgage there is a proviso, that in case the money be not paid by such a day, the mortgagee shall hold the land discharged, and not only so, but there is likewise an express covenant for further assurance....Secondly, that it was a maxim here, that an estate cannot at one time be a mortgage, and at another time cease to be so, by one and the same deed: and a mortgage

---

[1] *Bacon* v. *Bacon*, (1639) Tot. 133–4: "Where the mortgagee will suddenly bestow unnecessary costs upon the mortgaged lands, of purposes to clogg the lands, to prevent the mortgagor's redemption"; see *ante*, p. 29.

[2] 1 Vern. 7; see also 1 Vern. 214, 232.   [3] 1 Vern. 8.

THE EQUITY OF REDEMPTION 177

can no more be irredeemable, than a distress for a rent charge can be irrepleviable. The law itself will control that express agreement of the party; and by the same reason equity will let a man loose from his agreement, and will against his agreement admit him to redeem a mortgage.[1]

In this case it was decided that where the mortgagor had an estate in fee simple, the equity of redemption could not be limited to the heirs male of his body only, just as in the previous case it was held it could not be limited to his own life. Incidentally, both limitations could have been made in a roundabout way by subsequent settlement of the equity of redemption for a new consideration.

We may notice that Nottingham gives as his reason the principle he uses so often, that the mortgage is but a security. He appears to have decided the matter on this ground; but it seems from the argument in *Howard* v. *Harris* that he made no departure from the law as stated in *Newcomb* v. *Bonham*, and was merely strengthening his argument by an additional reason for his objection to "clogs", or else was merely stating a reason which had already been observed. A few years later clauses raising the rate of interest on non-punctual payment were held void as a clog on the redemption;[2] and likewise clauses restricting redemption for thirty years,[3] during the life of the mortgagor,[4] or providing for the pre-emption of the equity of redemption by the mortgagee.[5]

These rules protecting the mortgagor do not seem to have met with any opposition from his immediate successors; but these latter extended their operation by the frequent application of them which was found necessary, owing to the persistent attempts of mortgagees to limit in some manner this right to redeem, the tendency of both Roman and English equity in the formative period being to watch the interest of the debtor with care, on the assumption that he was at a disadvantage in his dealings with a prospective creditor. Thus, in their extended

[1] (1683) 1 Vern. 191.
[2] *Holles* v. *Wyse*, (1693) 2 Vern. 289; *Strode* v. *Parker*, (1694) 2 Vern. 316.
[3] *Talbot* v. *Braddill*, (1683) 1 Vern. 183.
[4] *Price* v. *Perrie*, (1702) 2 Freem. 258.
[5] *Jennings* v. *Ward*, (1705) 2 Vern. 520; *Orby* v. *Trigg*, (1722) 9 Mod. 2.

TER

178 THE THEORY OF CLOGGING

form these doctrines appear to have become hard and fast rules of the Court, before anyone thought fit to call this extended application in question.

Some general observations made by Hardwicke in *Mellor* v. *Lees*, 1742, suggest that he would have been disposed to confine the rule to cases of "Common mortgage", that is, apparently, mortgage by deed of land, and only then where there was an oppressive design on the part of the mortgagee. He said, "If, indeed, any fetters had been laid upon redeeming the mortgaged estate, by some original agreement...it would not avail, where it is done with a design to wrest the estate fraudulently out of the hands of the mortgagor".[1] In a case three years later, which is often referred to for a statement of the rule,[2] he again spoke of a "deed of mortgage"; but a few years after his death Lord Northington (then Lord Henley), in *Vernon* v. *Bethel*, laid down the law broadly in the following terms: "I take it to be an established rule, that a mortgagee can never provide at the time of making the loan for any event or condition on which the equity of redemption shall be discharged, and the conveyance absolute".[3] This judgment seems to have been conclusive.

The three subdoctrines established under this principle are well expounded in their modern form by Lord Davey in *Noakes* v. *Rice*. He says:

The 1st maxim presents no difficulty; [Once a mortgage always a mortgage,] it is only another way of saying that a mortgage cannot be made irredeemable. [He quotes *Northampton* v. *Salt*.[4]] The second doctrine to which I refer, namely, that a mortgagee shall not reserve to himself any collateral advantage outside the mortgage contract, was established long ago when the usury laws were in force. The Court of Equity went beyond the usury laws, and set its face against every transaction which tended to usury. It therefore declared void every stipulation by a mortgagee for a collateral advantage which made his total remuneration for the loan indirectly exceed the legal interest. I think it will be found that every case under this head of equity was decided either on this ground, or on the ground that the bargain was oppressive and unconscionable. The abolition of the usury laws has made an alteration in the view the

---

[1] 2 Atk. 494.
[2] *Toomes* v. *Conset*, 3 Atk. 261.
[3] (1762) 2 Eden 113.
[4] (1892) A.C. 1.

THE EQUITY OF REDEMPTION   179

Court should take on this subject, and I agree that a collateral advantage may now be stipulated for by a mortgagee, provided no unfair advantage be taken by the mortgagee which would render it void or voidable according to the general principles of Equity, and provided it does not offend against the third doctrine. On these grounds I think the case of *Biggs* v. *Hoddinott* (1898, 2 Ch. 307) in the Court of Appeal was rightly decided.

The third doctrine is really a corollary from the first, and might be expressed in this form: Once a mortgage always a mortgage and nothing but a mortgage. The meaning of that is that a mortgagee shall not make any stipulation which will prevent a mortgagor, who has paid principal, interest, and costs, from getting back his mortgaged property in the condition in which he parted with it.[1]

Or, as put by Lord Macnaghten two years later, "unaffected by any condition or stipulation which formed part of the transaction".[2]

These rules continued to develop without check until they became so extended that at one time there was a doubt expressed by more than one text-writer that the express power of sale given to mortgagees in the mortgage deed might perhaps offend against them as an attempt to clog the equity of redemption. However, with the industrial development of the last century, the manner in which these doctrines prevent a mortgagor who is a business man and in no way threatened with oppression from obtaining the best terms he can by agreeing to a restriction on his power of redemption has been much criticized. The abolition of the Usury Laws in 1854 has been eagerly seized upon as an opportunity to restrict their application, and during the last half century there has been a strong tendency to limit them as much as possible, without actually overriding the rules themselves. These latter appear to be far too settled for any direct judicial attempt to overrule them; but even if the Legislature does not interfere they may be whittled down in time by judicial legislation, until the cause for complaint against them has vanished.

In *Samuel* v. *Jarrah Timber Co.* 1904,[2] Lords Macnaghten, Lindley and Halsbury all quote Lord Northington's judgment

---

[1] (1902) A.C. 24.
[2] *Samuel* v. *Jarrah Timber Co.* (1904) A.C. 323.

180   THE THEORY OF CLOGGING

in *Vernon* v. *Bethel* as binding, though disapproving of the extent of the rule thus established. Lord Halsbury said:

I regret that the state of the authorities leaves me no alternative other than to affirm the judgement. A perfectly fair bargain made between two parties to it, each of whom was quite sensible as to what they are doing, is not to be performed at the same time a mortgage arrangement was made between them. If a day had intervened between the two parts of the arrangement, the part of the bargain which the appellant claims to be performed would have been perfectly good...but a line of authorities going back for more than a century has decided that such an arrangement as that which was here arrived at is contrary to a principle of equity, the sense or reason of which I am not able to appreciate, and very reluctantly I am compelled to acquiesce in the judgement appealed from.

Lord Macnaghten, who followed, said:

Having regard to the state of the authorities binding on the Court of Appeal if not on this House, it seems to me that they could not have come to any other conclusion, although the transaction was a fair bargain between men of business without any trace or suspicion of oppression, surprise, or circumvention.... The question here depends rather upon the rule that a mortgagee is not allowed at the time of the loan to enter into a contract for the purchase of the mortgaged property. This latter rule, I think, is founded on sentiment rather than on principle. It seems to have had its origin in the desire of the Court of Chancery to protect embarrassed landowners from imposition and oppression. And it was invented, I should suppose, in order to obviate the necessity of inquiry and investigation in cases where suspicion may be probable and proof difficult.[1]

The limitation which has been put upon the second doctrine as a result of the abolition of the usury laws is well illustrated by *Kreglinger* v. *New Patagonia Meat Co.*, 1913. The views of the House of Lords may be summarized thus: Equity considered that the mortgagor only needed protection while he was actually borrowing, when he was perhaps hard pressed for the money. The total remuneration of the mortgagee, inclusive of the collateral bargain, must not exceed the current rate of interest. Afterwards, the mortgagor might make what bargain he pleased, provided it was really independent and not part of

[1] (1904) A.C. (H.-L.), 323.

THE EQUITY OF REDEMPTION

181

the loan transaction. Since the repeal of the Usury Laws, as was said by Lord Parker in the Kreglinger case:

In every case in which a stipulation by a mortgagee for a collateral advantage has, since the repeal of the usury laws, been held invalid, the stipulation has been open to objection, either (1) because it was unconscionable, or (2) because it was in the nature of a penal clause clogging the equity on failure to exercise a contractual right to redeem, or (3) because it was in the nature of a condition repugnant as well to the contractual as to the equitable right.[1]

Thus, although a mortgagee cannot stipulate for any part of the property conveyed by the mortgage itself to remain his after the debt is satisfied, upon the principle that the mortgagor must be allowed to have his property back intact; a true collateral advantage may continue to be binding even after the loan is repaid. Hence, in the case before them it was held that an option of pre-emption on all sheep skins of the borrowing company for a period of five years, during which the loan was not to be called in, formed no part of the mortgage transaction, but was a collateral contract entered into as a condition of the company's obtaining the loan; that it was not a clog on the equity of redemption or repugnant to the right to redeem, and hence the lenders could exercise their right of pre-emption notwithstanding that the loan was paid off.

It is important to notice the difference between this case and *Bradley* v. *Carritt*, 1903,[2] where the mortgage contained a proviso that the mortgagor of most of the tea shares in a company would "always thereafter" induce the company to employ the mortgagee as its sole agent to sell tea, and pay damages if he were not so employed. In this case it was held that, as the shares themselves remained tied by a restriction which prevented free dealings with them, the mortgagor did not get back his property intact, and hence the proviso became void as soon as the mortgage was paid off. However, it is difficult to reconcile all the recent decisions as to what collateral advantages may and what may not be allowed.[3]

This modern view, that the rule making void every collateral advantage stipulated for by the mortgagee was founded upon

[1] (1914) A.C. 25.   [2] (1903) A.C. 253.
[3] See *Northampton* v. *Salt, supra,* and other cases.

182   THE THEORY OF CLOGGING

the usury laws, rests on very scanty authority. There is a reference to usury in Tothill,[1] but too vague to enable any inference to be drawn; and in the only case cited by Lord Parker in support of his view,[2] all that Lord Eldon says is that the Court will not allow compound interest "as tending to usury". There is no mention of usury in either *Newcomb* v. *Bonham* or *Howard* v. *Harris*, nor in the cases on the point which followed them.[3] In *Scott* v. *Brest*,[4] where there was a clause that on default the lender could appoint himself receiver of rents at a salary, the contract was held to be usurous; but this was in the nature of a clause raising the interest on non-payment, which has always been forbidden,[5] and not a stipulation for a collateral advantage perhaps lasting longer than the mortgage transaction itself. In other cases of a similar nature there is no mention of the subject of usury.[6] No! the objection to a collateral advantage arose as a subsidiary rule to the general determination on the part of the Courts of Equity to see the mortgagor was not unduly pressed, and did not directly or indirectly contract out of his equity of redemption. It was a corollary of the rule against clogging, enunciated in part by Nottingham as "once a mortgage always a mortgage".

The equity of redemption, then, is an estate in land which arises out of the mortgage agreement by operation of the law. In one sense it arises by contract, in that there must be a mortgage agreement, but really it is created by the Court of Equity contrary to the express agreement of the parties. Not only does equity imply terms in the agreement which totally alter its tenor, but these special terms cannot be excluded by the parties at the time the agreement is made.

The estate of the mortgagor, so created in equity, seems to be a future estate which arises only on forfeiture of the legal estate. This estate is peculiar in that it cannot be varied by the

---

[1] *Langford* v. *Barnard*, (1594) Tot. 134.

[2] *Chambers* v. *Goldwin*, (1804) 9 Ves. 271.

[3] *Talbot* v. *Braddill*, (1683) 1 Vern. 183; *Price* v. *Perrie*, (1702) Freem. Ch. 258; *Jennings* v. *Ward*, (1705) 2 Vern. 520; *Orby* v. *Trigg*, (1722) 9 Mod. 2.   [4] (1787) 2 T.R. 238.

[5] *Holles* v. *Wyse*, (1693) 2 Vern. 289; *Strode* v. *Parker*, (1694) 2 Vern. 316; *Wallingford* v. *Mutual Soc.*, (1880) 5 A.C. 685.

[6] *Langstaffe* v. *Fenwick*, (1805) 10 Ves. 405; *Davis* v. *Dendy*, 3 Madd. 190.

THE EQUITY OF REDEMPTION 183

instrument creating it; but it may be altered subsequently by further agreement between the parties. For instance, though at the time of the contract the right of redemption in equity cannot be restricted from running for the same length of time as the original estate mortgaged, yet by subsequent agreement any portion of that equitable right may be released, alienated, etc. Again, though no burden may be placed upon the equity of redemption by the mortgaged deed, yet by a subsequent agreement collateral advantages may be obtained by the mortgagee.[1] Once the mortgage bargain has been made, equity seems to consider the mortgagee capable of looking after himself. This reduces somewhat the force of argument that the present law as to clogging the redemption is unfair. Although it may be said that, by preventing the mortgagor from contracting out of his full right of redemption at the time the mortgage is made, equity has often prevented a man of business, perfectly capable of looking after his own interests, from obtaining the most advantageous terms he can. Yet, if he be trustworthy, he can surely sometimes attain in effect what he desires by means of a subsequent collateral agreement which was in view at the time the mortgage was made, but which was not made part of the mortgage transaction in order to avoid the stringent rules as to clogging.

D. THE MORTGAGOR AND THE FRANCHISE

The position of mortgagor and mortgagee as regards status qualifying them for the franchise seems always to have rested on possession. Cockburn, C.J., says of the mortgagor, "The commissioners are not bound to enquire whether the legal estate is in him. They find him in possession of the estate, and he 'hath or holdeth' the estate and thereby satisfieth the terms of the Statute of Henry VI".[2] If the mortgagee is in possession, he has the legal estate and also the possession; he is the owner of the land at law and is in receipt of the rents and profits.

---

[1] *Reeves* v. *Lisle*, [1902] A.C. 461; *Melbourne Banking Co.* v. *Brougham* (1882) 7 A.C. 307; *Cotterell* v. *Purchase*, (1735) Cas. t. Talb. 61.

[2] *R.* v. *Baker*, (1867) L.R., 2 Q.B. 621.

184 THE MORTGAGOR AND THE FRANCHISE

Hence, if the estate is of sufficient annual value, it has always been sufficient to confer the franchise upon him.[1]

The question of the eligibility of the mortgagor in possession was much discussed in the latter half of the eighteenth century, and seems to have been definitely settled after the Bedfordshire[2] and Buckinghamshire[3] cases, 1785, which decided, "that the interest upon a mortgage, the mortgagor still being in possession, is a charge upon the estate within the meaning of the Statute (8 Hen. VI, 7)"; and that if it was such as to reduce the value of the estate to less than 40s. per annum, "does invalidate the vote". In the same year there was a case of by no means so decided an authority,[4] but shortly afterwards a statute was passed confirming the former decisions.[5]

There seem no objections to mortgagors in possession as voters reported until 1755. It is possible that objections of this nature may have been made under the general objection of "not having a freehold in the said county of the value of 40s. per annum"; but the silence of the Journals and the opinions of subsequent reporters[6] point otherwise. In 1755 we find the first mention of evidence of a charge on the property being given as an objection. It was offered under the general objection of "not having a freehold, etc." Shortly afterwards special objections of charges upon the estate reducing the yearly value to below 40s. grew numerous. In this first case the vote was defended by denying the charge as a fact, seemingly admitting the legal effect of it in reducing the yearly value of the estate.[7] It might be imagined that perhaps the reason why no mention of objections to mortgagors by reason of reduced annual value is to be found in the reports before this date was that mortgagors had previously not had the right to vote, and that this right was silently established subsequently to Hardwicke's

---

[1] 2 and 3 Will. IV, c. 45, § 23; 6 and 7 Vict. c. 18, § 74.

[2] 2 Luder, 468; 40 Journ. 472.   [3] 2 Luder, 599; 40 Journ.

[4] *Cricklade Case*, 2 Luder, 323; 40 Journ.

[5] 28 Geo. III, c. 36, §§ 6, 9; see *Lee* v. *Hutchinson*, (1850) 8 C.B. 18, and *Copland* v. *Bartlett*, (1848) 6 C.B. 18, showing that "charge" in this connection is used to include mortgages, etc.

[6] Luder and Lutyer.

[7] *Dent's Case. Oxfordshire Case*, 25 Journ. 63; cited 2 Luder, 582.

THE MORTGAGOR AND THE FRANCHISE 185

announcement that the mortgagor had the estate and ownership of the land in equity, subject only to the security. This idea is clearly erroneous, for in 7 & 8 Will. III the legislature declared that, "the mortgagor or *cestui que trust* in possession shall and may vote for such estates, notwithstanding such mortgage or trust",[1] and this enactment seems to have been merely declaratory of the law and not a change in favour of the equitable owner.[2]

In the Bedfordshire and Buckinghamshire cases much attention was paid to the case of *Wetherell* v. *Hall*, 1782, where Lord Mansfield and a strong Court held that an equitable estate gave a qualification under the gaming laws; but that the clear yearly "value of £100" under 22 and 23 Car. II, c. 25, meant the value clear of all mortgages and incumbrances created by the owner or those under whom he claimed. He says, "The privilege is given to property; and the *cestui que trust*, the mortgagor, is really the owner. We consider the defendant's interest in this court just as it would be considered in a court of equity".[3] Here, in passing, we may notice once more Mansfield's words which have the semblance of importing equitable doctrines into the common law. He seems to be doing his best to make the common law recognize equitable interests in the interpretation of statutes of an economic nature, and in this instance he appears to have succeeded.

[1] c. 25, § 7.   See Argument in *Wetherell* v. *Hall*, Cald. 235.
[3] Cald. 230.

APPENDIX

It is frequently stated that with the coming into operation of the Law of Property Acts, 1922–6, the equity of redemption proper has ceased to exist. This is incorrect. Although the legal charge is now generally adopted as the form of landed security, it is still possible to grant a term of years to secure repayment of a sum of money at a fixed date. All legal mortgages in existence on the 1st January 1926 were converted into mortgages of this nature. When the date for payment is passed, the legal right to redeem has ceased. The mortgagor then has vested in him an equity to redeem the estate lost at law, subject to the same incidents as such, and exercisable in the same manner, as before the passing of the Acts.

It is true that the Legislature have in the first instance attached a legal reversion to every equity of redemption of a legal estate; but this does not mean that the equity of redemption has ceased. The mortgagor's right to redeem is exactly the same to-day as it was before 1926. The practice of granting long terms by way of mortgage has continued in general use over a considerable period as a method of securing portions to younger children, and such demises by way of mortgage have been in vogue from time to time for other purposes. At an early date the Chancellor extended to leaseholders, who had allowed the day for payment to pass, the relief granted to freeholders in similar circumstances, and this extension was so much a matter of course, that the fact of a mortgage being of a leasehold does not appear from the Reports to have been even argued as a reason against the granting of relief. This relief was named, both as to freehold and leasehold, the "equity of redemption".

Nor is the equity of redemption merged in the legal reversion, for they are of a different nature, the one an equitable right in the term of years granted to the creditor, the other a legal reversion subject to the term, a term which is unsatisfied. The rights of the mortgagee with regard to the term are those which he has by reason of his equity of redemption, enforceable as before under the rules of equity. The legal estate remaining in him does not come into possession until the equitable right to redeem has terminated by reason of the expiration of the term. An equitable estate, as the equity of redemption has been considered since the time of Hardwicke, merges in the legal estate only when they unite in the same person in the same right and are co-extensive and commensurate. Thus, an equitable estate tail, subject to an equitable interest expectant thereon,

APPENDIX 187

does not merge in a legal fee simple devolving by descent on the same person, since the legal and equitable estates are not of the same quality.[1]

Under the new Acts a freeholder can still assign a term of ten years to a creditor to secure a loan. After the day for payment is passed, the freeholder will have vested in him a legal reversion subject to the mortgage term, together with an equity to redeem the term itself. He can then create successive interests in the freehold reversion, life estates, estates tail, legal and equitable, and yet retain to himself the equity of redemption of the term. This equity is a separate estate in the land, distinct from the freehold reversion, and can be dealt with apart from such reversion as the owner desires. Any person interested in the equity of redemption, should successive interests be created therein, is entitled to redeem the mortgage; but a person interested in the freehold reversion, as distinct from the equity of redemption, may have no right to redeem. A similar position is found where a long term of years is granted by way of mortgage, or a term of 3000 years is created under the new Acts. The Law of Property Act, 1925, states that a mortgage of an estate in fee simple, or term of years, as the case may be, "shall only be capable of being effected at law" in certain ways, ways which result in a legal reversion being left in the mortgagor, and that any purported conveyance of the fee simple of assignment of a term by way of mortgage shall operate as if the prescribed methods were adopted. The Acts do not go on to enact that the legal reversion so created shall not be dealt with apart from the equity of redemption or that the latter merges in the reversion. Since legislation is presumed to alter the existing law as little as possible, there seems no reason why the mortgagor should not create successive interests in the legal reversion for what they are worth or even dispose of that reversion entirely, without parting with any portion of his equity of redemption of the term.

Just as there still remains under the amended law an equity of redemption of the legal term, so there still remains an equity of redemption on the mortgage of equitable estates. The conversion of estates tail and the beneficial interests of tenants in common into equitable estates and the provisions for safeguarding equitable interests must make mortgages of equitable interests still a commonplace. The term, "equity of redemption," is as correctly applied to equitable estates as to legal estates. It is an equity to redeem the mortgaged interest when the day fixed for payment has passed. Prior to 1926, on a second mortgage by the mortgagor, where both first and second mortgages were expressed to convey the whole

---

[1] *Merest* v. *James*, (1821) 6 Madd. 118.

APPENDIX

interest of the mortgagor in the property to secure payment of sums at fixed dates, after the dates were passed the mortgagor then had an "equity of redemption" of an equity of redemption, an equitable estate in the land.

The application of the Law of Property Act, 1925, to mortgages of equitable estates presents some difficulty. The vesting provisions of secs. 1 and 2 of Part vii, Schedule I of the Act, dealing with the conversion of the fee simple estates of mortgagees into long terms, expressly refer to "legal or equitable" estates. These words are also contained in sec. 2 of Part viii of the same Schedule, dealing with the position of subsequent mortgagees of leaseholds. Their omission from other sections of these two Parts calls for comment. They can probably be implied in secs. 3 and 4 of Part vii, dealing with the vesting of the fee simple in the mortgagor, by following on from the previous sections; but it is more difficult, in the face of their express insertion in the parallel section of Part vii, to imply them in sec. 1 of Part viii, thereby vesting an equitable subterm in a mortgagee by assignment of an equitable term of years. The occurrence of the words in sec. 2 of Part viii may assist the Court to do so. Their insertion in some cases and not others makes difficult the application of the doctrine, "Equity follows the law".

With regard to mortgages of an equitable fee simple since 1925, the position is even less clear. Subsec. 1, sec. 85 of the Law of Property Act, 1925, enacts that, "A mortgage of an estate in fee simple shall only be capable of being effected at law either by a demise...or by a charge... "; but subsec. 2 does not contain the words, "at law", enacting that, "Any purported conveyance of an estate in fee simple by way of mortgage" shall "operate as a demise". Similarly the side notes to the two subsections are worded respectively, "Modes of mortgaging legal estate in fee simple", and "Effect of mortgage of fee simple". The same inconsistent wording is to be found in sec. 86, concerning mortgages of leaseholds. A mortgage of an equitable fee simple in remainder is a commonplace. Hence the question whether the more liberal wording of subsec. 2 extends its application from legal to equitable estates, or whether, if it does not, the principle, "Equity follows the law", is to be applied, may become the subject of judicial decision.

Lastly, though the new Acts have created a legal charge with the supposed theoretical difference between it and the mortgage, in that the charge does not convey the property to the creditor; the legal charge is expressed to operate as if it were a mortgage, that is, the debtor is in the same position as if he had vested in him the equity of redemption of a term of years together with a legal reversion expectant on the mortgaged term. It would seem that a person who

APPENDIX 189

is at law in the same position as if he had a legal reversion, no more and no less, has in fact such a reversion; and similarly a person who is in equity in the same position as if he had an equity of redemption, has an equity of redemption in fact. Otherwise the creation of the legal charge may be likened to a decree that loaves may in future be made in the form of "Leavens", but that all "Leavens" shall be of the same size, shape and constituents as the former loaves.

INDEX

Abinger, C.B., 99, 102
Actio fiduciae, xv–lxiii *passim*
Actio in rem, 140, 146
Advowson, 167
Aequitas and *ius strictum,* xix–lxiii *passim*
  of Roman law, nature of, as contrasted with English equity, xix–lxiii *passim*
Ancient law, origin of some medieval and modern securities on property in, ix *seq.*
Anglo-Saxon gage of land, a conveyance on condition subsequent, xxx–xxxiv
Annuities, 133
Archaic features of early mortgage, xl
Arden, M.R., 71, 78, 85, 168
Ashhurst, J., 95, 96
Assets, equity of redemption as, 60, 163 *et seq.*
  not legal, 164
  interest of mortgagee as, 63
  trust as, 47, 60, 163 *et seq.*
    when legal, 166
  use not, 43
Attornment, 102
Austin, 138
Austinian School, 140 *et seq.*

Bacon, Sir F., 5, 10
  may have granted relief generally, 31 *et seq.*
Bailiff, *cestui que trust* as, 91, 106
  mortgagor as, 102, 104
Bankruptcy, 28, 55
  equity of redemption in assignee in, 82
  order and disposition clause, 71, 72
Best, C.J., 99
Blackburn, L.J., 78, 84
Blackstone, 14, 15, 109
Boethius quoted, lv
Bona fide purchaser for value, lviii–lx. *See* Purchaser
Bonae fidei negotium, fiducia as, xix–lxiii *passim*

Bond creditors, equity of redemption assets for, 163 *et seq.*
  trust assets for, 163, 166
Bonds, common law regain jurisdiction over, 33
  general relief of, 24, 25, 31, 32, 34, 36, 114
  limitation of action on, 97
  mortgage compared with, 33
  relieved when satisfied, 22, 23
Book-land, gages of, xxx–xxxiv
Borough English, 82
Bovill, C.J., 107
Bracton, 1, 2, 18, 87
Bractonian gage, xxix, xxxiv–xxxvi, xl
Bramwell, Lord, 118
Bridgeman, Sir O., 57, 58, 163
Britton, 2
Building Societies, 130
Buller, J., 96
Burnet, J., 72

Campbell, C.J., 123
Cary, 24, 25, 34
Challis, 4, 79, 85
Chancery, jurisdiction, significance of, in relation to proviso for redemption (reconveyance), xli *seq.*
Charge, *hypotheca* compared with, 111, 122
  legal, 131, 189
  meaning of, 135
  mortgagee's, lx–lxiii
  registered. *See* Registered charge
Chattels, mortgage of, 71, 72, 108
Chose in action, equitable interest not a, 46
  equity of redemption as a, 56, 57
  mortgagee has only a, 67
  no estate in a, 8
  use or trust formerly a, 9, 44, 52
Clarke, Sir T., 73
Clause of annulment or defeasance. *See* Defeasance
  in Roman law, 113
  raising rate of interest, 177

INDEX

191

Clog on redemption, 29, 175 *et seq.*
doctrine established, 62 *et seq.*
limited, 179 *et seq.*
questioned, 180
Cockburn, C.J., 183
Coke, 4, 5, 11, 27, 30, 33, 89, 90, 103, 141, 145, 146
quoted, xxxix
Collateral bargain, 113, 180
security-idea, viii–lxiii *passim*
Comparative legal history, studies in, ix–xiii, xxiv, lxii
" Condition " and " conditional limitation ", early history of distinction between, xxxvii–xl
Condition and covenant in "proviso " for redemption (reconveyance), xl–xlvii
mortgagor has at law a, 19
possibility, a, 19
strict performance required at law of, 20
Conditional gifts in medieval common law, xxix
Consolidation, 131
Contingent remainder, 5, 10
Contract and conveyance, combination of, in forms of security on property, xiv–lxiii *passim*
equity of redemption not created by, 53, 182
for sale, 133
mortgage a, 98
theory undeveloped when relief extended, 41
right *in personam*, a, 151
time the essence of, 41
trust created by, 51, 53
Conveyance and contract, elements of, in mortgage, xl–xlvii
on condition precedent as security, history of, xi, xxix, xxxiv–xxxvi, xl
on condition subsequent as security, history of, xxix–xxxvi, xxxvi–lxiii *passim*
to creditor: absolute in *fiducia* and conditional in mortgage, comparison of, xxvii–xxxvi, xxxvi–lxiii *passim*
Copyholder, 5, 39

Copyholder (*contd.*)
mortgage by, 127
Cotton, L.J., 125
Covenant. *See* Condition
Covenant to enjoy until default, 92, 93, 107, 108
Coventry, 19, 85, 100, 101, 106, 160, 161
Cowper, Lord, 47, 63
Culpa, xix
Curtesy, of equity of redemption, 66 *et seq.*, 82
of feoffment to uses, 43
of trust, 47
of trustee's interest, 57
Custodia, xix
Custom, 5, 46, 162

Davey, Lord, 178
Deadness, idea of, in mortgage, xxxviii n. 3
Debt claim, creditor's, viii–lxiii *passim*
Deed or Arrangement, 133
Deeds. *See* Documents
De ejectione firmae, writ of, 4
Defeasance of mortgagee's estate, history of, xxxvi–xl
Denman, C.J., 108
Denuntiatio, xvii, xviii
Deposit of deeds, 131
Determinable fee, early history of mortgagee's estate as, xxxvii–xl
Devise, general, by mortgagee, 62, 66
having other lands, 69, 157
passes legal estate, 158
by trustee, 157
mortgage revocation *pro tanto* of, 60, 67
Devisee, redemption by, 49
Diligentia, xix
Dingliche Kraft and *Wirkung*, xxviii, lii n. 5
Disseisin, equitable estate, of, 83
lease by mortgagor not, 92
lessee holding over, 103
mortgagor's possession not, 91, 100
mortgagee assigning, 92
Distraint, by mortgagee, 95
by mortgagor, 124
Documents, xvi–lxiii *passim*

INDEX

Dominium, xiv–lxiii *passim*, 117, 120
Dower, against feoffee to uses, 43, 45
  against trustee, 46, 47, 73
  redemption paramount to, 50, 52
  trust paramount to, 46, 51

Easement, no estate in, 8, 11
  registration of equitable, 133
Ecclesiastical courts, 17, 36
Eldon, Lord, 60, 83, 159, 182
Elegit, equity of redemption in fee not liable to, 161
  estate conferred by, 5
  freeholder's remedies conferred by, 4
  seisin not conferred by, 3, 68
  status not conferred by, 3
  writ of, must be registered, 133
Ellenborough, Lord, 83, 102, 123
Ellesmere, Lord, attitude to bonds of, 31
  dispute with Coke, 30
  ignorance of Roman law, 116
Entry, early history of mortgagor's right of, xxxvi–xl
Equitable estate, conception of, 74 *et seq.*
  disseisin of, 83
  limitation of action on, 84
  merger of, 186
  ownership and, 81, 83
  servitude, not an, 77
Equitable interest, not a chose in action, 46
Equitable rights, nature of, lix–lx
  of the common law, xi
Equitable waste by mortgagor, 154
Equity. See *Aequitas*
  acts *in personam*, 119, 146
  follows the law, 46, 68, 69, 72 *et seq.*, 84, 97, 162, 164, 188
    doctrine established, 57 *et seq.*
  law did not recognize, 76
  of the common law, xi
  stereotyped by doctrine of precedent, 60
Equity of redemption, appurtenant to an estate, 130, 185 *et seq.*
  as an equitable estate, vii–lxiii *passim*
  assets, as, 60, 163 *et seq.*
  chose in action, formerly a, 56, 57

Equity of redemption (*contd.*)
  contract, not created by, 53, 182
  curtesy of, 66 *et seq.*, 82
  dower, paramount to, 46, 51
  establishment of, 27 *et seq.*
    criticized, 118
  estate in land, as, 76, 82, 86
    dicta opposed, 82
    in statutes, 84
  executory interest and, 153
  expression appears, 55, 56
  fieri facias not against, 161
  interest in land, an, 51
  judgment creditor of, 52, 161, 162
  ownership and, 67 *et seq.*, 85, 103, 124, 128, 152 *et seq.*
  parallels to, in foreign laws, xii–xiii
  proprietary right, as, 53, 86
  realty, 49
  reversion at law, formerly not a, 124
    merger in, 186
  same estate in equity, the, 52, 54, 70, 77, 85, 99
  under new Acts, 130, 185 *et seq.*
Escheat, equity of redemption paramount to, 55
  trust paramount to, 73, 74
  use and, 43
Estate, chose in action, not in, 8
  conception of size of, 1
  easement, none in, 8, 11
  enjoyment of a thing, as, 11, 80
  evolved out of status, 1, 2
  interest limited in time, an, 3, 6, 10, 13, 77, 80, 109
  mortgagor's possession as an, 110
  ownership and, 6, 12, 13
  popular meanings of, 13
  proprietary right and, 1, 2, 3
  pur autre vie, 3, 9
  rent charge, in, 7
    not an estate in land, 76, 77
  right of entry and, 8, 11, 15, 76
  status and, 2, 3, 14, 15
  sufferance, by, 12, 14, 109
  trust, in, 7 *et seq.*
  use, in, 7 *et seq.*
  will, at, 2, 92 *et seq.*, 109
Executory interest, equity of redemption and, 153
  growth of, 5
  possibility, a, 86

INDEX

193

Eyre, C.B., 97
Eyres, C.J., 93

Faith, breach of, on part of mortgagee, xlv
"Feigned transactions" ("Scheingeschäfte"), *fiducia cum creditore* and mortgage as, liii–lv
Feoffment, on condition subsequent, history of mortgagor's, xxix, lxiii *passim*
 with livery of seisin, xxvii–lxiii *passim*
Fiducia, 111, 114 *et seq.*
 cum amico, xiv
 cum creditore and mortgage, comparison of, xii–lxiii *passim*
 cum creditore as a juristic entity, xiv n. 3
 cum creditore as *bonae fidei negotium*, xix–lxiii *passim*
 in law of France and Quebec, xiv n. 1
Fieri facias, equitable, allowed against trust, 47, 160
 not against equity of redemption, 161
Fine, 50
Foreclosure, 17, 27, 62, 85, 155, 156
 charge gives no remedy of, 136
 early days of, 90, 175
 extinguishment of right in equity, as, 57, 58
 first reported case of, 28, 49
 new Acts, under, 130
 Roman law, in, 111, 112, 114, 117
Forfeit-idea, viii–lxiii *passim*
 of pledged property on non-payment of debt, viii–lxiii *passim*
Forfeiture, for felony, 51
 equitable treatment of, 39
 use not liable to, 43
Forma donationis, xxxv
Formalism, xxv–lxiii *passim*
Formality and publicity of conveyances, xxv
Formula of fiduciary *mancipatio*, lvi
Franchise, *cestui que trust* entitled to, 80, 185
 mortgagee in possession do, 183
 mortgagor in possession do, 103, 155, 183 *et seq.*

Freebench, 47
Freeman, 1, 2
Friendly Societies, 130
Furtum, xx

Gaius quoted, xx, xxiii
Gaming laws, 185
Gavelkind, 82
Germanic and Roman legal thought, contrasts between, xxvii
Germanic conveyances on condition subsequent as security, xxxiii, xxxiv
 custom, xxx
 origin of mortgage, xxvii
Gierke quoted, x
Gift or Grant of Germanic and English law, xli, xlii
Glanvil, 12, 17, 18, 20
Glanvillian gage, xi, xxix, xxxiv–xxxvi
Grant. *See* Gift
Grant, Sir W., 78
Gray, Professor, 138
Greek pledge, 111
Guildford, Lord, 163, 165

Habendum, xliii n. 2
Hale, C.J., 33, 46, 48, 50 *et seq.*, 94, 162
 jealous of Chancery, 57
Halsbury, 179
Hardwicke, Lord, 7, 65 *et seq.*, 94, 111, 120, 128, 155 *et seq.*, 162, 166 *et seq.*, 174, 178, 184, 186
Herschell, Lord, 171
Historical development, stages of, of *fiducia cum creditore* and mortgage, xxv–xxvii
Holmes, C.J., 147
Holt, C.J., 93
Hypotheca, viii–xliii *passim*, 111, 114 *et seq.*
 charge compared with, 111, 122
 mortgage under new Acts compared with, 128, 130
Hypothecations in English law, x, xi, lx–lxiii
ὑποθήκη, *hypothek*, viii–lxiii *passim*

Infamia, xix, xx
In iure cessio, xiv–lxiii *passim*

TER

13

INDEX

Instruments of conveyance, xxv–lxiii *passim*
Italian and Anglo-Saxon securities on property, comparison of, xxxiii, xxxiv

Jekyll, Sir J., 157
Jewish pledge, 111
Jointress, redemption by, 49
Judgment creditor, *cestui que use*, and, 43
  equity of redemption liable to, 52
  feoffee to uses, and, 43
  heir of *cestui que trust*, and, 46
  redemption by, 161
    of whole estate, 162
  trust liable to, 47
  trust preferred against, 47
Judicial discretion, xv
Iura in rem and *iura in personam*, viii–lxiii *passim*
Jus in re, 141, 145
  aliena, lxi, 155
Justinian, 111

Kay, J., 173
Kekewich, J., 84
Kirkham, Robert, 35

Lambarde, 35
Land-book, conveyance by delivery of, as security, xxx–xxxiv
Leach, Sir J., 82, 161
Leake, 85
Lease, by *cestui que trust*, 106
  for years, great importance of, in history of English securities on property, xxxvi n. 1
  mortgagee, 126
  mortgagor at common law, 92, 96, 100, 126
    under express power, 103, 126
    under statute, 126
Legacies, Chancellor acquires jurisdiction over, 36
Legal *decorum*, liv
  rigour, mitigation of, in favour of debtors, xii *seq.*
Legatum per praeceptionem, xxii–xxiv
Lewin, 172
Lex commissoria, xv–xvii, xxii, xxvi
Licence, 93
  to consume, 108

Lien, 118
Lies permitted by the law, liv
Limitation of action, bonds, on, 97
  equitable estates, as to, 84
  mortgagee in possession, against, 101
  mortgage satisfied, 174
  redemption, for, 58
Lindley, Lord, 179
Lites pendentes, 133
Littleton, 4, 5, 13, 14, 18, 20, 37–9, 61, 89, 90, 113, 117, 122
Littletonian or common-law mortgage, xi–lxiii *passim*
Long term, 128, 187
Loughborough, Lord, 123, 159

Macnaghten, Lord, 179
Maitland quoted, xxxiii, xxxvii, lv
Mancipatio, xiv–lxiii *passim*, 114
Mansfield, Lord, 47, 73, 76, 77, 94–6, 98, 121, 185
Maxims:
  "Equity acts *in personam*", lx
  "Equity follows the law", lx
  "once a mortgage always a mortgage", xliv. *See also* Mortgage
Merger, 15
  equitable estate in legal, of, 186
  equity of redemption in reversion, of, 186
Monro, 24, 26
Mortgage, and *fiducia cum creditore*, comparison of, xii–lxiii *passim*
  as a form of hypothecation, development of, lx–lxiii
  as complex of two conveyances, feoffment in fee and lease for years, xxxv n. 4, xxxix, xl
  Littletonian or common law, xi–lxiii *passim*
  of fee, xxix–lxiii *passim*
  once a — always a, 175 *et seq.*, 182
  pre-Littletonian, xxix–xl *passim*
  under new Acts, 62, 128 *et seq.*
Mortgagee, accounts strictly, 86, 87, 154–6
  interest of, is personalty, 58 *et seq.*, 66
  position in Roman law of, 113
  possession of, formerly general, 88
    in Civil War, 90

INDEX

195

Mortgagee (*contd.*)
 reversioner, as, 99
 trustee, as, 83, 166 *et seq.*
  constructive only, 105, 173
  power of sale, of, 172
  under Trustee Relief Act, 174
Mortgages of estates tail, life estates,
 and terms for years, xxix n. 5
Mortgagor in possession, as bailiff,
 91
 as disseisor, 91
 as fraudulent, 89
 estate of, 110
 lease by, 92, 96, 100, 103, 126
 manor courts held by, 103
 prevalence of, 88, 90, 120
 proviso to leave, 89, 92, 107, 108
 restrain breach of covenant, may,
  125
 statutory powers of, 102, 124, 125
 sui generis, 87, 101 *et seq.*, 110
 tenant at will, 92 *et seq.*
 tenant by sufferance, 92 *et seq.*
 trespasser, remedies against, 123
 under new Acts, 105
Mortuum vadium, 17, 18, 20, 113

Natural justice, xii
Norburie, 31, 32
Norman Conquest, 1
North, Lord, 63, 161
Northington, Lord, 73, 178, 179
Nottingham, Lord, 38, 39, 46 *et seq.*,
 54 *et seq.*, 68, 73, 75, 77, 128,
 151, 157, 160 *et seq.*, 176, 177
Novel Disseisin, 17

Obligation of creditor in respect of
 res, xv–lxiii *passim*
Ownership, definition of, 153
 equitable estate as, 81, 83
 "estate" implied, 6, 12, 18
 Hardwicke's use of term, 77
 long term as, 155
 mortgagor has, 67 *et seq.*, 85, 103
  discussed, 152 *et seq.*
  reinforced by statute, 124
  under new Acts, 128
 of *fiduciarius*, nature of, l–lviii

Pactum fiduciae, xiv–lxiii *passim*
 de vendendo, xv–xviii, xxii, xxvi
Parke, B., 99, 102, 109

Parker, Lord, 170, 181, 182
Parker, Sir Thos., 71
Parol evidence to prove mortgage,
 62
Patteson, J., 102
Personal action, 13
 on debt claim, xiv–lxiii *passim*
Pfandrevers, xxxiv
Pignus, xiv–lxiii *passim*, 111 *et seq.*
Platt, B., 109
Pledge different from mortgage, 38,
 72
Pledge-idea, viii–lxiii *passim*
Plowden, 5, 10
Plumer, Sir Thos., 83, 97 *et seq.*, 169,
 174
Portion term, 129, 186
Possessio of gagee for a term, xxxiv,
 xxxv
Possession of *res*, xiv–lxiii *passim*
Possessory assizes, 3
Possibility, contingent remainder a,
 5, 10
 executory interest as, 86
 mortgage condition as, 19
 right of entry conferred by a, 8
Pound, Professor Roscoe, 147, 148
Powell, 100
Power of redemption, 49, 51, 55
Powers of sale, xxvi
Precarium, xv–xxvi *passim*, lx
Precedent, effect of, 36
 growth of, 162
Pre-emption, of collateral matter
 good, 181
 of equity of redemption invalid,
 177
Preston, 12, 15
Privity, 43, 44, 45, 51, 74
Profits *à prendre*, 76
Property Acts, recent, xxxii, xxxvi
 n. 1, lxii n. 1
Property-gage (substance-gage), ix–
 lxiii *passim*
Proprietary right, estate as, 1, 2, 3
 equity of redemption as, 53, 86
 right *in rem* as, 140 *et seq.*
Proscriptio, xviii
Proviso, for reconveyance, 18, 19, 21
 for redemption (=proviso for reconveyance), history of, xl–
  xlvii
 re-entry, 18

INDEX

Publicity. *See* Formality
Purchaser for value without notice, from mortgagee, 54, 55
  trustee, 43, 55, 140

Quare ejecit infra terminum, 4

Rainsford, B., 57
Raleigh, William, 4
Real action, 13, 100
Reconveyance, abolition of need for, 130, 132
  by *fiduciarius* and by mortgage, xv–xlvii *passim*
  common law may decree, 120
  unnecessary inconvenience of, 127
Recovery, equitable, 78
Redemption, comparison of fiduciary debtor's right of, with mortgagor's equity of redemption, xlviii–lx
  nature of fiduciary debtor's right of, xlix–lviii
Registered charge, 118
  ideal security, an, 118
  of chattels, 127
  of ships, 127
  under Land Transfer Acts, 127
  under new Acts, 133
Registration of title, 133
  in Middlesex and Yorkshire, 127, 133
  in nineteenth century, 133
  questioned, 134
Relationship, basis of English law, 148
Relief of mortgages, generally, 24, 27 *et seq.*
  under Commonwealth, 30, 52
  ground for extension of, 35 *et seq.*
  in cases of hardship, 25
  of right, 48
  of termors, 186
  satisfied, 21 *et seq.*
  under Ed. IV, 24
Rent charge, estate in, 7
  estate in the land, not an, 76, 77
  mortgagor cannot grant, 109
  ownership of land, not, 77
Rentenkauf, x
Reports, dates of publication, 56
  scanty in Chancery before Restoration, 56

Reservation to mortgagor void, 123
Reversion in fee, on leasehold mortgage legal assets, 165
  under new Acts in mortgagor, 128, 186
"Revert", "return", "remain", early history of terms, xxxvi–xl
Richards, C.B., 168
Right, meaning of, 138, 147
  in early law, 6
Right *in rem*, 138
  borrowed from Rome, 139
  mortgagor and, 143
  proprietary right and, 140
  rights of action and, 153
  secondary classification of a, 150
  trust and, 141
Right of entry, assignee of mortgagee has, 92
  mortgagor has at law a, 19, 89
  not an estate in land, 8, 11, 15, 76
"Right of redemption", 149
Rights, duality of, vii–lxiii *passim*
Roman and Germanic legal thought, fundamental contrasts between, xxvii
Roman equity, tends to protect debtor, 176, 177
  and common-law mortgage compared, 113 *et seq.*

Sabinians, opinion of, respecting legacy *per praeceptionem*, xxiii
St German, 2, 22
Sale, power of, 154
  clog distinguished, 179
  creditor's right of, xvi–lxiii *passim*
  mortgagee not trustee of, 172
  under new Acts, 130
  order of the Court, 162
  Roman law, 111, 114, 117
  Statute, 121
"Sale for repurchase" (*Verkauf auf Wiederverkauf, vente à rémére*), viii, xxxiv, xliv–xlvi
Sale-gage, xiv–lxiii *passim*
Satisfactio, xv, xviii, xix
Satisfied mortgage, mortgagee a trustee of, 167 *et seq.*
  presumption of, 97, 98
  relief of, 21 *et seq.*
Satzung, ältere and *jüngere*, of German law, x

INDEX

197

Saunders, 158
Seabanks, non-repair of, 103
Search, 134
Second mortgagee, powers of, 125
   redemption by, 50
   under new Acts, 125, 131, 134, 187
   under Roman law, 112
Securities on property, continuity
   and parallelism in history of,
   ix–xiii
   universal legal history of, viii–xiii
Security for money, mortgage as, 66,
   71, 85
   clogs and, 62 *et seq.*, 177
   extended relief and, 36 *et seq.*,
   90
   mortgagee trustee and, 167 *et
   seq.*
   mortgagee's interest personalty
   and, 59, 61
   Roman law and, 113, 117
   term of years as, 18
   test of mortgage, 62
Seignories, 76
Seisin, abeyance of, 10
   equitable, 66, 67, 77, 78
   statutory definition, 83
   freeholder has, 2, 4
   mortgagor has under new Acts,
   128
   ownership compared, 12, 43
   possession in early law compared,
   2, 4
   termor has no, 3
   tenant by *elegit* has no, 3, 68
   varied conception of, 11
Seisina, in fee, enlargement of termor's *possessio* into, xxxv
   ut de vadio, Glanvillian creditor's,
   xxxiv
Social and economic factors, influence of, in development of
   securities on property, viii,
   ix, xx, xxii, xlviii, xlix, lxi, lxii
Solutio, xv, xviii, xix
Springing use, 9
Status, Court favoured free, 1
   estate compared, 2, 3, 14, 15
   franchise and, 183
   freehold and, 1, 2, 3
   leasehold and, 3, 18
   personal condition and, 1
   proprietary right and, 1

Status (contd.)
   tenancy by *elegit* or statute gives
   no, 3
   tenure and, 1
Statute merchant, 3, 5, 68
Story, 85
Strange, M.R., 72
Sub-mortgage, 126, 128
Subpoena, adopted by Chancellor,
   43
   overrides common law, 30
Substance-gage. *See* Property-gage
Surety, relief of, 34

Tacking, 68
   doctrine of, vii n. 1
   under new Acts, 131
Tenant at will, assignment by, 107
   cestui que trust a, 91, 106
   cestui que use a, 91
   estate, has an, 109
   lessee of mortgagor a, 92
   limitation of action and, 174
   mortgagor a, 92 *et seq.*
     by agreement, 106, 108, 124
     by covenant to enjoy, 93
     death of, 107
     on satisfaction of mortgage, 105
     ownership and, 144
     right *in rem* and, 143
Tenant by sufferance, mortgagor as,
   92 *et seq.*, 124
   whether has estate, 12, 14, 109
Tenterden, C.J., 102
Thomasius quoted, li
Thurlow, Lord, 83, 97
Tort, 151
Tortious feoffment, 39
Tothill, 26, 182
Traditio, xiv–lxiii *passim*
Transfer of mortgage, 130
Trespass by relation, 143
Trespasser, mortgagor as, 99, 102,
   104
   mortgagor's remedies against, 129
Trust, analogy of, 48, 51, 53, 55, 65,
   106, 156 *et seq.*
   and analogy of use, 45, 73
   and *fiducia*, xiii, xiv n. 1
   and mortgage, vii, xi, xiii, lx
   as assets, 47, 60, 163 *et seq.*
   legal, 166
   chose in action, formerly a, 9, 44, 52

INDEX

Trust (*contd.*)
contract, created by, 51, 53
curtesy of, 47
not preferred to, 57
dower not preferred to, 46, 47, 51, 73
estate in, 7 *et seq.*
fieri facias not granted against, 76, 160
franchise conferred by, 80, 185
right *in rem* compared, 141
satisfied mortgage, of, 167 *et seq.*
Tyndal, 26

Ulpian, 112
Use, a chose in action formerly, 9, 44, 52
curtesy preferred to, 73
estate in, 7 *et seq.*
forfeiture, not liable to, 43
formerly not assets, 43
judgment creditor and, 43
tenancy at will and, 91
upon a use, 44
Usufruct-gage, xviii–lxiii *passim*
Usureceptio ex fiducia, xx–xxii, xlix
Usury, doctrine of clogging and, 178, 179
connection disputed, 182

Usury (*contd.*)
leasehold used as not savouring of, 3
mortuum vadium as, 17, 18

Vaughan-Williams, J., 102
Vifgage and *fiducia*, xviii
and *mortgage*, viii
Villein *status*, 1, 2
tenure, 1
Vivum vadium, English, xviii, 17, 20. See *Vifgage*
Roman law compared, 113
Von Ihering quoted, liv, lvi

Waste, mortgagor may commit, 103
writ of, 4
Watson, B., 102
Welsh mortgage, Chancellor's jurisdiction over, 48, 63
mortgagee took possession under, 91
vivum vadium compared, 20
Wigram, V.-C., 171
Williams, L.K., 31, 32, 33
Williams, P., 68
Wilshere, 85
Writ of entry *ad terminum qui praeteriit*, the mortgagor's remedy by, xxxv n. 4, xxxix
Wyld, J., 58

For EU product safety concerns, contact us at Calle de José Abascal, 56–1°, 28003 Madrid, Spain or eugpsr@cambridge.org.

www.ingramcontent.com/pod-product-compliance
Ingram Content Group UK Ltd.
Pitfield, Milton Keynes, MK11 3LW, UK
UKHW010900060825
461487UK00012B/1251